Passing into the present

MANCHESTER
1824

Manchester University Press

Contemporary American and Canadian Writers

Series editors:
Nahem Yousaf and Sharon Monteith

Also available

Passing into the present

Contemporary American fiction
of racial and gender passing

Sinéad Moynihan

Manchester University Press

Manchester and New York

distributed in the United States exclusively by Palgrave Macmillan

The right of Sinéad Moynihan to be identified as the author of this work has been asserted by her in accordance with the Copyright, Designs and Patents Act 1988.

Published by Manchester University Press
Oxford Road, Manchester M13 9NR, UK
and Room 400, 175 Fifth Avenue, New York, NY 10010, USA
www.manchesteruniversitypress.co.uk

Distributed in the United States exclusively by
Palgrave Macmillan, 175 Fifth Avenue, New York,
NY 10010, USA

Distributed in Canada exclusively by
UBC Press, University of British Columbia, 2029 West Mall,
Vancouver, BC, Canada V6T 1Z2

British Library Cataloguing-in-Publication Data
A catalogue record for this book is available from the British Library

Library of Congress Cataloging-in-Publication Data applied for

ISBN 978 0 7190 8229 0 *hardback*

First published 2010

The publisher has no responsibility for the persistence or accuracy of URLs for any external or third-party internet websites referred to in this book, and does not guarantee that any content on such websites is, or will remain, accurate or appropriate.

Typeset
by Florence Production Ltd, Stoodleigh, Devon
Printed in Great Britain
by MPG Books Group, UK

Contents

Series editors' foreword

This innovative series reflects the breadth and diversity of writing over the last thirty years, and provides critical evaluations of established, emerging and critically neglected writers – mixing the canonical with the unexpected. It explores notions of the contemporary and analyses current and developing modes of representation with a focus on individual writers and their work. The series seeks to reflect both the growing body of academic research in the field, and the increasing prevalence of contemporary American and Canadian fiction on programmes of study in institutions of higher education around the world. Central to the series is a concern that each book should argue a stimulating thesis, rather than provide an introductory survey, and that each contemporary writer will be examined across the trajectory of their literary production. A variety of critical tools and literary and interdisciplinary approaches are encouraged to illuminate the ways in which a particular writer contributes to, and helps readers rethink, the North American literary and cultural landscape in a global context.

Central to debates about the field of contemporary fiction is its role in interrogating ideas of national exceptionalism and transnationalism. This series matches the multivocality of contemporary writing with wide-ranging and detailed analysis. Contributors examine the drama of the nation from the perspectives of writers who are members of established and new immigrant groups, writers who consider themselves on the nation's margins as well as those who chronicle middle America. National labels are the subject of vociferous debate and including American and Canadian writers in the same series is not to flatten the differences between them but to acknowledge that literary traditions and tensions are cross-cultural and that North American writers often explore and expose precisely these tensions. The series recognises that situating a writer in a cultural context involves a multiplicity of influences, social and geo-political, artistic and theoretical, and that contemporary fiction defies easy categorisation. For example, it examines writers who invigorate the genres in which they have made their mark alongside writers whose aesthetic goal is to subvert the idea of genre altogether. The challenge of defining the roles of writers and assessing their reception by reading communities is central to the aims of the series.

Overall, *Contemporary American and Canadian Writers* aims to begin to represent something of the diversity of contemporary writing and seeks to engage students and scholars in stimulating debates about the contemporary and about fiction.

Nahem Yousaf
Sharon Monteith

Acknowledgements

This book evolved from a PhD project that I undertook in the School of American and Canadian Studies at the University of Nottingham from 2003 to 2006. As such, I owe a tremendous debt of gratitude to the academic and administrative staff there, as well as to my postgraduate peers. I would like to thank Sharon Monteith and Celeste-Marie Bernier, who co-supervised the project, and Sharon, in particular, for going above and beyond the call of duty to see it through to final publication. For their input and advice, I am grateful to Dave Murray at Nottingham and Helen Taylor at the University of Exeter. Stimulating discussions with academic friends – Susan Billingham, Joanne Hall, Lee Jenkins, Ruth Maxey, Catherine Mills and Simon Turner – were also invaluable.

For financial support during the writing of this work, I am grateful to the National University of Ireland and the Leverhulme Trust for providing doctoral and post-doctoral funding respectively. The British Association for American Studies and the Graduate School at the University of Nottingham also awarded additional funding which facilitated research trips to the United States.

Portions of chapters 2 and 3 originally appeared, respectively, in *Engaging Tradition, Making It New: Essays on Teaching Recent African American Literature*, ed. Éva Tettenborn and Stephanie Brown (Newcastle: Cambridge Scholars, 2008) and *Mother Tongue Theologies*, ed. Darren J.N. Middleton (Oregon: Wipf and Stock, 2009). I am grateful to the publishers for granting permission to reproduce this material here.

Acknowledgement is also due for the use of the following extracts: *Tracks* (1988) and *The Last Report on the Miracles at Little No Horse* (2001) by Louise Erdrich © HarperCollins Publishers Ltd; *From Caucasia with Love* by Danzy Senna (2001) © Bloomsbury Publishing; *The Human Stain* by Philip Roth (2000) published by Jonathan Cape, reprinted by permission of The Random House Group. Some material has previously been published in the chapter 'Native-Christian Syncretism in two Louise Erdrich novels', and is used by permission of Wipf and Stock publishers, www.wipfandstock.com.

Thanks, finally, to my family and friends – in Ireland, Britain and the USA – for supporting me throughout the process of researching and writing this book. Míle buíochas.

1

Introduction: 'passing' into the present: passing narratives then and now

Bette: I would never define myself exclusively as being white any more than I would define myself exclusively as being black. I mean, really, why is it so . . . wrong for me . . . to move more freely in the world just because my appearance doesn't automatically announce who I am?
Yolanda: Because it is a lie.

The L Word (2004)[1]

This exchange occurs not in a nineteenth-century American novel, nor even in one of the many racial passing narratives of the Harlem Renaissance,[2] but in Showtime's hit drama series, *The L Word*, in an episode first aired on 7 March 2004.[3] Bette (Jennifer Beals), who is of mixed race, and her partner, Tina (Laurel Holloman), who is white and is carrying their child, attend a support group in which the couple discuss their impending parenthood. An African American member of the group, Yolanda, takes issue with the couple over (what she mistakes for) their decision to use a white sperm donor in order that Tina will give birth to a white child. Yolanda reproaches Bette for talking 'so proud and . . . forthright about being a lesbian' while never once referring to herself as 'an African American woman.' Yolanda notes that the other members of the group are 'wondering what the hell we're talking about because they didn't even know you were a black woman.' At a subsequent meeting, Bette turns Yolanda's own critique against her, observing that *she* didn't realise Yolanda was a lesbian until she read a poem of hers. As Bette puts it, 'You're not exactly readable as a lesbian, and you didn't come out and declare yourself.'

Several interrelated issues arise from Bette and Yolanda's exchanges. First, and most obviously, is that Yolanda, in charging Bette with 'hiding so behind the lightness of your skin', is effectively accusing her of 'passing' as white.[4] As Yolanda perceives it, for Bette not to declare her blackness is dishonest, a 'lie.' Why is it that in March 2004, the metaphors of concealment, subterfuge and deception that have historically characterised passing are still pervasive in US culture? Why is it, in other words, that passing persists as a common trope in diverse cultural representations?[5] Passing is typically associated with a period stretching from post-Reconstruction to the Civil Rights Movement (the 1890s to the 1960s) or, even more specifically, yoked to the years of the Harlem Renaissance.[6] Juda Bennett locates the beginning of the black-to-white passing narrative in 'antebellum works . . . peaking with the literary output of the Harlem Renaissance.'[7] Werner Sollors observes that racial passing is 'particularly a phenomenon of the late nineteenth and the first half of the twentieth century' and adds that it was 'swept aside in social history by the civil rights movement, and in literature by the combined successes of Zora Neale Hurston and Richard Wright, who no longer employed the theme.'[8] According to Gayle Wald, by the time John Howard Griffin's memoir, *Black Like Me*, appeared in 1961, 'passing was already beginning to "pass" out of style for African Americans, going the way of Jim Crow buses and segregated lunch counters.'[9] It is a mistake to associate literary passing so closely with the socio-political context of twentieth-century America because, as Michele Elam observes, 'Narratives of passing are significant not because they gives [*sic*] us clues to actual extant practices but because they give us clues to extant cultural fretfulness about perceived practices.'[10] This book contests the traditional historiography of the passing narrative, questioning whether passing ever, in fact, went away. And, if it did recede, why is it back?

The Bette/Yolanda exchanges raise the question that if passing is back, how do recent manifestations of the theme engage with those of the past, and to what end? In other words, how self-aware are 'new' passing narratives? Beals's own career is an interesting case in point. Beals is of mixed race heritage, and has been accused on several occasions of passing as white. She has been criticised for not self-identifying as African American or for being a mixed race individual who 'use[s]' her 'minority' status 'to gain an advantage while stopping short of embracing . . . Black heritage and the Black community in general.'[11] According to *Ebony*, Beals claimed she thought she would never get into Yale University. But, as a minority, she was 'lucky': 'I'm not Black, and I'm not White, so I could mark "other" on my application, and I guess it's hard for them to fill that quota.'[12] From *Flashdance* (1983) in which, as a 'black' actress playing a 'white' character, she passes as white, as some would have it,[13] to *Devil in a Blue Dress* (1995), in which she plays a character passing as white, to *The L Word*, in which she plays self-consciously with her perceived previous engagements with passing, Yolanda's accusation that Bette is passing as white speaks to the multiple textual layers at which passing can operate even over the twenty or so years of Beals's career.[14]

Equally, the conversation Bette and Yolanda have reveals the contiguity of apparently distinct categories of identity and, by extension, the possibility that multiple types of passing – race, gender, sexual, religious – intersect and impinge upon one another. In this instance, as in Nella Larsen's *Passing* (1929), those categories are race and sexuality.[15] If Yolanda censures Bette for passing as white, then Bette retaliates by accusing Yolanda of passing as straight. Bette's claim that Yolanda is 'not exactly readable as a lesbian' speaks to Yolanda's point that Bette's own African American ancestry is not corporeally legible to the other members of the group. It is significant, however, that Bette's 'blackness' is visible to the only African American member of the group, Yolanda. Amy Robinson posits the narrative of passing as a triangular relationship between passer (here, this is Bette), duped (the other members of the group) and the in-group clairvoyant who can 'see' what/who the passer 'really' is (Yolanda). Robinson argues that '[t]hroughout the literature of racial and sexual passing, members of the in-group insist on a distinctive location that allows them to recognize a never truly hidden prepassing identity.'[16] However, in this case, the blackness of Bette's ambiguously raced body is legible to Yolanda in a way that Yolanda's sexuality is most decidedly *not* legible to Bette. Why is it that even in narratives that emphasise the interdependence and interaction of different identity categories, racial identity – especially if this corresponds to 'blackness' – seems to trump all others?[17]

Of supreme importance for the purposes of this book, therefore, is the fact that Bette does not realise Yolanda is a lesbian until she reads one of Yolanda's poems, in which Yolanda describes herself as 'a black, socialist, feminist lesbian, working to overthrow the white, male, capitalist patriarchy.' The text of Yolanda's poem thus replaces the text of her body in exposing her sexuality. One of my main concerns throughout this book is to interrogate the ways in which written texts serve, alternately or simultaneously, to fix or free up the identity categories that their authors, for whatever reasons, are seeking to conceal, evade or transcend. In other words, can one be 'given away' by a written text? Or, conversely, is it possible to disguise oneself through the disembodied act of writing? Is it significant, I wonder, that in novels that *thematise* passing, their authors frequently disguise the *form* of their novels? I examine texts in which protagonists not only play at racial and gender identities, but where authors play on the boundaries between novel and other types of textual production, between fiction and history, between novelistic genres, between author(ial persona) and protagonist. I analyse novels that pass as memoirs, a mock *Bildungsroman*, a 'mild genuflection to the detective form',[18] a novel-within-a-novel. I examine narratives whose dramatic impetus often derives from embedded documentation – letters, emails, poems, medical reports, dictionary or encyclopaedia entries. *All* of the novels I discuss challenge conventions of form which, in a postmodern context, one would imagine to be *de rigueur*. Why is it, then, that some of the authors of such texts have found themselves charged with 'inauthenticity'?

Déjà vu all over again?

If my discussion of *The L Word* makes a claim for the enduring popularity of tropes of passing in mainstream contemporary American culture, to unpack this assertion it is necessary to engage with the inverse relationship that supposedly exists between narratives of passing and scholarship on narratives of passing in the contemporary moment. In other words, there has been a proliferation of academic studies of the literature of passing just as the authors of such studies contend that passing is no longer a topic of interest for contemporary American writers. These studies authorise their marginalisation of contemporary narratives of passing by maintaining that they simply do not exist, an understandable elision given that the recourse to tropes of passing in the 1990s and beyond seems, at first glance, to be anachronistic in the extreme. Contemporary fictions of passing, then, do not seem to fit with the neat periodisation narrative that has been constructed around such stories. While some of these studies refer anecdotally to contemporary narratives of passing – Gayle Wald concludes *Crossing the Line: Racial Passing in Twentieth-Century U.S. Literature and Culture* with a brief discussion of Danzy Senna's *Caucasia* (1998) and Kathleen Pfeiffer references Philip Roth's *The*

Human Stain (2000) in closing her book – none explores recent passing stories to account for their resurgence at the end of the twentieth century.

A central claim of this book is that passing has resurfaced in fictions that are described as 'postmodern' because it is a useful meta-critical and meta-fictional tool. Contemporary American writers are attracted to the trope of passing because passing narratives have always fore-grounded the notion of textuality in relation to the (il)legibility of 'black' subjects passing as white. For instance, in one of the great narratives of unresolved racial ambiguity, William Faulkner's *Light in August* (1932), protagonist Joe Christmas is repeatedly described as 'parchmentcolored.'[19] Contemporary writers who invoke passing map such ideas self-reflexively on to the text itself. Indeed, from the beginnings of African American writing, the tropes of reading, authorship and passing have been interrelated, even with respect to the etymology of the word itself. The term is believed to be derived from the written pass given to slaves so that they might travel without being taken for runaways.[20] One of the reasons that most slaveholding states prohibited the teaching of slaves to read and write was the danger that such passes could then be forged.[21] For a mixed race slave, white skin could function as an additional kind of pass, enabling them to escape more easily with less risk of detection.[22]

The relationship between passing and controversies of authorship is borne out by the fact that the very first reference to racial passing in American literary history, Richard Hildreth's *The Slave; or, Memoirs of Archy Moore* (1836), was initially believed to be a slave narrative but was actually a novel written by a white abolitionist.[23] Meanwhile, James Weldon Johnson's *Autobiography of an Ex-Colored Man* was, according to Donald Goellnicht, Johnson's attempt 'to gain credibility and a market for his text by trading on the importance of autobiog-raphy in early African American writing.'[24] Published anonymously in 1912, complete with an authenticating preface by 'The Publishers' (reminiscent of those introducing slave narratives by William Lloyd Garrison and Lydia Maria Child), it purported to be an autobio-graphical account of a light-skinned African American man who definitively 'crosses the color line' to live as white. Many readers believed it to be a true story, what Johnson intriguingly calls 'a human document.'[25] It was reissued in 1927 with the author's name and an introduction by Carl Van Vechten. Johnson acknowledges in his actual autobiography, *Along this Way*, that his decision to write it was to some degree motivated by his readers' tendency to collapse author and character (the first-person narrator of *Autobiography*), and to conflate human writer with fictional document.[26]

A further, related reason for the appeal of passing among contemporary American writers is that while mixed race bodies may not be policed as rigidly as they have been in the past, they are increasingly defined and circumscribed according to the imperatives of the global marketplace. In her study of mixed identities in the USA and Latin America, Suzanne Bost identifies the contemporary 'fascination' with interracialism – as evidenced, for example, in the bid to have the category 'multiracial' added to the US census in 2000 – and notes that in the nineteenth century, such 'fascination with mixture corresponded with racial segregation, "sciences" of purity, and white supremacy; how do you know that history is not just repeating itself?'[27] While this remains an important open question, one undeniable consequence of the 'fascination' with interracialism in the 1990s, culminating in the decision to allow people to check more than one category on the census form, is that those of multiracial heritage suddenly became visible in the marketplace, both as a 'branding tool' symbolising the 'hip' and the 'new' (for, as industry reports estimate, forty-two per cent of all multiracials were born after 1982) and as a vast 'target market' in their own right.[28] Both positions are problematic: the first, because it implies a kind of millennialist 'newness' about mixed race identity that thoroughly dehistoricises the often exploitative and violent nature of interracial relationships in the USA; the second, because it involves identifying the putatively 'unique' characteristics and needs of this segment of the market, a worrying latter-day form of essentialism. Kimberly McClain DaCosta takes the example of Curls, a hair care company for 'multiethnic women', and argues that its advertisements suggest that mixed race women's hair 'is different *in a generalizable way* from the curly hair of *non*racially mixed women and girls', a claim that 'relies for its impact on the folk belief that there is an inherent bodily difference between the races.'[29]

There are several examples of the deployment of multiracialism as a branding tool. One of the earliest was Mattel's launch of a series of new 'ethnic' Barbie dolls in February 1991, which they promoted aggressively in Afrocentric publications such as *Essence* magazine and on Latin-oriented television shows. However, as Ann Ducille argues, 'these would-be multicultural dolls treat race and ethnic difference like collectibles, contributing more to commodity culture than to the intercultural awareness they claim to inspire.'[30] One of the key issues that Lauren Berlant identifies in relation to *Time*'s 'New Face of America' cover story of 1993, which has been discussed exhaustively by several scholars, is its status as commodity: 'When a periodical makes a "special issue" out of a controversy, the controversy itself becomes a commodity whose value is in the intensity of identification and anxiety the journal can organize around it, and this is what is happening to immigration as a subject in the U.S. mainstream.'[31] For sportswear giant Nike, the most important aspect of Tiger Woods's self-proclaimed 'Cablinasian' identity is that it has been able to market its products to a spectrum of black and brown subjects, as evidenced in its 'I am Tiger Woods' advertisement of 1996. As Henry Yu observes, 'the phrase, "I am Tiger Woods" could be translated by consumers as "My body is black and I am up and coming just like him", but more likely it meant "I want to wear what Tiger wears."'[32]

DaCosta argues that 'the contours of mixed race identification and community are increasingly being forged in the marketplace.'[33] In the texts I examine in this book, the prescriptions and proscriptions of the marketplace are also central. The relationship between issues of authorship by nonwhite or ethnic subjects and the cultural industries in which they work is a key concern, from the meta-critique offered in Percival Everett's *Erasure* (2001), whose author-protagonist discovers his non-racially marked novel in the African American Studies section of a Barnes and Noble bookstore, to comments made by Hollywood producer, Wiley Morgenstein, who wishes to option Stagg R. Leigh's ghetto novel for the big screen: 'They go to the movies now, these people. There's an itch and I plan to scratch it.'[34] Meanwhile, *The Bondwoman's Narrative*'s (2002) assertion of different kinds of disguise and passing is unintentionally ironic, given critics' and scholars' contemporary preoccupations with ascertaining the racial identity of its author. As Suzanne Bost argues, moreover, an 'important part of the marketing of *Caucasia* is the appearance of the light-skinned [author Danzy] Senna, whose photo accompanies some reviews of the best-seller.'[35] Equally, for *The White Boy Shuffle*'s Gunnar Kaufman, there is no escaping commodification in his twin sporting and artistic pursuits. Just as his basketball performances transform him into a 'commodity', so he becomes 'a human Hallmark card' through his composition of epithalamia and panegyrics.[36]

Passing and postmodernism

Broadly defined, to 'pass' is to appear to belong to one or more social subgroups other than the one(s) to which one is normally assigned by prevailing legal, medical and/or socio-cultural discourses. To pass as white, if one is 'black', or male, if one is 'female', is to challenge assumptions that the evidence of one's race and/or gender is always visually available by recourse to a set of physical characteristics considered immutable – skin colour, hair texture, fingernails, genitalia and so on. By contrast, to pass into a different class is more likely to be an invisible form of passing, predicated on the possibility of changing aspects of one's identity related to, but existing at one step's remove from, the body – dress, accent and so forth. The word 'appear' in my definition implies a degree of ambiguity between accident and design, between passing and being 'passed.' For some scholars, such as Randall Kennedy, 'passing requires that a person be consciously engaged in concealment.'[37] Contrary to Kennedy, I would argue that the origins of racial passing in American literary history are dominated overwhelmingly by (tragic) mulattas who *involuntarily* pass as white. In order to avoid dehistoricising the racial passing story, therefore, it is imperative not to discount subjects who pass unconsciously. Furthermore, it is ultimately impossible to distinguish between voluntary and involuntary passing for even where a conscious choice to pass is involved, as Wald puts it, 'such choice occurs within the context of a negotiation of categories that are authorized by racial ideology and quite literally mandated by the state.'[38]

I have just described the (f)act of passing. How, then, has passing been interpreted? Stephen J. Belluscio distinguishes very usefully between two understandings of passing. In the first, 'passing means to conceal a unitary, essential, and ineffaceable racial identity and substitute it with a purportedly artificial one, as in the oft-discussed case of a light-skinned black person passing for white.'[39] The second is an understanding of passing that is

> linked to performativity and that refers not to an assumption of a fraudulent identity but more broadly to 'the condition of subjectivity in postmodernity', in which our Lyotardian distrust of totalizing metanarratives, when applied to identity, has caused us to focus not so much upon identity as a unitary, essentialized entity, but rather as a process-oriented performance drawing upon a seemingly infinite number of cultural texts, 'ethnic' or otherwise.[40]

For Belluscio, the first perception of passing, associated with the studies of Gunnar Myrdal and St. Clair Drake and Horace Cayton in the 1940s, is rapidly, and understandably in a postmodern moment, giving way to the second.

I would argue that passing and postmodernism make compatible bedfellows not so much because passing has been appropriated by postmodernists as evidence of the possibility of endlessly deferring a stable identity but because passing so obviously enacts what Linda Hutcheon calls the 'postmodern paradox.'[41] In making a claim for the political power of postmodernism, Hutcheon observes that 'postmodernism ultimately manages to install and reinforce as much as undermine and subvert the conventions and presuppositions it appears to challenge.'[42] Postmodernism's political dimension is thus one of 'complicitous critique.'[43] This paradox is the passer's own: by 'crossing the color line', the passer *simultaneously* subverts and reinforces the racial binary. S/he subverts it by exposing its constructedness, its permeability, its instability. But in the very act of passing, s/he also reinforces it by granting authority and credibility to the mythical 'color line' as a real and true boundary to be transgressed. As Amy Robinson puts it, 'the social practice of passing is thoroughly invested in the logic of the system it attempts to subvert.'[44] For Phillip Brian Harper, this aspect of passing disqualifies it from carrying any political significance, though it may have critical value.[45] Hutcheon's construction reminds us, however, that Harper's opposition between critical and political is a false dichotomy. How can any phenomenon with the potential for critique not also be political?[46] Carole-Anne Tyler is closer to the mark when she describes passing as 'not quite not resistance', a concept that does manage to capture quite convincingly the paradox of passing.[47] In order to heed Gayle Wald's warning against the reproduction of 'a critical dualism of "subversive" or "complicit" passing that echoes the binary logic of race', Hutcheon's notion of 'complicitous critique' is the most convincing and helpful apparatus for interpreting the (f)act of passing.[48]

However, to return for a moment to Belluscio's two understandings of passing, he cautions against privileging the second at the expense of the first, observing that:

> while the latter notion of passing carries more critical currency in the postmodern era, we as critics cannot forget that many passing narratives written in the late nineteenth and early twentieth centuries are governed

by the logic of the first cultural notion, and our readings must be ever aware of this.[49]

I insist upon the importance of retaining an awareness of both cultural notions for an additional reason. That is, the authors of the contemporary passing narratives discussed in this book often exist in an ambivalent relationship to postmodernism. While their protagonists may (though not always) be permitted the luxury of an identity that is always already decentred, the same postmodernist principles are not often extended to the authors by publishers, critics and/or the reading public. Contemporary writers such as Louise Erdrich may deploy postmodernist techniques in their writing, but they have been roundly criticised in some quarters for doing so.[50] One of the reasons for which passing is back, if indeed it ever went away, is that even in this postmodern moment, expectations of 'authenticity' continue to be applied to authors who are considered 'marginal' for various reasons, but most often because of their ethnic background. This book emphasises the interrelationship of the theme of passing in contemporary novels and the issues of authorship that are addressed in those same novels. In other words, it considers the implications of viewing the acts of writing and passing as analogous.

What then are the particular kinds of passing under examination here? What of the privileged status of racial passing in this and, indeed, most studies of passing? As I suggested in my brief analysis of *The L Word*, this book is concerned with texts that thematise various forms of passing, particularly racial and gender passing, and the ways in which such narratives often contest other categories of identity, too, such as sexuality, religion and class. The danger is, of course, to set up racial passing as *the* 'authentic' form of passing, to suggest that other types of passing are significant only in the extent to which they relate to racial passing. In a US context, I would argue, it is impossible for it to be any other way. Where tales of cross-dressing and, indeed, many other forms of disguise are universal, racial passing is considered a uniquely American phenomenon. As Sollors observes, the term 'passing', as shorthand for 'passing for white', is an Americanism not listed in the first edition of the *Oxford English Dictionary*.[51] This situation is, as Wald and others have noted, attributable to the historical application of the one-drop rule, whose unilateral nature 'ensures that in the United States "black" people disproportionately bear the burden of racial representation.'[52] If, from its very etymological origins, the term 'passing' always implies 'racial passing' and 'racial passing' usually implies 'passing as white', it is understandable that an overwhelming number of studies of passing focus exclusively on this particular form of passing.

The only attempt to integrate discussions of racial, gender and other forms of passing in a single-author study occurs in the very earliest, Juda Bennett's *The Passing Figure: Racial Confusion in Modern American Literature* (1997).[53] Bennett gives over a chapter to examining 'the contemporary obsession with gender passing' and 'its relation to issues of race and racial passing.'[54] Building on Bennett's work, this book argues that in American literary history, gender passing has, from the outset, been inextricable from racial passing. Indeed, Hildreth's *The Slave; or, Memoirs of Archy Moore* (1836) is a case of *simultaneous* racial and gender passing.[55] Husband and wife Archy and Cassy flee their master (and father), Colonel Moore, when Cassy fears she will no longer be able to repel his incestuous advances. The couple's escape plan is to pass for white, and for Cassy to 'adopt a man's dress, and accompany [Archy] in the character of a younger brother.'[56] In Chapter 3 I focus on two novels by Louise Erdrich which testify to the importance of parallels and intersections between racial and gender passing by foregrounding two characters who pass in order to take up their Catholic vocations: one is a white woman who cross-dresses as a priest; the other a mixedblood woman who passes as white in becoming a nun.[57]

While I acknowledge from the outset the centrality of racial passing to this book, I also insist upon the importance of dislodging its predominance, though not in the ways that critics have previously sought to do so. Wald's solution is to examine examples of white-to-black masquerade alongside black-to-white passing stories. Equally, Baz Dreisinger's work centres on 'American narratives about white people who either envision themselves or are envisioned by others as being or becoming black.'[58] However, the white-to-black focus merely serves to reinforce the supremacy of the white–black racial binary, allowing a whole spectrum of white identities and *nonblack* communities of color to 'pass' out of the picture. Meanwhile, Belluscio argues that the 'critical apparatus of passing should be applied to the literature of white ethnic immigrant groups who came to the shores of the United States' from the 1880s to the 1920s.[59] His examination of black-to-white passing alongside novels written by Jewish and Italian Americans is certainly important. However, Belluscio's decision to discuss his chosen African American authors in separate chapters

from his Jewish and Italian American writers produces the same effect
as Wald's black-white/white-black focus, reinscribing at structural level
a fundamental white–black divide. Here, I emphasise the importance
of ethnic identity to discussions of whiteness, but also to discussions
of black and other nonwhite identities.

As Richard Dyer and others have argued, 'whiteness accrues power
precisely through its ability to "pass" as universal and invisible.'[60]
Historians such as David Roediger, Noel Ignatiev and Matthew Frye
Jacobson have shown that only by exposing the constructedness and
permeability of whiteness – including the existence of multiple
whitenesses rather than a monolithic Whiteness – can its hegemonic
power be overcome.[61] In chapters 4 and 5 I discuss two contemporary
novels, *Caucasia* (1998) and *The Human Stain* (2000), in which the
light-skinned African American protagonists pass not as straight-
forwardly white, but as Jewish. The bodies of Birdie Lee and Coleman
Silk testify to the *unknowability* and *invisibility* of racial difference.
Their existence thus suggests the possibility that difference does not
exist at all. So why do these characters paradoxically choose to *reaffirm*
their difference by passing into a group whose status has historically
oscillated between 'nonwhite', 'off-white' and 'white'?

Equally, I argue in this book that only by revealing the instability of
the category of blackness can the equation of 'race' with 'blackness' be
disputed and ultimately dismantled. Accordingly, a further way
in which this work challenges the overwhelming dominance of the
black-to-white trajectory in discussions of passing is not only to
interrogate whiteness as a fragmented category, but also blackness. If,
as Belluscio argues, a white ethnic subject must 'pass' in order to
become 'American', can a 'black' subject also 'pass' in order to become
'black'? In chapters 2 and 5 I offer passing as black(er) as an under-
theorised and increasingly common variation on the passing theme.
Dreisinger hints at the importance of this phenomenon when she asks
whether African American rappers are passing for black 'when record
executives encourage them to deliver exaggerated performances of
"authentic" blackness.' Whereas for Dreisinger, such 'moments of
black passing for black' are merely the 'starting point' for her work,
'which concerns those who, possessing not even "one drop" of black
blood, cross the color line', here they are a central concern.[62] I use the
unwieldy term 'passing for black(er)' rather than 'passing for blacker'
to indicate that there is nothing 'natural' or 'authentic' about the kind
of blackness such subjects perform. They are merely responding to

what society expects of them as visually 'black' subjects. This kind of passing, which I explore in relation to *Erasure* (2001) and *The White Boy Shuffle* (1996), also features in Spike Lee's film *Bamboozled* (2000). When Pierre Delacroix (Damon Wayans) fails in his attempt to pitch a Cosby-esque TV show to his boss, he comes up instead with *Mantan's New Millennium Minstrel Show*, which he assumes will lead to his dismissal and his release from his contract with the network. However, his boss loves the idea of African Americans blacking up, so the show is made and becomes a hit.

An incidence of passing in which a presumed member of the in-group must 'pass' in order to gain admittance to that in-group involves interrogating the categories traditionally questioned by an act of passing (black/white) *and* the definition(s) of racial passing itself (black-to-white, white-to-black). Passing as black(er) thus provides an opportunity to reconsider the rigid terms in which 'passing' itself has been conceived. In Wald's discussion of Eddie Murphy's 'White Like Me', she observes that the sketch represents 'a pointed inquiry into the visual protocols of racial classification', because it lays bare 'how whiteness is symbolized through an array of seemingly embodied signs, from "white" skin colour to "white" ways of walking and talking.'[63] Passing for black(er) reveals that there is a subtle, but important, distinction between the mythical 'embodied signs' of skin color (or hair texture, or fingernails) and those that can more easily be performed or assumed, such as walking and talking and, crucially, writing.

In *The White Boy Shuffle* (1996) and *Erasure* (2001), the protagonists are indisputably 'black' according to the visual economy of race, the most oft-deployed means of ascertaining racial identity. However, they are seen as 'white' or racially ambiguous in terms of their class background, cultural affiliations, modes of behaviour and so on. Passing for black(er) thus allows for the examination of the heretofore under-explored relationship between racial passing and blackface minstrelsy. After all, Gunnar's performance of exaggerated blackness while attending a predominantly white high school is imagined as 'rubbing burnt cork over our already dusky features' (Beatty, p. 170). In her discussion of Griffin's *Black Like Me*, in which the white journalist recounts his passing as black in the American South by using medications, cosmetics and a sunlamp, Wald does not once mention minstrelsy. Indeed, the term only appears on one occasion in her entire study, which is astonishing given that she focuses on instances of white-to-black as well as black-to-white passing. Although I may privilege racial passing here, then, I do not do so to the exclusion of other types of passing, as most other single-author studies do.[64] This book thus represents a unique attempt to integrate discussions of various typologies of passing (racial, gender, authorial) in a variety of contemporary American novels.

Like the novels' protagonists, their writers also come from diverse, or sometimes ambiguous, racial and/or ethnic backgrounds. I focus on writers who identify as white, African American or mixed race, but this book also explores fiction by authors of Jewish American, German American-Ojibway and Greek American ancestry. The diversity of authors is yet another way in which I challenge the overwhelming critical preoccupation with the black/white racial binary in narratives of passing. It also paves the way for an exploration of the ways in which passing operates at a formal level. The contemporary texts with which I am concerned are preoccupied with the issue of authorship: passing features as a plot device *and* as an authorial response to the demands of 'authenticity' placed upon their authors, the expectation or belief that certain writers are or should be treating the printed page as a stage upon which to describe their own personal experiences, even when their work is most emphatically fiction. It is no coincidence that among the novels of the eight contemporary authors explored in this work, six feature writer-protagonists, whether published authors (*Erasure, The White Boy Shuffle*), aspiring memoirists (*The Human Stain* (2000), *Middlesex* (2002)), a voracious letter-writer (*The Last Report on the Miracles at Little No Horse* (2001)) or a child writing a 'novel' as a homework project (*Caucasia* (1998)).

The diverse backgrounds of the authors studied here also facilitate the explosion of the enduring, and deeply problematic, assumption that African American writers – because of their racial positioning – simply write 'better' '(tragic) mulatto/a' characters and/or passing narratives. For example, despite Bost's professed reluctance 'to draw borders where borders are fluid', she finds that characters created by African American writers are 'more empowered and fluid' than the tragic mulatto heroines of white writers.[65] Meanwhile, Elizabeth Fox-Genovese claims that black women writers 'have informed [the trope of the tragic mulatta] with a complexity that no black man or white woman has easily appreciated.'[66] And Jean Fagin Yellin asserts that 'when African-American writers dramatize a woman of mixed race, she is very different from the Tragic Mulatto; this woman embraces her black identity, lives in the black community, and chooses a black man.'[67] Even Belluscio, who identifies the urgent need to move beyond 'the African American canon' in order to explode the 'black/white racial binary' surrounding passing narratives, only examines one black-to-white passing narrative written by a nonblack writer, William Dean Howells's *An Imperative Duty* (1891).[68] These generalisations on African American representations of passing and the '(tragic) mulatto/a', though understandable from a political standpoint, are quite simply misleading.

The structure of the book reflects my effort to destabilise the prominence of the black–white trajectory in existing discussions of passing, at the expense of other kinds of racial, ethnic and/or gender passing. Chapter 2 explores *The Bondwoman's Narrative* and Percival Everett's *Erasure* (2001), suggesting that in these texts the acts of passing and writing are inseparable, especially where the racial 'authenticity' of the author is in question. *The Bondwoman's Narrative* is a narrative of standard racial passing, featuring a legally black character who passes as white; Monk Ellison in *Erasure*, meanwhile, is passing as black(er). Chapter 3 offers an analysis of two novels by Louise Erdrich, in which race and gender collide with Christianity as a third, and less-studied, category of affiliation. While my interest in *Tracks* (1988) alongside *The Last Report on the Miracles at Little No Horse* (2001) may seem anomalous given the 1996–2006 focus of the rest of the book, it is impossible to discuss one Erdrich novel without the other for, as is the case with all of her reservation works, historical settings and characters overlap to such an extent that neither novel constitutes a stand-alone text.

In Chapter 4 I discuss a novel written in the first person which purports to be its protagonist's memoirs – *Middlesex* (2002) – and a second, *Caucasia* (1998), which, though fiction, self-consciously situates itself amid an array of mixed race memoirs published around the same time. Just as the protagonists' bodies are indeterminate, one in terms of her race, the other in terms of his/her gender, so the *form* of the novels and the writers' views on authorship remain ambiguous. Chapter 5 returns to the notion of passing for black(er) in Paul Beatty's *The White Boy Shuffle*, also a novel passing as its protagonist's memoirs, comparing it with Philip Roth's *The Human Stain* (2000) in terms of their protagonists' writerly and sporting pursuits. The conclusion draws together ideas from the entire book to interrogate the contemporary publishing phenomenon known as the 'misery memoir', and its relationship to passing. From Hildreth's *The Slave; or, Memoirs of Archy Moore* to Johnson's *Autobiography of an Ex-Colored Man*, to recent controversies involving J.T. LeRoy, James Frey and Margaret B. Jones, the issues of 'authenticity' and 'passing', as both plot device and authorial comment and strategy, remain inextricably linked.

Notes

1 TWIZ TV, *The L Word* Transcripts, www.twiztv.com/cgi-bin/thelword.cgi?episode=http://www.l-word.com/transcripts/tx/1x08listenup.html (26 May 2006).

2 Bette's question is remarkably similar, for example, to light-skinned Angie's query of her mother in Claude McKay's 1932 story, 'Near-White.' Angie asks: 'But if some colored people are light enough to live like white, mother, why should there be such a fuss? . . . Why should they live colored when they could be happier living white?', in *An Anthology of Interracial Literature: Black–White Contacts in the Old World and the New*, ed. Werner Sollors (New York: New York University Press, 2004), pp. 559–72 (p. 568).

3 'Listen Up', *The L Word*, Showtime (7 March 2004).

4 I place 'passing' in quotation marks in this first instance to indicate the scepticism with which I view the term, depending as it does on completely arbitrary designations of categories supposedly being transgressed. For ease of reading, however, I do not use quotation marks throughout this book, but ask that they be taken as read.

5 Some other recent examples of popular culture engagements with and variations upon the trope of racial and/or gender passing include the films *The Associate* (1996) and *White Chicks* (2004), and the FX reality TV show, *Black. White.* (2006).

6 This is the case in monographs by Kathleen Pfeiffer (covering the period 1892–1929), Mar Gallego (1912–32), Carlyle Van Thompson (1900–32) and Stephen J. Belluscio (1891–31). Kathleen Pfeiffer, *Race Passing and American Individualism* (Amherst: University of Massachusetts Press, 2003); Mar Gallego, *Passing Novels in the Harlem Renaissance: An Alternative Concept of African American Identity* (Munster: Lit Verlag, 2003); Carlyle Van Thompson, *The Tragic Black Buck: Racial Masquerading in the American Literary Imagination* (New York: Peter Lang, 2004) and Stephen J. Belluscio, *To Be Suddenly White: Literary Realism and Racial Passing* (Columbia: University of Missouri Press, 2006).

7 Juda Bennett, *The Passing Figure: Racial Confusion in Modern American Literature* (New York: Peter Lang, 1997), p. 1.

8   Werner Sollors, *Neither Black Nor White Yet Both: Thematic Explorations of Interracial Literature* (New York: Oxford University Press, 1997), pp. 247, 284.

9   Gayle Wald, *Crossing the Line: Racial Passing in Twentieth-Century U.S. Literature and Culture* (Durham, NC: Duke University Press, 2000), p. 23.

10 Michele Elam, 'Passing in the Post-Race Era: Danzy Senna, Philip Roth, and Colson Whitehead', *African American Review* 41.4 (2007), 749–68 (751).

11 Lynn Norment, 'Who's Black And Who's Not?: New Ethnicity Raises Provocative Questions about Racial Identity', *Ebony* (March 1990), 134–9 (136).

12 Ibid., 136.

13 See, for example, Leon E. Wynter, *American Skin: Pop Culture, Big Business, and the End of White America* (New York: Crown, 2002), p. 167.

14 Although the writers of *The L Word*, and not Beals, must be given credit for the complexities of Bette and Yolanda's exchanges, Beals herself reports that after agreeing to play Bette, she requested that show creator Ilene Chaiken write biraciality into Bette's character, which Chaiken did. Pam Grier's character, who was originally written as Bette's friend, was rewritten as Bette's half-sister. Adam Sternbergh, 'Back in a Flash', *New York Magazine* (21 February 2005) http://newyorkmetro.com/nymetro/arts/tv/11057/ (27 May 2006).

15 Deborah McDowell's claim that *Passing* is 'passing' as a tale of racial passing and that it is a veiled exploration of lesbian desire sparked a long-overdue renewal of interest in Larsen's neglected novella, ' "It's Not Safe. Not Safe at All": Sexuality in Nella Larsen's *Passing*', in *The Lesbian and Gay Studies Reader*, ed. Henry Abelove, Michèle Ana Barale and David M. Halperin (New York: Routledge, 1993), pp. 616–25.

16 Amy Robinson, 'It Takes One to Know One: Passing and Communities of Common Interest', *Critical Inquiry* 20.4 (1994), 715–36 (715).

17 Gish Jen, 'An Ethnic Trump', *New York Times Magazine* (7 July 1996), 50.

18 Michael T. Gilmore, *Surface and Depth: The Quest for Legibility in American Culture* (New York: Oxford University Press, 2003), p. 176.

19 William Faulkner, *Light in August* (1932; London: Picador, 1993), pp. 28, 91, 94, 113, 208.

20 Bennett, *Passing Figure*, p. 36.

21 Frederick Douglass recounts how he wrote passes for himself and four other slaves for their intended escape, which was subsequently foiled. *Narrative of the Life of Frederick Douglass, An American Slave* (1845), in *Narrative of the Life of Frederick Douglass, An American Slave and*

Incidents in the Life of a Slave Girl, ed. Kwame Anthony Appiah (New York: Random House, 2000), p. 84.

22 See, for example, William Craft, *Running a Thousand Miles for Freedom: The Escape of William and Ellen Craft* (1860), http://etext.virginia.edu/toc/modeng/public/CraThou.html (13 May 2009).

23 See Sollors, *Neither Black Nor White*, p. 255. Written in the first person, '[t]he book's acceptance as autobiography has been so complete that it has been discredited as false slave narrative; even twentieth-century critics have felt it necessary to point out that it is fiction.' Jean Fagan Yellin, *The Intricate Knot: Black Figures in American Literature, 1776–1863* (New York: New York University Press, 1972), p. 92.

24 Donald C. Goellnicht, 'Passing as Autobiography: James Weldon Johnson's *The Autobiography of an Ex-Colored Man*', *African American Review* 30.1 (1996), 18.

25 James Weldon Johnson, *Along This Way: The Autobiography of James Weldon Johnson* (1933; Harmondsworth: Penguin, 1990), p. 238.

26 Johnson, *Along This Way*, p. 239.

27 Suzanne Bost, *Mulattas and Mestizas: Representing Mixed Identities in the Americas, 1850–2000* (Athens: University of Georgia Press, 2005), p. 6.

28 Kimberly McClain DaCosta, *Making Multiracials: State, Family, and Market in the Redrawing of the Color Line* (Stanford: Stanford University Press, 2007), p. 162.

29 Ibid.

30 Ann Ducille, 'Dyes and Dolls: Multicultural Barbie and the Merchandising of Difference', *Differences* 6.1 (1994), 46–68 (53).

31 Lauren Berlant, 'The Face of America and the State of Emergency', in *Popular Culture: A Reader*, ed. Raiford Guins and Omayra Zaragoza Cruz (London: Sage, 2005), pp. 309–23 (p. 311).

32 Henry Yu, 'How Tiger Woods Lost his Stripes: Post-Nationalist American Studies as a History of Race, Migration, and the Commodification of Culture', in Guins and Cruz, *Popular Culture: A Reader*, pp. 197–210 (p. 200).

33 DaCosta, p. 155.

34 Percival Everett, *Erasure* (2001; London: Faber and Faber, 2004), p. 218. Subsequent references will appear in parentheses in the body of the text.

35 Bost, p. 188.

36 Tracy Curtis, 'Basketball's Demands in Paul Beatty's *The White Boy Shuffle*', in *Upon Further Review: Sports in American Literature*, ed. Michael Cocchiarale and Scott D. Emmert (Westport, CT: Praeger, 2004), pp. 63–73 (p. 64); Paul Beatty, *The White Boy Shuffle* (London: Minerva, 1996), p. 116.

37 Randall Kennedy, *Interracial Intimacies: Sex, Marriage, Identity, and Adoption* (New York: Pantheon, 2003), p. 285.

38 Wald, p. 187.

39 Belluscio, p. 9.

40 Ibid., p. 9.
41 Linda Hutcheon, *The Politics of Postmodernism* (London: Routledge, 1991), p. 10.
42 Ibid., pp. 1–2.
43 Ibid., p. 2.
44 Amy Robinson, 'Forms of Appearance of Value: Homer Plessy and the Politics of Privacy', in *Performance and Cultural Politics*, ed. Elin Diamond (London: Routledge, 1996), pp. 237–61 (p. 237).
45 Phillip Brian Harper, 'Passing for What? Racial Masquerade and the Demands of Upward Mobility', *Callaloo* 21.2 (1998), 381–97 (382).
46 In some instances, racial passing was carried out in some of the most highly charged political situations imaginable. Fair-complexioned Walter White, in his position as chief investigator of lynching for the NAACP in the 1920s, used his light skin to disguise his 'blackness', thus enabling him to go undercover in the South and expose the racial injustices taking place there. Zane Pinchback, the protagonist of the graphic novel *Incognegro* (2008) by Mat Johnson and Warren Pleese, is based on Walter White. Investigative or undercover passing is also undertaken by George Winston in Frank J. Webb's *The Garies and Their Friends* (1857) and Vera Manning in Jessie Fauset's *There Is Confusion* (1924).
47 Carole-Anne Tyler, 'Passing: Narcissism, Identity, and Difference', *Differences* 6:2–3 (1994), 212–48 (213).
48 Wald, p. 15.
49 Belluscio, pp. 9–10.
50 See Leslie Marmon Silko, 'Here's an Odd Artifact for the Fairy-Tale Shelf' (review of *The Beet Queen*), *Studies in American Indian Literature* 10.4 (1986), 178–84 (179).
51 Sollors, *Neither Black Nor White*, p. 247.
52 Wald, p. 14.
53 While Bennett's is the first full-length study of passing, earlier studies that deal with the literary mulatto and miscegenation also confront the subject of passing. See Judith Berzon, *Neither White Nor Black: The Mulatto Character in American Fiction* (New York: New York University Press, 1978) and James Kinney, *Amalgamation!: Race, Sex, and Rhetoric in the Nineteenth-Century Novel* (Westport, CT: Greenwood, 1985).
54 Bennett, *Passing Figure*, p. 2.
55 Sollors, *Neither Black Nor White*, p. 255.
56 Richard Hildreth, *The Slave: or Memoirs of Archy Moore* (1836; Upper Saddle River, NJ: Gregg, 1968), pp. 62–3. Ellen Craft engaged in real-life simultaneous racial and gender passing in 1848, inspiring comparable fictional escape scenes in Harriet Beecher Stowe's *Uncle Tom's Cabin* (1852) and William Wells Brown's *Clotel* (1853).
57 The term 'mixedblood' will be used throughout to denote subjects of mixed white and American Indian ancestry. Although not ideal,

reinforcing the blood quantum discourse, it is preferable to the alternatives 'half-blood' or 'half-breed.'

58 Baz Dreisinger, *Near Black: White-to-Black Passing in American Culture* (Amherst: University of Massachussetts Press, 2008), p. 2.

59 Belluscio, p. 2. Along similar lines, Catherine Rottenberg compares Jewish American texts and African American passing narratives published between 1912 and 1929 to consider 'how subjects have been compelled and encouraged to emulate dominant U.S. norms.' *Performing Americanness: Race, Class, and Gender in Modern African-American and Jewish-American Literature* (Lebanon, NH: University Press of New England, 2008), p. 3.

60 Wald, p. 166.

61 David Roediger, *The Wages of Whiteness: Race and the Making of the American Working Class* (London: Verso, 1991); Noel Ignatiev, *How the Irish became White* (New York: Routledge, 1995) and Matthew Frye Jacobson, *Whiteness of a Different Color: European Immigrants and the Alchemy of Race* (Cambridge, MA: Harvard University Press, 2000).

62 Dreisinger, p. 5.

63 Wald, p. 3.

64 This is true of studies by Wald, Pfeiffer, Van Thompson and Belluscio. See also M. Giulia Fabi, *Passing and the Rise of the African American Novel* (Urbana: University of Illinois Press, 2001). Edited collections on passing, however, do feature essays which interrogate both racial and other types of passing: Elaine K. Ginsberg (ed.), *Passing and the Fictions of Identity* (Durham, NC: Duke University Press, 1996) and María Carla Sánchez and Linda Schlossberg (eds), *Passing: Identity and Interpretation in Sexuality, Race, and Religion* (New York: New York University Press, 2001).

65 Bost, pp. 17, 22.

66 Elizabeth Fox-Genovese, 'Slavery, Race, and the Figure of the Tragic Mulatta, or, The Ghost of Southern History in the Writing of African-American Women', in *Haunted Bodies: Gender and Southern Texts*, ed. Anne Goodwyn Jones and Susan V. Donaldson (Charlottesville: University of Virginia Press, 1997), pp. 464–91 (p. 469).

67 Jean Fagan Yellin, *Women and Sisters: The Antislavery Feminists in American Culture* (New Haven: Yale University Press, 1989), pp. 197–8, n. 52.

68 Belluscio, pp. 1–2.

2

Living parchments, human documents: passing, racial identity and the literary marketplace

These marks are his signature, his physiological autograph, so to speak, and this autograph cannot be counterfeited, nor can he disguise it or hide it away, nor can it become illegible by the wear and mutations of time.

Mark Twain, *Pudd'nhead Wilson* (1894)[1]

Passing, it has been variously argued, no longer seems to engage contemporary novelists. Juda Bennett, for example, asserts in 2001 that the 'long list of authors from the first half of the twentieth century . . . is hardly balanced by the short list of contemporary writers who have addressed this figure of racial ambiguity.'[2] The 'short list' which Bennett provides consists of Charles Johnson's *Oxherding Tale* (1982), Danzy Senna's *Caucasia* (1998), Ralph Ellison's *Juneteenth* (1999) and Philip Roth's *The Human Stain* (2000).[3] Bennett argues that contemporary novelists, specifically Toni Morrison, evoke the passing myth 'without actually representing the phenomenon of passing, and in this way Morrison decenters and deforms the passing figure.'[4] This new kind of fiction, Bennett asserts, 'requires our participation, promising wonderful opportunities for epiphanies that are no longer about theme or character but about the reading process itself.'[5] Thus, Morrison's short story 'Recitatif' (1983) calls readers' attention to their preoccupation with reading race by revealing to the reader that one of the protagonists is white and the other black, but refusing to designate which is which.[6]

While texts such as Morrison's are 'about' reading, this chapter focuses on contemporary fiction that deploys passing plots in order to consider the act of *writing*. In other words, it extends Bennett's analysis by examining texts that invoke passing at both a narrative and meta-narrative level in order to reflect upon the politics of the literary marketplace. Indeed, in his recent work on African American writers and white publishers, John K. Young implicitly makes this connection when he claims that

> The American publishing industry ... has historically inscribed a mythologized version of the 'black experience' onto all works marked by race, in much the same way that, for much of the twentieth century, American jurists ascribed an innate blackness to all bodies marked as such, even if at the invisible and seemingly unknowable level of a drop of blood.[7]

The logic of passing is the logic of the one-drop rule: subjects can only be seen to be passing if they are legally and socially defined as black despite their 'invisible blackness', to borrow Joel Williamson's term.[8] Young returns to the legal shift instituted by the Plessy v. Ferguson decision of 1896, arguing that it has its cultural analogue in 'a similar duality for African American authors, who are marked in advertisements, prefaces, and other paratextual material as black, even when their texts themselves might belie such strict classification.'[9] If, as Amy Robinson puts it, the racial passer exposes the fallacy that 'appearance is assumed to bear a mimetic relation to identity, but in fact does not and can not', so publishers, readers and reviewers often demand that African American authors' work 'bear a mimetic relation' to their racialised experience, based on their own assumptions regarding what this experience entails.'[10] In this chapter, then, racial passing and writing emerge as analogous pursuits. Narrative passing prompts readers to question the degree to which the passer can control (and/or transcend) his or her (raced) body and how this body is perceived by others. Meta-narrative passing involves the self-reflexive exploration of the extent to which the author is in control of the text that s/he produces and how it is received and marketed.

While Young's insightful study focuses on the literary marketplace in the twentieth century, the demands made of African American writers by publishers, critics and readers at the beginning of the twenty-first century cannot be fully historicised without reference to the nineteenth-century publishing industry. The discussion that follows foregrounds a nineteenth-century African American text 'discovered' at the turn of the twenty-first (Hannah Crafts's *The Bondwoman's Narrative*) and a contemporary African American novel (Percival Everett's *Erasure*) in order to reveal the extent to which continuities exist between nineteenth-century and contemporary representations of passing, and to argue that such continuities are inextricably bound up with the issue of authorship and the act of writing. Examining *Erasure* (2001) alongside *The Bondwoman's Narrative* (2002) enables a consideration of the ongoing expectations of white and black publishers, reviewers and readers regarding African American writing from the mid-nineteenth century, to the mid-twentieth (Irving Howe's views on Richard Wright, Ralph Ellison and James Baldwin) to the turn of the twenty-first (Oprah's Book Club). It is for these reasons that I open with a quotation from Mark Twain's *Pudd'nhead Wilson*, a work notable for its Janus face. Set predominantly in 1853 but published in 1894, its plot, featuring a murder case solved by recourse to fingerprints, now appears almost prescient. Twain's evocation of the 'signature', the 'autograph' and its (il)legibility in relation to fingerprints resonates with conceptions of authorship and authenticity, and the connections between the two. A signature serves to authenticate a document, confirming the identity of its author and/or the veracity of its content. In this chapter, the novels I examine foreground such a slippage between body and text, particularly as this pertains to the idea of authorial authenticity implied by the 'signature' or 'autograph.'

In opening with a quotation from *Pudd'nhead Wilson*, I echo Percival Everett, who begins *Erasure* by referring epigraphically to the same work, but in a slightly more oblique way: 'I could never tell a lie that anybody would doubt, nor a truth that anybody would believe.' Although this is a quotation from Twain's *Following the Equator* (1897), in that work, Twain attributes his chapter heading quotations to the fictional character Pudd'nhead Wilson. Apart from succinctly capturing the novel's preoccupation with the slipperiness of notions of truth/falsehood and authentic/fake, Everett's early reference to Twain also anticipates his use of *mise-en-abîme* in *Erasure*'s novel-within-a-novel structure.

In *Erasure*, the twelfth novel of seventeen by Everett, black experimental novelist Thelonious Ellison, nicknamed 'Monk', is lacking in recent publishing success because, as his agent tells him, his writing is 'not black enough' (p. 49). Finding himself suddenly responsible for caring for his aging mother and struggling financially, he pens a satirical ghetto novel under the pseudonym of Stagg R. Leigh. In deciding to do so, he draws his inspiration from the success of Juanita Mae Jenkins, whose *We's Lives in Da Ghetto* is promoted on the Kenya Dunston Show, a thinly veiled parody of Oprah's Book Club, and is proving a lucrative publishing phenomenon. As Stagg R. Leigh, middle-class Monk thus passes for black(er). Taken at face value, the novel – initially called *My Pafology* but later retitled *Fuck* – is an updated version of Wright's *Native Son* (1940) and enjoys both critical and popular acclaim. *Erasure* ends on the cusp of Monk's exposure, when *Fuck* is adjudged the winner of a literary prize by a panel of experts on which he himself sits, despite the fact that Monk, his identity still a secret, inveighs against his own novel. The 'erasure' of the title thus refers to Monk's own identity, which disappears with his complicity in maintaining the media phenomenon of his pseudonymous other. It also concerns the act of writing itself which, as Kathleen Pfeiffer argues, is 'like passing, an act of self-generation; both are independently and willfully creative acts.'[11] In *Erasure*, however, writing is presented ambivalently as a form of simultaneous invention *and* destruction, creativity *and* erasure.

Fuck is not Monk's first attempt at writing naturalistic fiction. In 1988 he enjoys some mild success with a 'realistic' novel called *The Second Failure*, 'about a young man who can't understand why his white-looking mother is ostracised by the black community' (p. 69). After his mother commits suicide, the protagonist 'realizes that he must attack the culture and so becomes a terrorist, killing blacks and whites who behave as racists' (p. 70). Monk 'hated writing', 'hated reading' and 'hated thinking about' *The Second Failure* (p. 70). Of course, the novel is aptly named, for *Fuck* is nothing if not a 'second failure' for Monk, a text that exploits a *different* though equally widespread, popular and easily recognisable stereotype of black life and which, like *The Second Failure*, also sells well. Through *The Second Failure* Everett connects the over-determination of the tragic mulatta in African American fiction to the contemporary literary stereotype comprised of Van Go Jenkins, the protagonist of *Fuck*, and his ilk. By engaging in an act of authorial (and thus invisible) passing, Monk hopes to transcend his raced body and simultaneously expose and explode the commodification of degrading racial stereotypes. In so doing, Everett explores whether such incorporeal passing might be more liberating and perhaps empowering than the embodied passing of countless literary tragic mulattas, or whether one's textual output can ultimately be detached from its author's body.

The Bondwoman's Narrative describes the attempted escape of two mixed race women, one slave and the other free, from a plantation in the antebellum South. When Hannah, the light-skinned slave-narrator, discovers that her beautiful new mistress has black ancestry and is being blackmailed by the ruthless lawyer, Mr. Trappe, who knows her secret, the two women flee their home, Lindendale, together. In this novel, therefore, there are two mulattas – Hannah's beautiful mistress, the conventional 'tragic mulatta', and Hannah, a feistier, more proactive version. Born into property and privilege as a free white woman, Hannah's mistress is unable, in both mind and body, to endure the prospect of being sold into slavery that attends her reversal of fortune and suffers an untimely death less than half way through the novel.[12] The slave, Hannah, on the other hand, passes up the opportunity to pass on at least one occasion (p. 116). Not conventionally beautiful (she is described as 'excessively homely' (p. 103)), Hannah can more easily deflect the lustful white male gaze. She eventually escapes to freedom, is reunited with her mother, marries and becomes a writer. Believed by many to have been penned by a fugitive slave, 'Hannah Crafts', some time between 1855 and 1861, *The Bondwoman's Narrative* was published by Warner Books on 2 April 2002, some fourteen months after Henry Louis Gates, Jr. acquired the manuscript at auction for eight hundred dollars in February 2001. In his introduction to the novel, Gates recounts his meticulous campaign to determine the author's race, sex and legal status (slave or free). The novel provides an opportunity to analyse the degree to which the contemporary literary scene is dominated by similar concerns to those which characterised the 1850s, particularly if the novelist is, or might be, African American.

Before continuing, it is necessary to explain precisely what is meant by some of the terms that arise in the discussion that follows. This chapter pivots upon *Erasure* because it allows for the articulation of two under-theorised dimensions to passing. The first is the notion of passing as black(er). Phillip Brian Harper elucidates two types of racial passing in the US context – the 'standard racial pass', in which 'a light-skinned person legally designated as black passes for white', and the 'reverse racial pass', in which 'a person legally recognized as white effectively functions as a non-white person in any quarter of the social arena.'[13] The passing as black(er) in which Monk Ellison is engaged thus offers a potential solution to or, at the very least, a different perspective on, the 'problem' that passing tends to reinscribe the categories it purports to explode. By passing as black(er), he exposes the arbitrariness of racial categories based on physical appearance in the same way as the 'standard' or 'reverse' racial pass. Passing as black(er) also facilitates an assessment of the ways in which what Michael Rogin calls America's two tropes in race mixing – blacking up and the tragic mulatta who tries to pass – intersect.[14]

Second, Monk's passing as black(er) is not effected in a *physical* sense. In other words, Monk does not, initially at least, present himself in person as something other than his 'true' self, as the racial passer does in conventional passing stories. His passing is carried out through the act of writing. He assumes an authorial disguise, offering Stagg R. Leigh's novel as a text to be read in place of Monk's own body. This is what I mean when I distinguish between 'incorporeal/disembodied' versus 'corporeal/embodied' passing. That Monk subsequently finds himself obliged to incarnate Stagg R. Leigh speaks volumes about the degree to which passing is an act that collapses body and text as one and the same, no matter how much Monk endeavours to separate them by substituting his written text for his material body.

Searching for Hannah Crafts

Hannah, the narrator of *The Bondwoman's Narrative*, also attempts to transcend her body through writing and, indeed, reading. The key issue for both Monk Ellison and Hannah is the relationship between the black body that *generates* a text to be read (the African American author) and the black body that, in white America, has *constituted* (and still constitutes) a text to be read. Thus, publishers, critics and the reading public alike demand that Monk explore subjects that *they* deem appropriate to his racial affiliation because they have seen and *read* the author's photograph on one of his book jackets (*Erasure*, p. 49). Everett thus highlights the tendency within the publishing industry to reduce the African American author to his or her race(d body). For Hannah, literacy becomes a strategy for taking command of the gaze that would otherwise control her white-looking slave body. In the novel's opening, she immediately anticipates accusations that she does not have the requisite learning to attempt 'to write these pages' by positing her skills at 'observing things and events' (*Bondwoman*, p. 5). Instead of books, Hannah studies 'faces and characters' (p. 27). If the mulatta protagonist often finds herself the *object* of an inquisitive gaze, here the mulatta protagonist usurps this gaze, scrutinising 'faces and characters' in order to produce a piece of writing.

Subsequently, Hannah juxtaposes a body-as-text motif alongside her own desire to acquire literacy. In one paragraph, she bemoans the injustice of a society that condemns those of African ancestry to a life of slavery, especially since her 'complexion was almost white, and the obnoxious descent could not be readily *traced*' (p. 6, emphasis added). Here, she posits her body's resistance to being read as black. A few lines later she expresses her earnest wish to learn how to read. She is thus attempting, firstly, to avoid being read as black and to shift the focus away from her body altogether and secondly, to empower herself by acquiring literacy. She wishes to be the agent and not the object of an act of reading. Just as the passer conceals, wittingly or unwittingly, his or her African American heritage, Hannah (in a self-reflexive nod from the author) hides the book she is using to teach herself to read (p. 7).

Hannah's white slave body disrupts the comfortable correspondence (black equals slave, white equals free) constructed by white, antebellum America, and exposes the fallacy that one's race is bodily inscribed. The myth that certain physical clues – such as dark skin or kinky hair – can provide categorical evidence of one's racial identity is a recurring motif in nineteenth-century narratives of racial passing, of which *The Bondwoman's Narrative* in an example. The absence of such markers on the white-but-legally-black body enabled the passer to transcend his or her socially prescribed status. In legal terms, the white-looking black body was thus conceived as a 'forgery by nature.'[15] Of course, the passer's apparent freedom to choose his or her race and by extension, social status, is double-edged because in order to erase his or her legal blackness, the passing figure must always depend on the evidence of his or her physical whiteness. In other words, the body still constitutes a *text* but in order to pass, he or she relies on being read as white rather than black. The passer can thus transcend his or her social status, but can never transcend his or her body.[16] Hannah's efforts to call attention to her acquisition of literacy and simultaneously de-emphasise her body-as-text reveal the intimate connection between the contemporaneous (nineteenth-century) and contemporary (twenty-first century) contexts of the book's composition and publication respectively. First, they are reminiscent of the circumstances surrounding the production of nineteenth-century slave testimony, in which the ex-slave's *narrative* focus on his or her acquisition of literacy is counterbalanced by his or her *actual* post-publication treatment as a type of text by the reading (in both senses) public. Second, Hannah's attempt to privilege text over body emerges as unintentionally ironic, given the contemporary preoccupation with ascertaining the racial identity of *The Bondwoman's Narrative.*

In the nineteenth century it was not enough for a former slave to *describe* in writing his or her acquisition of literacy (and by extension, confirm his or her authorship of the text) or, indeed, for his or her learning to be verified by a white sponsor. His or her body was summoned as an additional source of evidence of the truth of the slave experiences reported, often in the form of bodily inscribed proof such as scars or welts inflicted through whippings and physical abuse. Literacy is an important skill for the slave to acquire, but it in no way guarantees the autonomy that it may, on the surface, appear to promise. This point is quite forcefully made in *The Bondwoman's Narrative* when Hannah is obliged to transcribe a letter dictated to her by her would-be mistress. Mrs. Wheeler is attempting to acquire Hannah at a knock-down price, so she writes to her owner and claims that he should sell her because she is tearful and over-religious and 'would be likely to run away the first opportunity' (p. 153). Hannah hesitates 'to pen such a libel' on herself but although she is doing the writing, she has no control over what she is writing. Thus, any agency that the ex-slave subject acquires by producing an account of his or her life experiences is tempered, and even negated, by the reading public's repeated denial of such subjectivity through the objectification of the slave body, a seemingly required companion text to his or her written narrative.[17]

Of course, the necessity of the bodily presence of ex-slave authors on the lecture circuit was a situation that arose largely of the abolitionists' own making. As Laura Browder argues, the power of slave testimony lay in its *representative* rather than in its individual value, the message being that the institution of slavery itself is inherently wrong, not just the mistreatment of individual slaves at the hands of individual slaveholders. For this to be understood, slave narratives needed to be written in a form which is recognisable to and comfortable for a white readership. Thus, while the value of a slave narrative rested on its authenticity, 'authenticity depended on strict adherence to a set of generic conventions.'[18] The treatment by abolitionists of the ex-slave body as a type of text was an effect of their fear of passing: the very real possibility that black or white writers would impersonate ex-slaves by producing ersatz slave testimony. To ensure the effectiveness of their political agenda, abolitionists depended on the absolute veracity of slave narratives, for a narrative written by white abolitionists could

quickly be dismissed as propaganda by slaveholders and their sympa-
thisers.[19] False testimony could irreparably damage their campaign.
To circumvent the risk of slave narrative hoaxes, abolitionists encouraged ex-slave authors to present themselves on the lecture circuit to
be interrogated by an audience about their experiences, and to display
their scarred bodies as evidence of the torture they endured as slaves.[20]
The inhumane institution that was slavery could thus literally be read
upon the bodies of fugitive slaves and their corporeal presence became
the most effective means of authenticating their written tales.

Similarly, in *Erasure*, various interested parties express a desire
to meet Stagg R. Leigh in the flesh. In the case of Paula Baderman,
his Random House editor, Monk declines, preferring the disembodied disguise offered by the telephone. However, when Hollywood
producer Wiley Morgenstein offers him three million dollars for the
film rights to the book, he agrees to a meeting. He also appears on the
Kenya Dunston Show, Everett's nod to the Oprah Winfrey Show, but
is interviewed behind a screen. Despite his best efforts at authorial
disembodiment, therefore, Monk finds himself obliged to incarnate
Stagg R. Leigh. This culminates in the ceremony for the literary
award which Monk attends as both a judge and, as Stagg R. Leigh, the
winner.

What Hannah attempts to avoid *within* the text of *The Bondwoman's Narrative* is the kind of speculation *surrounding* the publication of the text: the obsession with posthumously circumscribing the
body of its author. While Monk sees himself as a 'hermeneutic sleuth'
(*Erasure*, p. 31), the publicity surrounding the publication of a series of
recovered novels by black women writers in the past few decades,
including *The Bondwoman's Narrative*, demonstrates the degree to
which the author of a text may find himself or herself the object, rather
than the subject, of an investigation. Henry Louis Gates, Jr. has long
been at the forefront of this effort to find and reprint long-forgotten
manuscripts by African American women, having in 1982 successfully
authenticated the autobiographical novel *Our Nig* (1859) as the earliest
novel published by an African American woman, Harriet E. Wilson,
and the first African American novel to be published in the United
States. Yet the detective work both of ascertaining the race of
these long-dead writers and of evaluating their originary nature is a
collaborative effort in which new 'finds' often displace previous ones.

In another well-publicised recent case, the controversy surrounding
the authorship of *The Bondwoman's Narrative* was followed, in

February 2005, by a debate on the racial identity of Emma Dunham Kelley-Hawkins, author of *Megda* (1891) and *Four Girls at Cottage City* (1895). These novels, long out of print, had been published in 1988 as part of Oxford University Press's forty-volume *Schomburg Library of Nineteenth-Century Black Women Writers*, a series edited by Gates. However, in the process of researching Kelley-Hawkins's life in preparation to write a biographical entry on the author for *African American National Biography*, Brandeis doctoral student Holly Jackson discovered convincing evidence of Kelley-Hawkins's lack of African American ancestry. For Jackson, a likely reason that Kelley had been received as a black author was the photograph of her that has circulated with *Megda* since its first edition in 1891, providing 'final assurance that the work constitutes African American literature.'[21] Jackson's claim bears out Young's assertion regarding the importance of paratextual material in establishing authors as 'black', just as it substantiates Monk's suspicion that his novels are not well-received because their non-racially marked content appears to contradict his racially marked author photograph.

Finally, even when an author's race is not in doubt, issues of genre are still debated. For example, after the publication in October 2006 of Julia C. Collins's novel, *The Curse of Caste*, originally serialised in the *Christian Register* in 1865, the editor and eminent critic William Andrews argued that Collins's work deserves to be recognised as the first novel published by an African American woman, displacing both *Our Nig* and *The Bondwoman's Narrative*, because the autobiographical content of the last two prevents their being categorised as fiction. Obviously, this argument rests on the assumption that these texts are, in fact, autobiographical; however, given the ongoing investigation into Crafts's identity, this cannot be said to be more than a provisional claim.

In Warner Books' press release Gates is cast as a kind of sleuth by his fellow scholars, credentials established by his previous authenticating endeavours. Nellie Y. McKay says: 'Once again, the field of black literature and culture is the beneficiary of Professor Gates's incredible investigative [*sic*]' and David Brion Davis calls the novel a 'spectacular discovery' and an 'astonishing tale of meticulous research and detective work.'[22] Gates himself, writing in the *New York Times*, describes his investigation into the author's identity, the relationship of which to sleuthing is underlined by the expertise offered by Dr. Joe Nickell, 'an historical-document examiner' who has also worked as a private investigator (Crafts, p. 284).[23] Excerpts from Nickell's report, which is appended in full at the end of *The Bondwoman's Narrative*, are quoted by Gates in his introduction to the novel.

Gates also includes an essay by Nickell in *In Search of Hannah Crafts: Critical Essays on The Bondwoman's Narrative*, in which Nina Baym and Katherine E. Flynn respectively pursue the two possible lines of inquiry initiated by Gates, one leading to Hannah Vincent, the other to Jane Johnson.[24] In 'Searching for Hannah Crafts', Nickell reinforces the notion of the author as the subject of a criminal investigation, an idea which is present in the title of the collection and the almost identical title of Nickell's essay. He offers 'an updated profile of "Hannah Crafts." We are still looking for a female writer, who was relatively young at the time of composition, which dates from between 1855 (the escape of Wheeler's slave, Jane Johnson) and 1861 (the advent of secession and war).'[25] What is also fascinating about Nickell's essay is the degree to which he personifies the manuscript of *The Bondwoman's Narrative*, introducing a slippage between author and text. Gates and Laurence Kirschbaum of Time Warner Trade Publishing gave him 'a wonderful opportunity to meet the mystery author when they commissioned me to authenticate the manuscript' and Nickell 'lived with it for six weeks.'[26] In the absence of the author's material body which can be read, the author's race and gender are read through his or her textual output.

The significance of *The Bondwoman's Narrative*, as Gates would have it, is that, if authenticated as authored by a fugitive slave, the novel may represent a unique opportunity to read a nineteenth-century African American text unmediated by white editors and sponsors:

> Between us and them, between a twenty-first-century readership and the pre-edited consciousness of even one fugitive slave, often stands an editorial apparatus reflective of an abolitionist ideology, to some degree or another; here, on the other hand, perhaps for the first time, we could experience *a pristine encounter*. (*Bondwoman*, p. xxxiii, emphasis added)

Gates is referring to white abolitionists' tendency to print authenticating documents before and after the slave narrative itself. A frontispiece portrait and testimonial letters declared that the subject existed and was who he said he was. According to Raymond Hedin, in the slave narrative such editorial intervention 'relegates the narrator's words to the status of middle, defined, as all literary middles are, by its relationship to the beginning and the end, thus creating the impression that the narrative proper is a "means" serving its white audience's "ends." '[27]

Ironically, the framework of the Gates-edited *Bondwoman's Narrative* reproduces exactly such an effect of mediation. The two-hundred-and-thirty-four-page novel is sandwiched between Gates's introduction at the start (one hundred pages) and textual annotations, Joe Nickell's report on Crafts's handwriting, appendices and other items at the end (a further seventy-eight pages). In other words, the reader of the Gates-edited *Bondwoman's Narrative* has about as much chance of 'a pristine encounter' as with any African American-authored text published in the nineteenth century. As Benjamin Soskis argues, 'Gates has, in a way, inherited the role of the white abolitionists whose introductory remarks assured the reading public as to the authenticity of slave testimony.'[28] Gates's term 'pristine encounter' is an interesting turn of phrase, implying that a text may be pure or, indeed, impure, just as the 'blood' of the passer is not, despite appearances, 'pristinely' white.

Suffering biographies

Nineteenth-century slave narratives evidence a tension between the demand that each individual's autobiography be true and verifiable and that it also be representative of 'an undifferentiated sameness of existence' under slavery.[29] This conflict between individuality and representative sameness persists today in the expectation that African American authors – and, arguably, all 'ethnic' writers and writers of color – should at once write from personal experience (autobiography) *and* of 'the' African American (or 'ethnic') experience in general (sociology). In *Erasure* these demands – and, indeed, the tension between them – emerge in two ways. First, by evoking the Kenya Dunston Show, Everett elucidates one of the key means by which such demands are made manifest in the contemporary literary marketplace: through book clubs, especially the phenomenon that is Oprah's Book Club.[30] Second, through allusions to Ralph Ellison's *Invisible Man* (1952), Everett reminds readers that such debates have a long history in African American letters.

In *Erasure* the attempt to resolve the seemingly incompatible demands of autobiography and sociology and the facility with which 'authenticity' may be faked are evident in the publicity surrounding the appearance of Juanita Mae Jenkins's book, *We's Lives in Da*

Ghetto, the novel which serves, in part, as Monk's motivation in writing *My Pafology*.[31] When Monk sees Jenkins on the Kenya Dunston Show, she reveals that she is from neither the (rural) South nor from (urban) Harlem, the acceptable bastions of an authentic African American identity, but from Akron, Ohio (*Erasure*, p. 61). Her inspiration for the novel derives from having spent 'a couple of days' in Harlem with relatives when she was twelve years old. But despite the fact that biographical details do not accord with 'authentic' African American identity, as may be perceived by the reading public, this does not disqualify her from praise for writing convincingly and representatively of 'the' African American experience. Thus, one reviewer extols the 'verisimilitude' of Jenkins's novel, noting that 'one can actually hear the voices of her people as they make their way through the experience which is and can only be Black America' (p. 46). ✈

Oprah's Book Club is known for emphasising the redemptive possibilities of reading (auto)biography or, indeed, reading fiction *as* (auto)biography. Oprah Winfrey, who launched the book club in 1995, testifies to such potential when she describes the experience of reading the first volume of Maya Angelou's autobiography, *I Know Why the Caged Bird Sings* (1969): 'I was a colored girl, raised by my grandmother, living in an impoverished town just like her. Maya Angelou grew up to be Maya Angelou. It was my life – it was the possibility for *my* life.'[32] Reading Angelou's autobiography, Winfrey appears to suggest, affected the course of her own life story. This emphasis on factual experience is, in turn, the cornerstone for Winfrey's book club shows, applying to all the authors she chooses, and not just the African American ones.[33] By encouraging her audience to read the novels she selects as, to some extent, autobiographical, her readers are, according to Eva Illouz, 'solicited to actively incorporate the novels in their lives.'[34] What is significant about Angelou's book, moreover, is that it is not only an autobiography but is, like the majority of novels chosen for the book club, what Illouz would term, a 'suffering [auto]biography.'[35] As D.T. Max, among others, has argued, an Oprah-type book is easily identifiable: 'the narratives she has chosen are overwhelmingly by women – 22 out of 28. In eight novels, young women are abused, raped or murdered. A dozen men commit adultery or act abusively toward their families. Women nurture, men threaten.'[36]

Yet as Max subsequently acknowledges, Winfrey did not invent the kind of fiction she promotes: 'Publishers have been selling it for 15 years with some success, especially since the breakthrough of

The Color Purple.[37] Alice Walker's 1982 novel is one of Winfrey's favourite books.[38] Indeed, she plays Sofia in Steven Spielberg's 1985 adaptation of the novel for the screen. It has also been the subject of much condemnation by black male writers and critics. In his novel *Reckless Eyeballing* (1986), Ishmael Reed indicts black women writers, such as Walker, who, he feels, allowed themselves to be conscripted to a white feminist agenda in their unforgiving representations of African American men. In so doing, he echoes African American columnist and critic Stanley Crouch, who, in 1979, condemned 'black female writers who pay lip service to the women's movement while supplying us with new stereotypes of black men and women.'[39] For novelist Charles Johnson, writing in 1988, *Reckless Eyeballing* is 'a novel I'd have been too chicken to write', although since then he, too, has not been slow to criticise Walker.[40] The Thelonious Monk/Juanita Mae Jenkins pairing also recalls the ideologically opposed black writers of Trey Ellis's 1988 novel *Platitudes*, Dewayne Wellington, a failing experimental novelist, and Isshee Ayam, his radical feminist counterpart, modelled at least in part on Alice Walker.

As Monk is writing *My Pafology*, he is spurred on by passages remembered from *Native Son*, *The Color Purple* and, intriguingly, *Amos and Andy* (*Erasure*, p. 70). The explicit link established between Wright's and Walker's novels and the long-running radio and television minstrel show suggests that the mimicking of so-called black mannerisms and speech patterns and the performance of cultural stereotypes associated with blackface may equally be effected through writing as on the vaudeville stage.[41] Of course, the minstrel show was primarily a commodity, with blackface itself as 'the metaphor for the commodity' as Susan Willis puts it. 'It is the sign of what people paid to see', she continues, 'the image consumed, and it is the site of the actor's estrangement from self into role.'[42] If *My Pafology* might be interpreted as a kind of literary minstrelsy, its selection by Kenya Dunston reinforces the notion of the book as commodity just as it confirms Monk's 'estrangement' from self (Monk) into role (Stagg R. Leigh). In applying metaphorical burnt cork, Monk registers his own upper-middle-class protest against the alienation he feels when he reads texts such as *We's Lives in Da Ghetto*. To the characters in novels who shout '*dint, ax, fo, screet* and *fahvre*', Monk wants to scream that 'I didn't sound like that, that my mother didn't sound like that, that my father didn't sound like that' (p. 70).[43] However, although Monk resents the racist stereotyping evident in Jenkins's book as much as he would 'a display of watermelon-eating, banjo-playing darkie carvings and a pyramid of Mammy cookie jars', because of his own privileged class position and Harvard education, he is often guilty of succumbing to similar stereotypes himself (p. 35). On a visit to his sister's women's clinic he has a discussion with one of her patients about Zora Neale Hurston and Jean Toomer. Monk is surprised at the woman's knowledge and is forced to admit that he 'had expected this young woman with the blue fingernails to be a certain way, to be slow and stupid, but she was neither' (p. 26).

Returning to the politics of book clubs, Oprah's Book Club has met with the disdain of white male writers, most famously in the *furor* involving Jonathan Franzen that unfolded towards the end of 2001. Franzen's novel *The Corrections* (2001) was Oprah's forty-third book club selection in September of that year. After he registered in several interviews his unease with his book's being branded with the 'Oprah' logo and adjudged his novel unsuitable for the book club because his work belongs 'solidly in the high-art literary tradition', Oprah withdrew her invitation to Franzen to appear on the show because he was 'seemingly uncomfortable and conflicted about being chosen as an Oprah's Book Club selection.'[44] Some women writers reacted with anger to Franzen's snub, interpreting his comments as a judgement on the artistic abilities of the other (predominantly women) authors of Oprah's selections.[45]

However, in Franzen's essay on the controversy, in which he recounts the visit of Oprah's television crew to his childhood home of St. Louis, Missouri, to shoot background material for the show, he attributes his impatience with Oprah's Book Club to its insistence on the autobiographical content of his novel. Although he has been living in Manhattan for twenty-four years, for the benefit of Oprah's viewers he pretends 'to arrive in the Midwestern city of his childhood [and the setting for the novel] and reexamine his roots.'[46] He is also filmed at a local Museum of Transportation:

> I have no particular fascination with trains and I've never been to the museum, but a transportation museum makes a cameo in *The Corrections*, and one of the novel's main characters is a railroad man. So my job is to stand or walk near trains and look contemplative. I do this for an hour.[47]

He does, however, draw the line at being filmed in front of his old family home, despite the producer's offer to obtain permission from the current owners. What the Franzen affair shows is the near impossibility of determining whether the male author's derision is directed towards Oprah's insistence on (auto)biography over 'art', or whether it is a gendered response to the predominantly feminine leanings of the book club's authors and readers. To what extent, then, is the disapproval of Ishmael Reed, Trey Ellis, Charles Johnson and Stanley Crouch (of Alice Walker), of Monk Ellison (of Juanita Mae Jenkins) and of Jonathan Franzen (of Oprah's Book Club) less about art (and, in the cases of Ellis, Reed, Johnson Crouch and Monk Ellison, about race) than gender?[48]

The two are linked. For with 'major' white male writers – such as Philip Roth – the use of autobiographical material in their fiction does not preclude their work from being considered 'literary' or their themes universal.[49] On the other hand, for those white male writers such as Franzen, less established than Roth at the time the controversy erupted, or, in an even more profound way, for authors who are women, 'ethnic' and/or writers of color, the assumption that their work must be autobiographical stems from the conviction that marginal(ised) authors must write as an act of testimony, and their fictionalised individual experiences can never be of universal significance. When Oprah's film crew shot footage of him in the Midwest, what Franzen was objecting to, I suspect, was not that they drew attention to the autobiographical details in *The Corrections per se* (for Roth too mines his own life but is still 'solidly in the high-art literary tradition') but the *association* of this true-life material with the suffering biographies of Oprah's Book Club.

Black boys and native sons

If Monk's *My Pafology* is a reaction to Juanita Mae Jenkins's *We's Lives in Da Ghetto*, it is also an updated version of Richard Wright's *Native Son* (1940). *Native Son* was itself a Book-of-the-Month selection, the first novel by a black writer to be so chosen.[50] In fact, Wright's novel was subjected to white vetting to ensure it contained 'appropriate' material for its Book-of-the-Month readership. As John K. Young elucidates, Wright's original manuscript 'included an early scene in which Bigger and Jack masturbate in a movie theatre and then watch a newsreel featuring Mary Dalton consorting with a well-known radical while on vacation in Florida.' On the advice of Edward Aswell, his Harper and Brothers editor, Wright revised this scene and also altered the relationship between Bigger and Mary so that 'Mary's sexual interest in Bigger in the original manuscript is largely absent from the published version.' After the changes had been made, the book club accepted the novel, as did the British publisher, Gollancz.[51] Thus, from the novel's initial publication in 1940 until Arnold Rampersad's Library of America edition of Wright's *Early Works* appeared in 1991, there was no masturbation scene in print.[52] For Young, this example 'indicates the aesthetic limits for African American writers created by the economic power of mainstream publishers and, in this case, by the Book-of-the-Month Club.' Although this power imbalance affects almost all writers, there is 'a particular difficulty in representing "the black experience" in terms which depart too far from the mythologized version most often reinforced by mainstream presses.'[53] Monk's experience in the novel satirises the idea that, some sixty years later, very little has changed for African American writers.

Given the fact that Wright's presence haunts *Erasure* – at both a narrative and a meta-narrative level – it is obviously significant that the novel's protagonist is named Thelonious Ellison. In evoking both Ralph Ellison and Wright, Everett refers to and resurrects critical debates from the 1950s and 1960s, suggesting that they are of ongoing relevance in relation to African American fiction and the literary marketplace.[54] James Baldwin's claim in his essay 'Everybody's Protest Novel' – itself an indictment of *Native Son* – that 'literature and sociology are not one and the same'[55] provoked a rebuttal from Irving Howe, who counter-argued that the sociology of a Negro's existence 'formed a constant pressure on his literary work, and not merely in the way this might be true for any writer, but with a pain and ferocity that nothing could remove.'[56] Upon the literary work of the Negro writer, Howe appears to suggest, the anguish of Negro life is indelibly inscribed. In Howe's construction, any novel by an African American author is, by definition, a 'suffering [auto]biography', to borrow Illouz's phrase. Howe's essay, 'Black Boys and Native Sons', in turn precipitated an exchange with Ralph Ellison, who writes in 'The World and the Jug' that 'the question of how the "sociology of his existence" presses upon a Negro writer's work depends upon how much of his life the individual writer is able to transform into art.'[57]

What is particularly striking about Ellison's essay is that, on two occasions, he mentions racial passing. First, he notes that, 'although the sociologists tell us that thousands of light-skinned Negroes become white each year undetected, most Negroes can spot a paper-thin "white Negro" every time simply because those who *masquerade* missed what others were forced to pick up along the way.'[58] Quite apart from Ellison's fascinating conflation of 'paper' and 'passing' – once again evoking the pale-skinned black body as a type of text – his use of the verb *masquerade* is an interesting choice because Ellison's interpretation of Howe's essay is that 'in addition to a hero, Richard Wright, it has two villains, James Baldwin and Ralph Ellison, who are seen as "black boys" *masquerading* as false, self-deceived "native sons." '[59] Howe, as Ellison would have it, sees Baldwin and Ellison as 'masquerading' (or 'passing') for American writers, 'phonies' who are 'guilty of filial betrayal' because they are 'actually "black boys." '[60] Ellison, in his second reference to passing, draws together the notions of 'passing', 'masquerade' and 'writing', and thus turns Howe's critique against him, indicting intellectuals (such as Howe) for 'their facile, perhaps unconscious, but certainly unrealistic, identification with what is called the "power structure." Negroes call that "passing for white"' (p. 173).

Everett's invocation of these literary debates from the 1950s and 1960s is reinforced by *Erasure*'s nods to Ellison's novel *Invisible Man* (1952). Towards the end of Everett's novel, Monk sees a billboard saying 'Keep America Pure', echoing the Liberty Paint slogan from *Invisible Man* (*Erasure*, p. 272).[61] There are also a number of references to Ellison's chameleon character, B.P. Rinehart.[62] Monk decides to unmask himself at the awards ceremony because: 'I had to defeat myself to save my self, my own identity. I had to toss a spear through the mouth of my own creation, silence him forever, kill him, press him down a dark hole and have the world admit that he never existed' (p. 287).[63] This passage draws attention to itself through its use of racially inflected language ('spear-chucker') and through its overt reference to *Invisible Man*, in which the narrator succeeds in silencing Ras the Destroyer by locking his jaws with a spear.[64] Of course, *Invisible Man* is not a passing narrative, but its tropes of seeing, blindness and invisibility, along with the protagonist's putting on masks, are strongly reminiscent of the passing tradition in African American literature.

Passing/writing

My Pafology recalls one of the great passing narratives *and* African American literary hoaxes of the twentieth century, James Weldon

Johnson's *Autobiography of an Ex-Colored Man* (1912). Given its notoriety and the mystery surrounding its authorship, it is unsurprising that Johnson's novella is an important intertext for Everett. When Monk first encounters *We's Lives in Da Ghetto* in Borders bookstore on a quest to locate one of his own books, it is described in terms of a search for his reflection in a mirror: 'I went to Literature and did not see me. I went to Contemporary Fiction and did not find me.'[65] This episode is evocative of black-to-white passing narratives, in which the protagonist's encounter with his or her mirror image represents a crisis of racial identity. In *The Autobiography of an Ex-Colored Man*, after his schoolteacher publicly designates him as nonwhite, the narrator rushes home to peer at himself in the looking glass.[66] Monk eventually 'finds himself' in African American Studies, which foreshadows his subsequent attempt to manipulate such racial and marketing categories in writing *My Pafology*.[67] The opening lines of *Erasure* are overtly reminiscent of those of Johnson's novella, in which the secret of passing and inscribing that secret become inseparable. Johnson's narrator begins by acknowledging, 'I know that in writing the following pages I am divulging the great secret of my life.'[68] Meanwhile, *Erasure*'s protagonist, Monk, commences in a similar confessional tone: 'My journal is a private affair, but as I cannot know the time of my coming death, and since I am not disposed, however unfortunately, to the serious consideration of self-termination, I am afraid that others will see these pages' (p. 3).

The permanence and indelibility of a written record thus serves to highlight the comparative fragility of the body. The notion that Monk's journal may incriminate him or expose him after his death foreshadows the novel's subsequent revelations regarding Monk's father, who takes his own life some time before the novel opens. After suffering four strokes, Monk's father (a doctor) eventually shoots himself (p. 13). He leaves instructions with his wife to burn some of his papers, which turn out to be letters he received from a white nurse with whom he had an affair while they were both serving in the Korean War. The evocation of this interracial relationship recalls the conventions of nineteenth-century passing fiction, in which the death of the heroine's father brings about the exposure of her mixed racial heritage, the revelation that her mother had black ancestry and that her parents' connection was thus not a legal marriage between two white people, but unsanctioned miscegenation. The light-skinned heroine is then invariably remanded into slavery.

In the nineteenth-century stories, the mulatta's racial and legal status is determined by her father's success or failure at arranging for documentation to be drawn up during his lifetime: manumission papers for his wife, in order that his marriage licence will be legally binding, a will and so on. His daughter's identity, indeed, her very body, will be defined and circumscribed according to what is contained within these papers. Significantly, the father's good intentions and genuine attempts to regulate his irregular affairs during his lifetime are often posthumously foiled by the legal establishment, which has the final say in interpreting and authenticating the documents presented.[69] Thus, in *The Bondwoman's Narrative*, the aptly named Mr. Trappe becomes executor to Hannah's mistress's father's will and, having access to his papers, discovers 'some important secret' therein (p. 34). The secret is that the beautiful mistress is the daughter of a slave and, since slaves inherited the condition of the mother, is herself legally a slave. It is fitting that Trappe, a lawyer who makes his living from linguistic ambiguity, is frequently depicted as surrounded by texts (pp. 35, 45). Of course, *Erasure* is not a black-to-white passing story but this explicit reference to his father's interracial relationship is nonetheless significant because, as in the nineteenth-century narratives, Monk's discovery of his father's affair and of the existence of a half-sister is framed in terms of the sudden appearance of heretofore unseen documents. Western society's profound investment in and dependence on the power of writing to record faithfully ensures that the message contained within a document, accurate or not, is nevertheless often accorded the status of absolute truth. Under the pseudonym of Stagg R. Leigh, Monk attempts to operate in the space between a text's capacity to incriminate or exonerate, enslave or liberate.

In treading this very fine line, writing emerges, in *Erasure*, as profoundly ambivalent through its repeated juxtaposition with the ultimate act of self-annihilation, suicide. For example, Monk recalls:

> Throughout my teens and twenties I had killed myself many times, even made some of the preparations, stopping always at the writing of the note. I knew that I could manage nothing more than [sic] a perfunctory scribble and I didn't want to see that, have my silly romantic notions shattered by a lack of imagination. (p. 159)

Here, Monk claims, presumably with tongue in cheek, that the only thing that prevented him from committing suicide was the pressure of composing an adequate note. Later still, Monk admits that *My Pafology* is not a work of art, 'but more a thing to mark, a warning perhaps, a gravestone certainly' (p. 234). Equally, *reading* as well as writing can give rise to extreme bodily reactions conceived in almost fatal terms. Monk experiences severe physical incapacity each time he is exposed to Jenkins's *We's Lives in Da Ghetto*: reading the opening paragraph, he thinks he is 'going to throw up' (p. 34). As he reads a review of the novel on an aeroplane, the woman seated beside him is prompted to ask, 'Is something wrong?' (p. 46). When he sees a copy of the book on Marilyn Tilman's nightstand, he loses his erection (p. 212) and he wonders why Jenkins sends him 'running for the toilet' (p. 240).

The ambivalence of writing is reflected in a perceptible shift in Monk's depiction from writer to doctor after he pens the ghetto novel. Monk comes from a long line of doctors – grandfather, father, uncle, brother and sister – and his occupation as a writer initially sets him apart as a family anomaly. Lisa tells him he is 'different' (p. 31), and when he is still alive, his father is persistent in his claims that Monk is 'an artist. He is not like us' (p. 163). Before writing *My Pafology*, in other words, there is a clear delineation between those members of the Ellison family who (re)construct bodies, on one hand, and texts, on the other. Monk, possessing a kind of artistic vision, has a special way of seeing things (pp. 9, 12). Whereas writing is, initially, portrayed as unequivocally 'creative', medicine is alternately associated with life and death. The funeral of Monk's father, who dies by his own hand, is attended by hundreds of people 'claiming to have been delivered into this world by the great Dr. Ellison, this in spite of most of them being clearly too young to have been born while he was still practicing' (p. 7). His life-giving abilities thus provide a counterpoint to his own self-murder. Furthermore, Monk's sister, Lisa, is brutally (and ironically) murdered by Pro-Life activists because she performs abortions at her women's clinic. The death of Monk's sister is counterbalanced by his subsequent discovery that he has another sister, albeit a half-sister, the issue of his father's affair (p. 171).

Meanwhile, Monk, in writing *My Pafology*, unconsciously begins to emulate his remaining sibling, his brother Bill. A plastic surgeon in Scottsdale, Arizona, Lisa resents Bill because 'he practiced medicine for no reason other than the accumulation of great wealth' (p. 5). This anticipates Monk's subsequent abandonment of his own professional integrity to write a novel that will be a commercial success. Bill's decision to remove the mask he has been wearing for many years, the front of heterosexuality (he is married with two children), is paralleled by Monk's adoption of the literary mask that is Stagg R. Leigh. Bill's occupation as a plastic surgeon testifies to the slipperiness of bodily inscribed signs, the capacity of modern medical science not only to treat ailing bodies but to make them new, which is exactly what Monk does in generating Stagg R. Leigh.[70]

With Monk's creation of this writer and his literary spawn, *My Pafology*, the dichotomy earlier established between doctor and writer collapses. Monk's literary *alter ego* and his book are depicted in terms of a medical cloning experiment, the implication being that Stagg R. Leigh cannot be divorced from Monk's body. Monk wryly refers to himself as an engineer, implying that he has genetically engineered Stagg R. Leigh (p. 273). As one of a panel of judges for the literary prize, he reads some five hundred novels and proclaims himself jaded: 'I was familiar with novels the way a surgeon is familiar with blood' (p. 255). He tells the other judges, who do not know he is Stagg R. Leigh, that *My Pafology* is 'a failed conception, an unformed fetus . . . a hand without fingers, a word with no vowels' (p. 289), the gynaecological metaphors reinforced by the text-within-a-text presentation of *Fuck*. Ultimately, *My Pafology*, as embodied by Stagg R. Leigh, becomes Monk's grotesque offspring, his monster to Monk's Frankenstein. Such gothic import is suggested when Monk's agent, Yul, admits after reading *My Pafology*: 'This thing scares me' (p. 151). The evocation of death, suicide and murder alongside the act of writing foreshadows Monk's subsequent fear that in masquerading as Stagg R. Leigh, he has inadvertently killed off a part of himself and that it will be necessary 'to defeat myself to save my self' (p. 287).

The coexistence of tropes of erasing and generating is reflected in the acts of naming and unnaming that are undertaken by Everett, by Monk and also by Stagg R. Leigh in the novel. Naming and unnaming is a recurring trope in African American literature beginning with the slave narrative. For example, after becoming a free man, Frederick Douglass retains his Christian name 'to preserve a sense of [his] identity' but changes his surname, from Bailey to Johnson and then to Douglass.[71] (Douglass is present in *Erasure* as Monk's childhood friend, Doug Glass.) In so doing, he affirms at once 'autonomy and identification in relation to the past.'[72] In naming and unnaming, the African American subject expresses his or her selfhood while registering his or her suspicion that all labels formulated by the master society are 'enslaving fictions.'[73] In *Erasure*, a similar ambivalence towards naming is evident, whereby the names chosen by Everett (Thelonious Ellison) and Monk (Stagg R. Leigh) seem to be richly allusive, but on closer inspection may be empty signifiers. Everett calls his protagonist Thelonious Ellison, who goes by the moniker Monk, thus conjoining a jazz musician and a giant of African American literature. However, when one remembers that Ralph Ellison is the author of *Invisible Man* (1952), 'black literature's most memorable cipher of the nameless', it is more tempting to conclude that the name 'Ellison', despite evidence to the contrary, in fact connotes absence and emptiness.[74]

The invocation of jazz musician Thelonious Monk offers a sense of continuity between Monk's 'real' name and the pseudonym under which he writes *My Pafology*. In choosing the *nom de plume* Stagg R. Leigh, Monk is paying tribute to the mythical African American figure known as Stagolee. The subject of countless musical tributes – in ballad, blues, jazz, epic, folk song and rap – the folk anti-hero is believed to have been one Lee Shelton, a pimp, who, in 1895, shot his friend William Lyons in a saloon in St. Louis during an argument over Lee's hat. That the Stagolee legend has survived primarily through oral traditions offers an intriguing counterpoint to Monk's ultimately unsuccessful quest for textual disembodiment.[75] However, the sheer profusion of versions of the Stagolee myth (he appears variously as Stagolee, Staggerlee and Stack Lee) raises the question of whether such over-determination actually connotes a lack or absence of meaning.

From Thelonious Ellison, to Stagg R. Leigh, to Van Go Jenkins, the surname of *My Pafology*'s protagonist is a sardonic homage to Juanita Mae Jenkins, whose *We's Lives in Da Ghetto* in part inspires its composition. The choice of Van Go is most probably explained by a bizarre nightmare that occurs towards the end of the novel, in which Monk dreams of seeing Nazi soldiers lancing Van Gogh's *Starry Night*, an episode which is the culmination of numerous narrative digressions emphasising Hitler's obsession with artistic purity (p. 283). In italicised passages throughout the novel, Everett explicitly links the myths of artistic and racial purity through the insertion of several imagined conversations between artists persecuted in Hitler's Germany in the 1930s (Paul Klee, Ernst Barlach and Kaethe Kollwitz, among others) – notes for a novel that Monk never writes, at least within the timeframe of *Erasure* (pp. 45–6).

This ambivalence regarding writing in *Erasure*, whether it represents an act of self-generation or a kind of self-murder, is characteristic of standard racial passing narratives, in which passing and death are always closely bound up. In the nineteenth-century narratives the mulatta who passes invariably meets a tragic and untimely end. In subsequent stories the death of a visibly black or mixed race parent facilitates the protagonist's decision to pass.[76] Alternatively, passing is imagined as symbolic death, the death of blackness as the passer melts into white society. To say a loved one 'passed' can mean that s/he died or that s/he passed as white. Often the effect is the same, for deciding to pass permanently was to commit to never seeing one's family again. In *The Human Stain* the passer's repudiation of his black family is portrayed in terms of matricide. As Coleman Silk perceives it, he is '[m]urdering [his mother] on behalf of his exhilarating notion of freedom!'[77] If passing and death are closely aligned and, in *Erasure*, writing and death are intimately related, Everett's novel suggests a connection between passing and writing that is, ultimately, borne out in the other contemporary narratives of passing examined in this book. Whereas passing was, historically, undertaken to advance one's social and economic opportunities in a racist society, Everett suggests that the conditions of the contemporary literary marketplace foster different kinds of 'passing' which, like the more conventional form, can offer a pointed, though limited, critique of those conditions.

Notes

1   Mark Twain, *Pudd'nhead Wilson* (1894; London: Dover, 1999), p. 115. Subsequent references will be included in parentheses in the main body of the text.
2   Juda Bennett, 'Toni Morrison and the Burden of the Passing Narrative', *African American Review* 35.2 (2001), 205–17 (205).
3   Ibid., 214, n. 1. Meanwhile, Suzanne Jones isolates John Gregory Brown's *Decorations in a Ruined Cemetery* (1994) and Donald McCaig's *Jacob's Ladder* (1998) as two of 'the few contemporary novels about passing.' The latter of these, like Barbara Chase-Riboud's *The President's Daughter* (1994) and E.L. Doctorow's *The March* (2005), thematises passing through the vehicle of the historical novel. All three are set in the nineteenth century. Suzanne W. Jones, *Race Mixing: Southern Fiction Since the Sixties* (Baltimore: Johns Hopkins University Press, 2006), p. 220.

4 Ibid., p. 205.
5 Ibid., p. 214.
6 Toni Morrison, 'Recitatif', in *Norton Anthology of American Literature*, Vol. 2, 2nd ed., ed. Nina Baym et al. (1983; New York: Norton, 1998), pp. 2078–92.
7 John K. Young, *Black Writers, White Publishers: Marketplace Politics in Twentieth-Century African American Literature* (Jackson: University Press of Mississippi, 2006), p. 4.
8 Joel Williamson, *New People: Miscegenation and Mulattoes in the United States* (New York: Macmillan, 1980), p. 103.
9 Young, p. 4.
10 Robinson, 'Forms of Appearance', p. 250.
11 Pfeiffer, p. 139.
12 Hannah Crafts, *The Bondwoman's Narrative*, ed. and introd. Henry Louis Gates, Jr. (London: Virago, 2002), p. 100. Subsequent page references appear in the body of the text.
13 Harper, 'Passing for What?', 382.
14 Michael Rogin, *Blackface, White Noise: Jewish Immigrants in the Melting Pot* (Berkeley: University of California Press, 1998), p. 29.
15 Eva Saks, 'Representing Miscegenation Law', in *Interracialism: Black–White Intermarriage in American History, Literature, and Law*, ed. Werner Sollors (New York: Oxford University Press, 2000), pp. 61–81 (p. 73).
16 The fact that the very coinage of the term 'miscegenation' in 1864 was bound up with a controversy of authorship adds yet another twist to the construction of the miscegenous body as forgery. David Goodman Croly and George Wakeman – journalists at the quasi-Copperhead newspaper, the New York *World* – authored an anonymous pamphlet entitled *Miscegenation*, which advocated interracial marriage and was in wide circulation from early in 1864. Until the appearance of this pamphlet, amalgamation was the term used to describe interracial sexual relations. Purportedly originating from the Republican, anti-slavery camp, the fraud was an attempt to damage Abraham Lincoln's re-election campaign. Neither man ever acknowledged responsibility for his role in the hoax. Sidney Kaplan, 'The Miscegenation Issue in the Election of 1864', in Sollors, *Interracialism*, pp. 219–65.
17 The importance of authenticity was not always imposed exclusively by a white sponsor. Some former slaves saw the potential for their own empowerment in the provability of their tales. James Pennington, for example, proclaims that 'The facts in this case are my private property.' Conversely, Monk Ellison is a man 'without a decent lie to call my own' (p. 58). James Pennington, *The Fugitive Blacksmith; or Events in the History of James W. C. Pennington* (1849), quoted in Ann Fabian, *The Unvarnished Truth: Personal Narratives in Nineteenth-Century America* (Berkeley: University of California Press, 2000), p. 79.

18 Laura Browder, *Slippery Characters: Ethnic Impersonators and American Identities* (Chapel Hill: University of North Carolina Press, 2000), pp. 20–1.

19 Ibid.

20 Fabian, pp. 84–112. In *My Bondage and My Freedom* Frederick Douglass recounts how his 'overseer had written his character on the living parchment of most of their [slave] backs, and left them callous.' As a free man, Douglass is introduced as 'a graduate from a peculiar institution' with 'my diploma written on my back.' *My Bondage and My Freedom*, ed. and introd. John David Smith (1855; New York: Penguin, 2003), p. 130.

21 Holly Jackson, 'Identifying Emma Dunham Kelley: Rethinking Race and Authorship', *PMLA* 122.3 (2007), 728–41 (732–3).

22 Time Warner press release, *The Bondwoman's Narrative* by Hannah Crafts (2 April 2002) www.twbookmark.com/books/48/0446530085/press_release.html (22 November 2004).

23 Henry Louis Gates, Jr., 'Borrowing Privileges', *New York Times* (2 June 2002), 18.

24 Nina Baym, 'The Case for Hannah Vincent', and Katherine E. Flynn, 'Jane Johnson, Found! But Is She "Hannah Crafts"? The Search for the Author of *The Bondwoman's Narrative*', in *In Search of Hannah Crafts: Critical Essays on The Bondwoman's Narrative*, ed. Henry Louis Gates, Jr. and Hollis Robbins (Cambridge: Perseus, 2004), pp. 315–31 and 371–405.

25 Joe Nickell, 'Searching for Hannah Crafts', in Gates and Robbins, pp. 406–16 (414–15).

26 Nickell, p. 406.

27 Raymond Hedin, 'Strategies of Form in the American Slave Narrative', in *The Art of the Slave Narrative: Original Essays in Criticism and Theory*, ed. John Sekora and Darwin T. Turner (Macomb: Western Illinois University Press, 1982), pp. 25–35 (p. 25).

28 Benjamin Soskis, 'Freedoms and Fictions', *New Republic* (3 June 2002), 36–40 (37).

29 John Sekora, 'Black Message/White Envelope: Genre, Authenticity, and Authority in the Antebellum Slave Narrative', *Callaloo* 32 (1987), 482–515 (497).

30 Several commentators have been tempted to equate Percival Everett with Thelonious Ellison and to see *Erasure* as a fictionalised autobiographical piece. For example, the subtitle to an interview with Everett reads: 'His new novel satirises ghetto culture and white attitudes – but Percival Everett's books still end up on the Black Fiction shelf.' Sean O'Hagan, 'Color Bind' (interview with Percival Everett), *Observer* (16 March 2003), http://books.guardian.co.uk/departments/generalfiction/story/0,6000,9 14871,00.html (11 August 2005). Everett's own playfulness has (probably intentionally) contributed to such interpretations: the paper delivered by Monk at the *Nouveau Roman* Society conference in *Erasure* was published

under Everett's name in *Callaloo* in the winter of 1999. Percival Everett, 'F/V: Placing the Experimental Novel', *Callaloo* 22.1 (1999), 18–23.

31 Juanita Mae Jenkins's novel is itself likely referencing *Push*, a 1996, award-winning novel by Ramona 'Sapphire' Lofton. *Push* is the story of Claireece Precious Jones, HIV-positive and the mother of two children by her own father at the age of seventeen. Like Stagg R. Leigh, whose novel earns him a large advance from Random House, Sapphire received a $500,000 dollar advance from Alfred A. Knopf. William Powers, 'Sapphire's Raw Gem', *Washington Post* (6 August 1996), B1–4. The parallels between *Push* and *The Color Purple* are striking, and indeed Sapphire cites Alice Walker's 1982 novel and Toni Morrison's *The Bluest Eye* (1970) as major influences on her work. Sapphire, 'Sapphire's big push' (interview with Mark Marvel) (June 1996) www.findarticles.com/p/articles/mi_m1285/is_n6_v26/ ai_18450196 (31 October 2004).

32 Quoted in D.T. Max, 'The Oprah Effect', *New York Times Magazine* (26 December 1999), 36–9 (39).

33 For example, in the show devoted to Janet Fitch's *White Oleander* – which describes protagonist Astrid's adolescence in multiple foster homes after her mother is imprisoned for murdering her lover – the four guest readers of the novel were two women who had grown up in troubled homes, one foster-care parent and one social worker. Chris, the foster-care parent, asserted: 'All the self-help books and books on foster care I've read in my whole life didn't do it for me . . . I can't believe this book is fiction (qtd. in Max, 39).

34 Eva Illouz, *Oprah Winfrey and the Glamour of Misery: An Essay on Popular Culture* (New York: Columbia University Press, 2003), p. 143.

35 Ibid., p. 103.

36 Max, 37–8.

37 Ibid., 40.

38 Ibid., 38.

39 Stanley Crouch, 'Aunt Jemima Don't Like Uncle Ben', *Notes of a Hanging Judge: Essays and Reviews, 1979–1989* (New York: Oxford University Press), pp. 29–34 (p. 29).

40 Charles Johnson, *Being and Race: Black Writing since 1970* (London: Serpent's Tail, 1988), p. 58. For Johnson's critique of Walker, see his introduction to the 1995 Plume edition of *Oxherding Tale* (1982).

41 W.T. Lhamon Jr., *Raising Cain: Blackface Performance from Jim Crow to Hip Hop* (Cambridge, MA: Harvard University Press, 1998), p. 56.

42 Susan Willis, 'I Shop Therefore I Am: Is There a Place for Afro-American Culture in Commodity Culture?', in *Changing Our Own Words: Essays on Criticism, Theory, and Writing by Black Women*, ed. Cheryl A. Wall (London: Routledge, 1990), pp. 173–95 (p. 189).

43 Many critics have argued that blackface has always been inflected with class concerns. Lhamon notes that in its very early manifestations,

disempowered young white workers applied blackface as an act of social protest, 'as a defiant measure of their own distance from those arguments among enfranchised interests. Youths in blackface were almost as estranged from the bourgeois inflections of the slavery quarrel as were the blacks whom they therefore chose to figure their dilemma and emphasize their distance' (p. 43). David Roediger, Eric Lott and Michael Rogin also foreground the issue of class in their studies of blackface performance.

44 'Oprah's Book Club 43rd Selection *The Corrections*' (22 October 2001), www.oprah.com/obc/pastbooks/jonathan_franzen/obc_user_communica tion.jhtml (28 July 2005).

45 See, for example, Angela Long, 'The Idea of the Home as a Safe Place is Lost to us Now – in the US More than in Other Places' (interview with Sue Miller), *Irish Times* (18 March 2002), 12. Like Franzen, Sue Miller has written autobiographically of her father's struggle with Alzheimer's and her sixth novel, *While I Was Gone*, was an Oprah's Book Club selection in May 2000.

46 Jonathan Franzen, *How to be Alone: Essays* (London: Fourth Estate, 2002), p. 259.

47 Ibid., p. 270.

48 African American literary critics have also been divided along gender lines. I think it is reasonable to assume that, as a faculty member in the Department of English at the University of Southern California who teaches courses on creative writing, American Studies and critical theory, Everett is familiar with a particular moment in the 1980s during which African American men and women critics clashed over the deployment of poststructural theory in readings of works by black authors. African American women commentators claimed that the use of post-structural theory dehistoricised texts by black women which could only fruitfully be read and appreciated with reference to their historical context. Interestingly, the 'tragic mulatta' played a key role in such disputes. In his introduction to *Workings of the Spirit*, for example, Houston A. Baker delineates what he terms Black Power (theoretical) versus Black Studies (historical) approaches to African American women's writing and implicitly creates a three-way analogy between turn-of-the-twentieth-century writers (such as Pauline Hopkins), their mulatta protagonists and non-theorising African American women scholars, all of whom Baker claims 'worry, worry, worry about the approbation of a white other.' *Workings of the Spirit: The Poetics of Afro-American Women's Writing* (Chicago: University of Chicago Press, 1991), p. 19.

49 On the reception of Roth's work as autobiographical, and Roth's response to this, see David Brauner, *Philip Roth* (Manchester: Manchester University Press, 2007), pp. 9–11.

50 Addison Gayle, *Richard Wright: Ordeal of a Native Son* (New York: Doubleday, 1980), p. 119.

51 Young, *Black Writers, White Publishers*, p. 15.

52 Ibid., p. 16.

53 Ibid., p. 17.

54 The burden of the name of Everett's fictional protagonist has its real-life counterpart in Ralph Ellison's own name, Ralph Waldo Ellison, after the preacher-philosopher Emerson. According to Kimberly Benston, Ellison, 'having struggled against the "trouble" caused him by social rituals of self-declaration', followed 'Emerson's call for "self-reliance" and ironically contracted his middle name [. . .] to the singular letter, "W." This minor gesture of unnaming was Ellison's private act of naming.' 'I Yam What I Yam: The Topos of Un(naming) in Afro-American Literature', in *Black Literature and Literary History*, ed. Henry Louis Gates, Jr. (New York: Methuen, 1984), pp. 151–72 (p. 159). Emerson, of course, appears as a character in *Invisible Man* (1952) as the last of the prospective employers to whom the narrator presents himself in New York. The narrator only meets the younger Emerson, who reveals the actual content of Bledsoe's letter of introduction. Interestingly, Ellison is known to have signed letters as B.P. Rinehart, the chameleon character from *Invisible Man*. See Timothy L. Parrish, 'Ralph Ellison: The Invisible Man in Philip Roth's *The Human Stain*', *Contemporary Literature* XLV.3 (2004), 421–59 (436).

55 James Baldwin, 'Everybody's Protest Novel', *Collected Essays* (New York: Library of America, 1998), pp. 11–18 (p. 15).

56 Irving Howe, *A World More Attractive: A View of Modern Literature and Politics* (New York: Horizon, 1963), p. 100.

57 Ralph Ellison, 'The World and the Jug', *The Collected Essays of Ralph Ellison*, ed. John F. Callahan (New York: Modern Library, 1995), pp. 155–88 (p. 159).

58 Ellison, *Essays*, p. 171, emphasis added.

59 Ibid., p. 156, emphasis added.

60 Ibid., p. 160.

61 Ralph Ellison, *Invisible Man* (1952; Harmondsworth: Penguin, 1965), p. 16.

62 Ibid., pp. 184, 238, 242, 245.

63 In these passages, Everett is referring to and engaging with the theories of Roland Barthes, problematising Barthes's advocacy of 'the birth of the reader' at the cost of 'the death of the Author' by making Monk's readership a racist one. 'The Death of the Author', *Image, Music, Text* (New York: Hill and Wang, 1977), rpt. http://faculty.smu.edu/dfoster/theory/Barthes.htm (29 October 2004).

64 Ellison, *Invisible Man*, p. 450.

65 James Weldon Johnson, *The Autobiography of an Ex-Colored Man* (1912; New York: Dover, 1995), p. 34.

66 Ibid., pp. 7–8.

67 Incidentally, the packaging of *The Bondwoman's Narrative* and *Erasure*
    respectively aptly illustrate the tools used to market these novels. John
    Bloom notes that *The Bondwoman's Narrative* was designed 'to exude
    authenticity', with a cover 'made to look like someone's idea of a yellowed,
    frayed-edge manuscript tied with twine.' 'Literary Blackface? The Mystery
    of Hannah Crafts', in Gates and Robbins, pp. 431–8 (p. 431). Similarly,
    Celeste-Marie Bernier and Judie Newman observe that such a cover
    encourages the reader to '[c]ut the string, [. . .] open the book, and release
    Hannah from her symbolic bondage.' '*The Bondwoman's Narrative*: Text,
    Paratext, Intertext and Hypertext', *Journal of American Studies* 39.2
    (2005), 147–65 (150). Meanwhile, the Faber and Faber editions of *Erasure*,
    both hardcover and paperback, silhouette the title of Stagg R. Leigh's
    novel, *Fuck*, against the title of Everett's novel, *Erasure*, with the common
    'u' acting as the point of overlap. On the paperback cover there is a
    photograph of a young African American boy holding a gun to his head,
    anticipating the novel's preoccupation with suicide. In the American
    Hyperion edition, the title *Erasure* appears alongside the novel's page
    numbers, with the letters comprising 'Erasure' crossed out. The prepon-
    derance of Xs in this edition suggests, appropriately, both erasure and
    intersection.
68 Johnson, *Autobiography of an Ex-Colored Man*, p. 1.
69 See, for example, Dion Boucicault, *The Octoroon; or, Life in Louisiana*
    (1859; Upper Saddle River, NJ: Literature House, 1970). See also Frances
    Harper's *Iola Leroy* in *Three Classic African-American Novels*, ed.
    and intro. Henry Louis Gates, Jr. (New York: Random House, 1990),
    pp. 267–463 (p. 304).
70 According to Sander L. Gilman, 'The model of "passing" is the most
    fruitful to use in examining the history and efficacy of aesthetic surgery.
    Taken from the history of the construction of race, not gender, it provides
    the most comprehensive model for the understanding of aesthetic
    surgery.' *Making the Body Beautiful: A Cultural History of Aesthetic
    Surgery* (Princeton, NJ: Princeton University Press, 1999), p. 22.
71 Douglass, *Narrative*, pp. 102–3.
72 Benston, p. 153.
73 Ibid., p. 151.
74 Ibid., p. 159.
75 Cecil Brown, *Stagolee Shot Billy* (Cambridge, MA: Harvard University
    Press, 2003) p. 8.
76 See, for example, Johnson's *Autobiography of an Ex-Colored Man* (1912),
    Jessie Fauset's *Plum Bun* (1928) and Nella Larsen's *Passing* (1929).
77 Philip Roth, *The Human Stain* (2000; London: Vintage, 2001), p. 138.

3

The way of the cross(-dresser): Catholicism, gender and race in two novels by Louise Erdrich

> The woman shall not wear that which pertaineth unto a man, neither shall a man put on a woman's garment: for all that do so *are* abomination unto the Lord thy God.
>
> Deuteronomy 22:5[1]

> The real question comes down to whether we are godly creatures or a mass of differentiated cells. That's the ultimate identity question.
>
> Louise Erdrich, interview with Mark Anthony Rolo (2004)[2]

This chapter examines the enduring significance of religion as a category of identity in contemporary US society, analysing the ways in which religious discourse overlaps with raced and gendered identities in two novels by contemporary German American-Ojibway writer Louise Erdrich. In so doing, I wish to highlight the fact that in identity politics, certain categories have been, and still are, scrutinised more than others. Perhaps because of scholars' profound commitment to anti-essentialism from the 1980s on, race and gender, as categories which have been historically conceived as rooted in the body, have received the most attention. However, many would argue that the critical impulse to deconstruct race and gender, while undeniably important, has been pursued at the expense of less visible, but equally, if not more, powerful categories, especially that of class. For instance, Walter Benn Michaels claims that 'race has turned out to be a gateway drug for all kinds of identities, cultural, religious, sexual, even medical' and that 'we love race – we love identity – because we don't love class.'[3] In fact, by focusing too closely on race and gender, critics risk reproducing unwittingly the logic of legibility by which these categories have derived their hegemonic power and thus enabling

those categories that are less corporeally visible – such as class and religion – to 'pass' out of the picture. While a rich and illuminating body of work exists on the *interdependence* of race/class and gender/ sexuality in American Studies, religious identity is without question the most overlooked category – either by itself, or interlocking with other categories – in identity politics scholarship. This is in spite of the obvious centrality of religious rhetoric to American political discourse in general – and specifically, during the George W. Bush era – as well as its ongoing importance among ordinary Americans. In the American Religious Identification Survey, carried out among adults in 2001, for example, 81 per cent of those surveyed claimed to have a religious affiliation and 77 per cent of these identified that affiliation as Christianity.[4]

In this chapter I unpack the ways in which Erdrich's novels privilege religious belief over her characters' raced and gendered identities (though they are connected) by challenging readers to consider the possibilities and limitations of Native/Christian (specifically, Catholic) syncretism. If, as Dennis Walsh asserts, the clear opposition Erdrich draws between Catholicism and shamanic religion in her first novel *Love Medicine* (1984) yields to a perceptible blurring of the two in *Tracks* (1988), published four years later, I take Walsh's hypothesis further to argue that the figure of Father Damien Modeste in *The Last Report on the Miracles at Little No Horse* (2001) represents the ultimate crisis in the categories of Native versus Catholic.[5] Erdrich's preoccupation with religious identity is mapped upon the bodies of two women who pass in order to take up their Catholic vocations. Pauline Puyat, a mixedblood woman who passes as white in becoming a nun (Sister Leopolda), is one of two narrators in *Tracks*.[6] She also features as a conspicuous absent presence in *The Last Report*, which dramatises the life of Agnes DeWitt/Sister Cecilia/Father Damien Modeste, a former postulant nun who subsequently passes as a priest. Erdrich thus asks readers to reflect upon the ways in which raced and gendered identities overlap with religious affiliation as a third category of identification and prompts scholars to question how race and gender have served to mask the importance of religion in contemporary American society and culture.

In *Tracks*, two narrators – Nanapush and Pauline Puyat, who becomes Sister Leopolda – chart the decline of the Ojibway way of life on a North Dakota reservation through the combined forces of Old World diseases, harsh winters and the General Allotment (Dawes) Act of 1887.[7] *The Last Report*'s sympathetic portrayal of Father Damien, who appears as a minor character in *Tracks*, could be seen as Erdrich's counteraction of the (self-) destructiveness of Leopolda. Spanning the years 1910 to 1996, *The Last Report* traces through flashbacks the life of Agnes DeWitt. After a brief and unsuccessful spell as Sister Cecilia, a postulant in a Minnesota convent (1910–12), Agnes embarks on a romantic relationship with farmer Berndt Vogel, who is subsequently killed while attempting to rescue his lover from bank robbers who have taken her hostage. Following Berndt's death, Agnes takes on the identity of Father Damien Modeste, a Catholic priest who dies in a flood while en route to the Indian mission of Little No Horse. Agnes lives as Father Damien, dispatching regular epistles to the Pope on various matters of importance to reservation life, until her suicide by drowning in 1996.

In *The Last Report*, historical settings are juxtaposed with a contemporary story, reflecting the growing fascination with Native/ Catholic syncretism over the past twenty years or so. Francis Cree, former Tribal Chairman of the Turtle Mountain Band of Ojibway in North Dakota, of which Louise Erdrich herself is a member, confirms this when he observes in a 1991 interview that 'the Catholic spirituality, looking back, is beginning to understand what they dropped.' Most of the Catholic people 'are turning here, back to their traditional ways, those that's part Indian. Even some of those that are not Indian. They're looking back and saying "Look, by gosh, there is something there. There is something in the native spirituality. We see it."'[8] The combination of *Tracks* and *The Last Report* can thus be read as a timely intervention into debates on 'a new evangelism' emerging from a Roman Catholic Church 'no longer so concerned with the Christianization of Indians as with the Indianization of Christianity.'[9]

While Erdrich's novels are undoubtedly concerned with Native and Catholic religious practices, they may also be interpreted, more generally, in the context of contemporary philosophical, theological and literary debates on postsecularism. As Henry Goldschmidt argues, the events of 11 September 2001 had the effect of both shaking 'the once popular faith in the inevitable secularization of "modern" society' and of 'highlighting the inseparability of racism from religious persecution.'[10] On the first issue, scholars such as John McClure and Andrew Tate claim that a new 'postsecular' impulse is evident in contemporary fiction by writers as diverse as Thomas Pynchon, Toni Morrison, Jon McGregor, Jim Crace, Michèle Roberts and Douglas

Coupland. For McClure, who focuses on North American writers, including Erdrich, this body of fiction may be termed 'postsecular' because

> the stories it tells trace the turn of secular-minded characters back toward the religious; because its ontological signature is a religiously inflected disruption of secular constructions of the real; and because its ideological signature is the rearticulation of a dramatically 'weakened' religiosity with secular, progressive values and projects.[11]

For Tate, whose discussion extends to British as well as American writers, such narratives include 'improbable stories of faith healing, fulfilled prophecy and experiences of epiphany . . . many writers, both sceptical and devout, have re-imagined the life of Christ; ghosts, angels and mystics are now common figures in serious literary fiction.'[12] The recent scholarly attention to the postsecular in contemporary fiction begs the same question as is posed with regard to passing in the introduction to this book. Why is a 'new' religious sensibility emerging once more in contemporary fiction? Could it be that it never, in fact, went away?

On the second issue, religious belief has itself helped to produce 'race' as a category. As Goldschmidt puts it, 'religion has been inextricably woven into both racial and national identities, to such an extent that "race", "nation", and "religion" have each defined the others.'[13] Thus, the suggestion that racial prejudice 'can be attributed solely to bad *science*'[14] or that race is simply 'a fiction of *law* and custom' (Twain, p. 7), is to ignore the ways in which religious discourse has informed race as an abstract idea and racism as a social reality. As Richard Dyer and others have argued, whiteness derives its power from promoting itself as a normative, non-raced, invisible state, a standard from which the bodies of all people of colour are deemed to deviate. Christianity is directly implicated in the construction of whiteness in this way because it 'is founded on the idea – paradoxical, unfathomable, profoundly mysterious – of incarnation, of being that is in the body yet not of it.'[15] Christianity 'maintains a conception of a split between mind and body, regarding the latter as at the least inferior and often as evil.' Hence, by reducing nonwhite individuals 'to their bodies and thus to race', white people become, by contrast, 'something else that is realised in and yet is not reducible to the corporeal, or racial.'[16]

Theorising the cross-dresser

How does cross-dressing fit into all this? Is cross-dressing a form of passing? For Judith Halberstam, writing on female masculinity:

> the notion of passing is singularly unhelpful. Passing as a narrative assumes that there is a self that masquerades as another kind of self and does so successfully; at various moments, the successful pass may cohere into something akin to identity. At such moments, the passer has become. What of the biological female who presents as butch, passes as male in some circumstances and reads as butch in others, and considers herself not to be a woman but maintains distance from the category 'man?'[17]

I quote Halberstam at length because I believe she underestimates the typical passer, who may operate with a greater level of self-consciousness than she gives him or her credit for. Often, the *passer* does not necessarily believe s/he 'really' belongs in a group other than the one into which s/he is (tres)passing, but recognises that *society* views him or her in that way. Because, as Halberstam sees it, 'female masculinity seems to be at its most threatening when coupled with lesbian desire', she focuses in her book on 'queer female masculinity almost to the exclusion of heterosexual female masculinity.'[18]

From Halberstam's remarks and the work of other theorists, it seems clear to me that within Gender and Sexuality Studies, a hierarchy has been established which accepts that certain manifestations of gender ambiguity are *more* subversive than others: male-to-female cross-dressing is more subversive than female-to-male transvestism; queer subjects are more subversive than heterosexual subjects. Those who subscribe to such assumptions could learn from the work of a growing body of critics of passing, who recognise the redundancy of the subversive versus complicit debate and wonder what *else* passing could signify in the contexts in which it occurs.[19] Indeed, even Judith Butler, whose *Gender Trouble* many have credited with conferring on drag its supposed subversive status, questions in a subsequent book 'whether parodying the dominant norms is enough to displace them; indeed whether the denaturalization of gender cannot be the very vehicle for a reconsolidation of hegemonic norms.'[20] In a field so concerned with the deconstruction of binaries and with advocating multiplicity in all its manifestations, it is remarkable that the transgendered subject remains locked in exclusively queer interpretations.

In her comprehensive study of tranvestism, Marjorie Garber warns against restricting discussions of cross-dressing 'to the context of an emerging gay and lesbian identity.' For Garber, this is 'to risk ignoring, or setting aside, elements and incidents that seem to belong to quite different lexicons of self-definition and political and cultural display.'[21] However, since Butler identified drag as a cultural practice that 'reveals the distinctness of those aspects of the gendered experience which are falsely naturalized through the regulatory fiction of heterosexual coherence', the temptation to interpret incidents of cross-dressing or female masculinity as significant only in so far as they appear to denote queerness has been too great for many commentators to resist.[22] For Leslie Feinberg, this correlation between the cross-dresser's gender and sexuality 'is based on the fact that uni-gender lesbian and gay cross-dressers were socially visible and organized at a time when most bi-gender, heterosexual cross-dressers were isolated or members of "underground" organizations.'[23] Ignoring Garber's advice, most theorists – including Halberstam – have followed Butler in empha-sising cross-dressing as a process that relates almost exclusively to queer, at the expense of heterosexual, subjects.

Butler's analyses of drag, cross-dressing and the sexual stylisation of butch/femme identities are only marginally useful for my discussion of *The Last Report on the Miracles at Little No Horse*. The female-to-male cross-dressing protagonist of *The Last Report* is a priest who remains celibate for most of his/her vocational life, apart from a brief period during which s/he enjoys an affair with a fellow (male) priest. Thus, the significance of the gender passer in this context is more complex than a strictly queer interpretation will allow. Instead, my reading of *The Last Report* draws heavily upon Garber's observation that:

> the apparently spontaneous or unexpected or supplementary presence of a transvestite figure in a text (whether fiction or history, verbal or visual, imagistic or 'real') that does not seem, thematically, to be primarily concerned with gender difference or blurred gender indicates a category crisis elsewhere, an irresolvable conflict or epistemological crux that destabilizes comfortable binarity, and displaces the resulting discomfort onto a figure that already inhabits, indeed incarnates, the margin.[24]

This chapter, then, following Garber, is written in response to Feinberg's rhetorical question: 'Wouldn't it be wonderful if we could all support the understanding that gender expression does not determine sexuality, and then open up a discussion between our communities?'[25] For Garber, the cross-dresser represents a 'third term' which 'questions binary thinking and introduces crisis.' Three 'puts in question the idea of one: of identity, self-sufficiency, self-knowledge.'[26] In *Tracks* and *The Last Report*, the category in crisis is Catholicism. Subject to external appropriation of its teachings to support widely divergent ends and overlapping with apparently contradictory faiths, Catholicism is the belief system that is constantly threatening to collapse.

Beyond the veil: passing from nun to priest

In her work on Catholic women writers, Jeana DelRosso identifies Louise Erdrich as one of several writers who address 'the conflicts between Catholicism and their individual cultures with an internally divided attitude . . . that is informed in part by the fact that Catholicism was imported into those cultures through colonialism.'[27] In *Tracks* and *The Last Report*, Erdrich makes the Catholic clergy the starting point for her interrogation of whether Catholicism's colonialist function necessarily distances it irreconcilably from Native beliefs, or if the two might, in some contexts, prove compatible. In so doing, she draws upon a popular – but mostly forgotten – genre of nineteenth-century American literature, the escaped nun's tale. Although converting Native Americans to Christianity is the express aim of both Father Damien and Sister Leopolda, by appealing to this tradition, Erdrich's nun and priest figures emerge as immediately more complex than this imperialising impulse would suggest. In her study of anti-Catholic literature of the nineteenth century, Susan Griffin identifies some of the characteristic tropes of the nuns' tales:

> women were being kidnapped from confessionals, imprisoned and raped in convents; Inquisitors continued to maintain and use hidden torture chambers; Jesuits practiced their time-honored treacheries; nuns posing as governesses corrupted Protestant children; priests hovered over deathbeds, snatching away family fortunes; Papal emissaries plotted to overthrow government power; Mother Superiors tyrannized over helpless girls, barring all parental intervention.[28]

The most famous of the escaped nuns' narratives, Maria Monk's *Awful Disclosures of the Hôtel Dieu Nunnery* (1836), which purported to be a 'true' account of the author's abuse at the hands of cruel nuns and priests at the Hôtel Dieu convent in Montreal, was the bestselling book in the United States prior to the appearance of *Uncle Tom's Cabin* in 1852.

The salacious, titillating tales of convent life which began to appear in the 1830s are deeply embedded in a more general 'othering' of Catholicism throughout United States history.[29] In particular, the appearance of escaped nuns' tales coincided with a sharp increase in the number of predominantly Catholic German and Irish immigrants to the United States. This ambivalence towards the convent and women religious is thus reflective of the ambiguous position occupied by Catholicism, as opposed to other Christian denominations, in the United States. For while Catholicism has undoubtedly performed a colonising function in its mission to christianise Native Americans, it has itself always been considered 'other' in the United States through its association with various immigrant groups. From the mid-nineteenth century onwards, Catholic Germans and Irish arrived in great numbers, succeeded by Italians and Poles, and today, by Hispanics.[30]

The escaped nuns' tales evince not only anxieties about the growing influence of Catholicism in the United States in the nineteenth century, but also unease about the changing role of women in society, particularly with respect to American religious life. As David Hackett observes, it is significant that the protagonists of the nuns' narratives were young Protestant women who had converted to Catholicism and become nuns. With men and women operating in increasingly 'separate spheres' in the nineteenth century, Protestantism 'played an important role in shaping the idea of the true woman.'[31] With the consequent 'predominance of women in Protestant churches and new theological interpretations of a nurturing and self-sacrificing Christ', Protestantism was, in the nineteenth century, seen to be becoming more and more 'feminized.'[32] In a period during which there was some concern about women's growing power in religious matters, Griffin argues very persuasively that the escaped nun's story served to undercut her possible authority by illustrating the 'young [Protestant] woman's incapacity to be trusted: her testimony is essential to unveiling the truth, but it also proves her vulnerability and fallibility.'[33] The Catholic nun persists as a locus of fears regarding gender, or as Sara Maitland puts it: 'Nuns, precisely because they do not belong – as daughters, wives or mothers – to any individual man, can be used safely as a projection of a misogyny which is far more general.'[34]

The nun thus emerges from nineteenth-century cultural representations as a vexed figure in terms of ethnicity, gender and Catholicism,
and indeed, colonialism. If American convent captivity narratives such
as Monk's are 'connected to the older, more established genres of the
gothic, Indian captivity narratives and a long European tradition of
anti-Catholic literature', they also look forward to more recent versions
of the convent story.[35] Nancy Lusignan Schultz cites Toni Morrison's
Paradise (1998) as a contemporary example of the convent story.[36] To
this, I would add the reservation novels of Louise Erdrich. Schultz's
observation regarding the nuns' tales indebtedness to Indian captivity
narratives relates the othering of Native Americans to that of Catholics
through their perceived violence and brutality. As James R. Lewis
points out, a majority of Puritan captivity tales were set in the French
and Indian War, 'causing Indians and Catholics to become associated
with each other in the Puritan mind.'[37] It is not surprising, given this
historical context, that Erdrich draws upon – sometimes seriously,
sometimes playfully – the escaped nuns' tales in her novels,
capitalising on the legacy of the literary nun as a vexed figure.

This is most apparent in the postulant Marie Lazarre's encounter
with the brutal Sister Leopolda in Erdrich's first novel, *Love Medicine*.
Like the Protestant girls in the nineteenth-century stories, Marie is
seduced by the iconography and symbolism of Catholicism, imagining
herself becoming a saint 'carved in pure gold. With ruby lips. And my
toenails would be little pink ocean shells, which they would have to
stoop down off their high horse to kiss.'[38] That a Native girl might be
so devout echoes *Awful Disclosures*, in which Monk claims that 'Many
of the Indians were remarkably devoted to the priests, believing
everything they were taught.'[39] At the convent, however, Leopolda, who
is Marie's mother although Marie does not know it at this time,
subjects Marie to relentless abuse in the name of holiness – pouring
boiling water on her back and stabbing her with a fork. Having failed
to 'run back down the hill' after the first violent incident, Marie finally
decides to 'Rise up and walk!', escaping the nun and the convent (*Love
Medicine*, pp. 49, 56). In *The Last Report* Erdrich also recalls the
conflation of convent and brothel in the nineteenth-century nuns'
tales. When Sister Cecilia (Agnes DeWitt) leaves the convent and
arrives at Berndt Vogel's farm, Berndt thinks at first that the stranger
'must be a loose woman, fleeing a brothel.'[40]

The references to the escaped nuns' stories in Erdrich's novels
reflect the enduring potential of the figures of the nun and priest, and

the space of the convent, to operate as a locus for anxieties and/or desires regarding the imbrication of discourses of race, gender and Catholicism. The nun and priest – even disregarding the racial and gender ambiguity of Leopolda and Damien – are already ambivalent figures. In Erdrich's novels the act of passing becomes an appropriate metaphor for the subjects' (in)ability to negotiate what are, apparently, opposing categories which are, in this case, Native versus Christian beliefs. Central to Erdrich's interrogation of Christianity, therefore, is her construction of Agnes DeWitt/Father Damien Modeste and Pauline Puyat/Sister Leopolda as narrative doubles. Like Pauline Puyat, who becomes Sister Leopolda, Agnes also begins her religious life in a convent as the novice nun Sister Cecilia. Recalling the conventions of many passing narratives, both Pauline and Agnes undergo symbolic deaths in undertaking their Catholic vocations, their rebirths demanding changes of nominal and physical identity. Pauline becomes Sister Leopolda and has her hair 'chopped from [her] head with a pair of shears.'[41] Agnes assumes the name Father Damien Modeste, and a masculine identity. Agnes keeps Leopolda's 'secret' (that she murdered Napoleon Morrissey) in order that her own secret identity will not be revealed. A section of the novel entitled 'Leopolda's Passion' (pp. 336–41) is followed directly by a chapter called 'Father Damien's Passion' (pp. 342–51). The identities of Father Damien and Sister Leopolda are thus intimately bound up with one another. By offering the reader two alternative – one 'positive', one 'negative' – embodiments of Native/Christian alliances, Erdrich's view of religious syncretism emerges as ultimately ambivalent.

The theology of the body

The contemporary (1996) narrative concern of *The Last Report* is to establish the now-deceased Sister Leopolda's suitability for sainthood based upon the miracles she allegedly performed during her lifetime. This inquiry into Leopolda's blessedness, undertaken by Father Jude Miller, a priest sent from the Vatican, is a process in which Father Damien establishes himself as a 'crucial witness' in order to refute the 'miracles' (*Last Report*, pp. 50–1). *The Last Report*'s preoccupation with miracles is significant because the Christian miracle is, historically, one of the issues which blurred the distinction between Native and Christian beliefs. If, according to David Murray, '[p]rimitive religions saw the gods at work in nature as an integral part of it, and therefore saw them as capable of being induced to make things happen', then the Judaeo-Christian God 'was seen as absolute, sovereign and outside of, and prior to, nature.' In this construction, which opposes 'Primitive' and 'Judaeo-Christian' traditions, Christian miracles, which imply that God could be influenced directly through prayer, emerge as deeply 'problematic.'[42] The 'report' of the novel's title, then, is Damien's final attempt to set the Vatican straight regarding the falseness of Leopolda's 'miracles' and her consequent ineligibility for sainthood. The struggle that is wrought between Leopolda (posthumously) and Damien over the miracles reflects a deeper conflict which stems from the fact that they experience the encounter between Christianity and Native beliefs in widely divergent ways. In this conflict, the body is the principal battleground. In Catholic teaching, of course, the body emerges as a site of profound ambivalence. On the one hand, it appears to be preoccupied with circumscribing and delimiting the body; on the other, it seems to affirm the possibility of transcending one's body.

The Catholic hierarchy – intervening through Canon Law and papal encyclicals – seeks to regulate the body, sex and reproduction, issues that in some other Christian religions are considered matters of individual conscience. The Catholic Church's opposition to and prohibition of pre-marital sex, artificial methods of contraception, abortion and homosexuality are well known. In fact, the basic symbol of Christianity, the cross, is 'the shape of an object whose significance is the body that was nailed to it.'[43] This image is remarkable for evoking the body as a fixed, immobile entity – contained by and within the cross shape – and is thus an effective metaphor for the Catholic Church's attempts to impose bodily boundaries. Father Jude Miller is the mouthpiece for some of these views when he claims that 'Intercourse outside the boundaries of marriage hurts the order of things. Creates disorder. Breaks traditions, vows, families. Creates such . . . problems' (*Last Report*, p. 135).

Agnes's cross-dressing as Father Damien thus appears to contravene several key tenets of Catholic dogma. Most obviously, she assumes the role of priest, a vocation still denied to Catholic women. Formerly a novitiate nun, Agnes's decision to cross-dress as a priest in 1912 coincides roughly with the circumscription of the autonomy of the women's orders in 1917. Indeed, Agnes, in her priest's garb, immediately notices that Kashpaw, who meets her off the train to take her to the reservation, 'treated her with much more respect as a priest than she'd ever known as a nun' (p. 62). The Catholic Church's persistent refusal to ordain women, even as other Christian Churches do, is one of the reasons for which many feminists find the Church inherently misogynistic. Interestingly, the Church's justification for refusing to ordain women is predicated not only upon its assumption that Christ is male, but also, by implication, upon its disapproval of homosexuality:

> It is *the Eucharist* above all that expresses *the redemptive act of Christ the Bridegroom toward the Church the Bride.* This is clear and unambiguous when the sacramental ministry of the Eucharist, in which the priest *acts 'in persona Christi',* is performed by a man.[44]

If the Eucharist were performed by a woman priest, this would be equivalent to a union of two feminine entities – the Church and the priest.

The issues of priestly celibacy, the ordination of women and homosexuality become interlinked in *The Last Report* when Father Damien enjoys a brief affair with Father Gregory Wekkle. Before he learns that Damien is biologically female, Gregory fears he is 'one of those whom the Church darkly warned against, the ones who lay with men as with women.' For Gregory, homosexual intercourse is akin to the 'sin of murder, one of those sins crying out to heaven for vengeance' (p. 200). While the Catholic Church is undoubtedly opposed to homosexuality, in nineteenth-century anti-Catholic discourse, Protestants' mistrust of celibacy in the clergy focused upon the supposed 'spiritual marriage' between the priest and Christ which, for Protestants, contained a 'barely veiled theme of homoeroticism.'[45] Where the Church's disapproval of homosexuality is now considered deeply *conservative*, in a specific US climate of anti-Catholicism, one of the ways in which the Church's *subversive* potential was depicted was in terms of the perceived homoeroticism of priestly celibacy. In *The Last Report*, then, the cross-dresser's ambiguity – uniting the issues of homosexuality, priestly celibacy and the ordination of women – reinforces yet again the ambivalence with which Catholicism has been viewed in the United States.

In ostensible contradistinction to this obsession with containing the body as symbolised by the crucifix, in English language usage, *cross* and *crossing* often evoke the very opposite connotations of bodily mobility and transgression. Furthermore, Catholicism embraces a non-essentialist conception of the self that is not contained *in* or *by* the body. The 'self' in Christianity is intangible, indefinable, and is usually called 'the soul.' It is the soul that accedes to eternal life after the earthly body has expired. In *The Last Report* it is this more liberating theology of the cross that (in Agnes's case) Erdrich seeks to explore, privileging the receptiveness of Catholicism to notions of bodily transformation and finding therein the potential for reconciling Agnes's lifelong gender disguise with the proscriptions of her religious faith. Of course, disguise is far from anathema to the Catholic faith. In reminding adherents that God is omnipresent and to encourage them to see God in all his creatures, Catholicism teaches that God may appear in many guises. For Agnes, Mary Kashpaw, her long-time, faithful housekeeper, is such a figure (p. 123).

The coexistence of these apparently incongruent conceptions of the body enables Erdrich to interrogate Catholicism, and the potential for a melding of Catholic and Native beliefs, through the bodies of Sister Leopolda and Father Damien. A war is waged over the extent to which each can exert corporeal control, master their bodies, become subjects rather than objects. Leopolda's marriage of the two belief systems leads to paralysis; Damien's to mobility. Leopolda's conversion to Catholicism is accompanied by attempts at bodily mortification; Damien's Catholicism enables bodily transformation. Leopolda ultimately strives for bodily containment, Damien for bodily transcendence; while Leopolda wishes for visibility – to be seen, Damien wants vision – to be able to see.

As in all passing narratives, the passer's ambiguously gendered or raced body is often presented in terms of his or her mobility between places, races, genders and cultures. If Damien is 'welcome where no other white man was allowed' (p. 276), Pauline is aware that if she never sees Nanapush, Fleur or the Kashpaws again, they will not miss her (*Tracks*, p. 196). Damien's association with mobility is evident from his very first appearance in *Tracks*. Ravaged by disease and freezing conditions, Nanapush appears to suggest that the Ojibway people have become fixed in a historical moment, relics of an almost forgotten past. Although he saves Fleur, Nanapush fails to revive the other members of her family, 'quiet forms' that are 'stone cold' (p. 3). During the harsh winter of 1912, Fleur and Nanapush almost become frozen statues themselves: 'the slivers of ice began to collect and cover us. We become so heavy, weighted down with the lead gray frost, that we could not move' (p. 6). Significantly, the pair are liberated from their immobility by the arrival of Father Damien, who bursts through their cabin door, 'causing that great crack of light to interfere with death' (*Last Report*, p. 80). By contrast, Pauline Puyat is associated throughout with immobility, which is similarly wrought in terms of congealing, particularly after she enters the convent. During a cold winter spent there, her blood 'never thawed', which she views, however, as something of an achievement which enables her to grow strong (*Tracks*, p. 136). When Nanapush tempts her with hot, sweet tea in an effort to force her to urinate and thus violate her self-imposed twice-a-day rule, she tries to resist by making herself 'into a block of ice' (p. 150).

Elsewhere in *Tracks* her immobility takes the form of paralysis, notably when she witnesses Fleur's rape at the hands of the men with whom they both work (p. 26). After they return to the reservation and Fleur, pregnant with her second child, enters premature labour, Pauline again undergoes a type of paralysis, claiming that 'the Lord overtook my limbs and made them clumsy', ensuring that she cannot work her arms, hands or fingers properly (p. 157). In contrast, when she is inflicting violence on others, she is finally able to overcome her paralysis. In strangling her former lover, Napoleon Morrissey, 'the only things left of intelligence' are her hands: 'What I told them to, then, they accomplished' (p. 202). While Pauline is all 'angles and sharp edges, a girl of bent tin' (p. 71), she longs for the fluidity that marks the bodies of the lovers, Fleur Pillager and Eli Kashpaw, who 'swelled and shrank' in relation to each other (p. 72). Pauline envies greatly Fleur's mobility and the power that accompanies it. In mediating between Misshepeshu, the water monster, and the people, Fleur is 'the one who closed the door or swung it open' (p. 139). Pauline hopes that through converting the Ojibway people to Christianity, she will fulfil a similar intermediary function: 'There would have to come a turning, a gathering, another door. And it would be Pauline who opened it, same as she closed the Argus lockers' (p. 139). But if Fleur is the 'hinge' (p. 139) then Pauline is merely 'a piece of wall', attempting to shore up boundaries rather than sidestep them (p. 76). By contrast, Agnes's mobility between genders and cultures is most explicitly depicted through Damien's friendship with Nanapush, named for the Ojibway trickster.[46] Agnes's cross-dressing – which becomes a metaphor for her ability to transcend linguistic and cultural barriers (her command of the Anishinaabe language, her bonds with the Native people) – recalls the trickster's 'transformational powers to escape from difficult situations' and his/her 'control over . . . physical boundaries.'[47]

To gain some mastery over her body in the name of serving God, Pauline imposes limits upon herself and engages in punishing acts of bodily mortification. As part of this campaign she deprives herself of food, wears her shoes on the wrong feet and denies herself daytime urination. Despite this, she is still incapable of exercising any self-control. As Nanapush observes, 'once Pauline's mouth started it couldn't stop. It was as if she took the first drink and from then on the drinks took her' (p. 52). In another episode, she describes how she halves her bread allowance every time she sits down to eat (*Tracks*, p. 147). Subsequently, she pays a visit to Fleur's cabin and hungrily devours the food generously offered to her before realising that Margaret and Fleur deny themselves in order that their loved ones, Nanapush and Lulu, do not go without (p. 145). In contrast, the priest derives, or imagines he derives, actual nourishment from the Eucharistic bread and wine: 'Did their part of the sacrament transubstantiate in real as well as metaphorical terms? Had the dry thin consecrated Host turned into a thick mouthful of raw, tender, bloody, sweet-tasting meat in the mouths of the sisters? And the wine to vital blood?' (*Last Report*, p. 69)

Another of the many forms of penance which Pauline performs involves plunging her arms into boiling water. As they are recovering and she is having the bandages changed, she 'shed[s] a skin with the dirty wrapping. Every few days I shed another, yet another' (*Tracks*, p. 195). Pauline does not move easily in her own skin, and thus attempts to shed it by whatever available means. In contrast, although there are 'times that she missed the ease of moving in her old skin', Agnes slips relatively effortlessly into the skin of the dead priest (*Last Report*, p. 65). Even Pauline's acquisition of spiritual acuity is depicted in terms of violence inflicted on the skin. As God reveals himself to her, 'Skins were stripped from [her] eyes' (*Tracks*, p. 137). Like all passing narratives, *Tracks* and *The Last Report* are preoccupied with the interrelated concepts of seeing, not seeing and being seen, *hyper*visibility and *in*visibility. 'I have never seen the truth', Damien tells Jude Miller, 'without crossing my eyes' (*Last Report*, p. 135). In his last note to the Pope before committing suicide, Damien claims that 'All I ever wanted to do is see' (p. 344). As Rita Ferrari argues, 'invisibility signifies cultural oppression but can also signify access to the transcendent when invisibility inverts and expands into vision.'[48] Thus, while Damien's 'true' gender identity is invisible, he achieves the transcendence of vision: he *sees* (by crossing his eyes). By contrast,

Pauline merely *watches*, unable to transform her invisibility into vision, opting instead for voyeurism. Angry with Fleur's lover, Eli Kashpaw, for rejecting her romantic advances, Pauline wreaks revenge on him by procuring a love medicine that will lead him to seduce her adopted cousin, Sophie Morrissey. Pauline thus wields control over these external bodies while remaining incapable of ruling her own. She experiences vicarious sexual pleasure by watching the two engage in intercourse, but her own sexual encounters with Napoleon Morrissey are totally unfulfilling. In *The Last Report*, after she confesses to the murder of Napoleon, she reveals that she has been spying on the priest and thus knows his secret: 'I have waited outside your window after the ox, Mary Kashpaw, is snoring in the ironing shack. I've seen you undress' (*Last Report*, p. 274).

This scene from *The Last Report* depicts Pauline's attempts to wrest power from Damien in two ways, first, by the act of looking itself (taking control of the gaze) and second, by telling Damien about it (the act of speaking), both of which reflect Pauline's struggles in *Tracks*, in which neither Pauline's voyeurism nor her narrative voice translates into a corresponding level either of mastery over herself or influence over others. It is significant, moreover, that this confrontation takes place in the context of Catholic confession because, as Chris Weedon argues, after Michel Foucault, Catholic confession illustrates the profound limitations of speaking: 'To speak is to assume a subject position within a discourse and to become *subjected* to the power and regulation of the discourse.'[49] To interpret the sections Pauline narrates in *Tracks* as her confessions, spoken to those who have the authority to judge and chastise her for her transgressions, Pauline emerges as impotent even though she narrates. On the other hand, Damien subverts the traditional gender power relations of confession, power relations that inhere in the fact that the hearer is always male while the speaker may be male or female.[50] It is notable that '[m]ore than any other blessed sacrament, Father Damien enjoyed hearing sins, chewing over people's stories, and then with a flourish absolving and erasing their wrongs, sending sinners out of the church clean and new' (*Last Report*, p. 5). While in *Tracks* Pauline may have the ability to construct a story, in *The Last Report*, Damien has the power to change or undo it.

In *Tracks*, Pauline's voyeurism is her attempt to take control of the gaze under which she has always been invisible. The erasures that Nanapush describes in the opening of *Tracks* – the diminishing

Ojibway population due to disease and exile, the end of the traditional way of life, the loss of Ojibway land – are subsequently symbolically enacted upon Pauline's mixedblood body, thus consigning her to an object status which belies her narrative voice. Although he tells Lulu that she is 'the child of the invisible, the ones who disappeared' (*Tracks*, p. 1), it is in fact Pauline who is 'invisible' (p. 15).[51] In the subsequent section, Pauline remembers her father's reaction upon her decision to leave the reservation for the nearby town of Argus. He warns her: 'You'll fade out there', reminding her that she is lighter than her sisters. 'You won't be an Indian once you return', a prospect that initially appeals to her (p. 14). However, her light skin actually serves to render her invisible: she 'blends' into walls, 'fades' into a corner, 'melts back to nothing' (pp. 16, 19). She is a 'moving shadow' (p. 22), 'unnoticeable' (p. 39).

In an effort to acquire visibility and, by extension, subjectivity, Pauline decides to become a nun, which demands she pass for white. The order will not admit any Indian girls so Pauline conveniently reports that God tells her in a dream that 'despite my deceptive features, I was not one speck of Indian but wholly white' (p. 137). However, the black habit of the nuns only serves to make her 'more invisible than ever' (p. 75). Indeed, Pauline's association with absence and erasure is compounded by her job assisting Bernadette Morrissey in washing and laying out the dead and she comes to cut a Grim Reaper figure: 'when people saw me walking down the road, they wondered who was being taken, man, woman, or child' (p. 75). Bernadette's daughter, Sophie, calls Pauline 'death's bony whore' (p. 86). Pauline's association with death is reinforced by her affinities with crows (*Tracks*, p. 54; *Last Report*, pp. 54, 318), a medieval Christian symbol signifying a bad omen and a bringer of misfortune and death. The transition from Pauline Puyat to Sister Leopolda is described in terms of her symbolic death as an Ojibway and rebirth as a white Christian. After falling asleep in a tree, with her head 'tucked . . . beneath the shelter of [her] wing' (the Ojibway bury their dead in trees), Pauline awakes knowing she is different: 'I became devious and holy, dangerously meek and mild' (*Tracks*, pp. 68–9).

Ultimately, Pauline's quest for corporeal control manifests itself in violence directed at others. Unable to establish any self-mastery, she (mis)directs her force at external targets. Significantly, her victims are those people (Napoleon Morrissey, her former lover, and Marie Lazarre, the child she bears as a result) who manage, at one time or another, to penetrate her body. Just as she frequently provides divine justification for her actions (she kills Napoleon, she claims, because he was 'the devil in the shape of the man' (*Last Report*, p. 273)), the nature and instruments of her violence betray the extent to which she has distorted the trappings of Catholicism: she strangles Napoleon Morrissey with a rosary made of barbed wire (*Tracks*, pp. 201–2; *Last Report*, p. 163). After stabbing Marie Lazarre with a fork, she claims that the stigmata were miraculously bestowed upon Marie (*Last Report*, p. 136; *Love Medicine*, pp. 55–6). Damien, on the other hand, reserves acts of violence for his own body: to avert the danger of posthumous exposure, he exerts the definitive form of bodily control (in gross violation of Catholic doctrine, of course) by taking his own life.[52]

Damien and Leopolda: passing between Native and Christian beliefs

Damien's at-oneness with his ambiguously gendered body and Pauline's alienation from her racially mixed body are reflected in the ways in which they fuse Catholic and Ojibway traditions. While Damien begins to practise a mixture of faiths, discovering that '*The ordinary as well as esoteric forms of worship engaged in by the Ojibwe are sound, even compatible with the teachings of Christ*' (*Last Report*, p. 49), Pauline can only substitute one for the other. For Damien, Ojibway and Christian figures can coexist with no apparent difficulty: '*Saint Augustine, Nanabozho, whoever can hear me, give me a little help now,* he prayed' (p. 266). For Pauline, by contrast, this is an uneasy alliance, signalled by her attempt to dispel her nightmares by hanging a Native American dreamcatcher alongside the crucifix above her bed. But this 'only spun the dreams through, thicker, faster, until I ceased to sleep at all' (*Tracks*, p. 66). Pauline sees Native and Christian beliefs in completely oppositional terms, claiming that 'Indians were not protected by the thing in the lake or by the other Manitous who lived in trees, the bush, or spirits of animals' and they should thus turn to the Lord (p. 139).

Her rejection of Ojibway practices in favour of Christianity is symbolically evoked when she shoots a bear who invades Fleur Pillager's cabin while Fleur is giving birth to her daughter, Lulu (p. 60). Among the Ojibway, bear hunting was conducted according to complex religious procedures. As Sam Gill notes, treatment of the bear 'approached the level of veneration.'⁵³ Although she does so to protect the inhabitants of Fleur's cabin, in shooting the bear Pauline fails to respect the procedures by which Ojibway bear-hunting rites ought to be conducted. Significantly, Father Damien, en route to Fleur's cabin to baptise Lulu, encounters the banished bear and by instinct, splashes it with holy water (*Last Report*, p. 183). Performing the ritual of baptism, an important Christian ceremony for initiating infants into God's community, Damien (somewhat comically) registers his respect for the bear, and by extension, Ojibway customs.

The most obvious and effective way in which Erdrich reveals the compatibility of Christian and Native traditions is through Damien's embodiment of the cross-dresser-as-spiritual-leader. When Kashpaw first encounters Damien, he mistakes the priest for a (male) two-spirit figure:

> The priest was clearly not right, too womanly. Perhaps, he thought, here was a man like the famous Wishkob, the Sweet, who had seduced many other men and finally joined the family of a great war chief as a wife, where he had lived until old, well loved, as one of the women. (*Last Report*, p. 64)

In fact, none of the Native American characters in the novel is ever convinced by Agnes's passing. Mary Kashpaw, Damien's faithful housekeeper, eventually discovers the priest's secret when he spends a month in a coma and fails to grow any facial hair in that time. Damien eventually realises that Fleur Pillager, too, 'had known his secret from the beginning, and it hadn't mattered' (pp. 263–4). Similarly, Nanapush perceives that Father Damien is 'oddly feminine' (p. 91). Many years later, in a strategic attempt to distract Damien from their game of chess, he asks: 'Are you a man priest or a woman priest?' (p. 230). It is not so much that these characters are complicit with Damien (with the possible exception of Mary Kashpaw, who prevents his posthumous exposure by ensuring that the dead priest's female body is buried at the bottom of a lake) as that her sex is irrelevant to them. Only Leopolda threatens to write to the bishop and expose '*Sister* Damien' (p. 273).

Of course, rather than the better-known male-to-female role in certain Native traditions, Father Damien recalls, more accurately, the existence of a female cross-gender – or 'two-spirit' – role in at least thirty-three Native American tribes.⁵⁴ Unsurprisingly, the notion of Father Damien as a kind of 'two-spirit' figure dominates existing interpretations of the novel.[55] What is interesting about this role is the extent to which it mirrors the priest's duties and responsibilities in Catholicism, including priestly celibacy and its concomitant childlessness. Female two-spirits eschewed marriage and, like a priest, cross-gender females did not bear children once they assumed their masculine occupations: 'Their kin considered them nonreproductive and accepted the loss of their childbearing potential, placing a woman's individual interests and abilities above her value as a producer.'[56] Most significantly, the role of the female two-spirit often comprehended a spiritual element. Cross-gender females 'were inspired by dreams or visions, had shamanic powers, or were sanctioned by tribal myths.'[57] For Protestant missionaries, for whom Natives and Catholics were both Other, 'the greater use of ritual and ritual objects on the part of the Catholics made them seem more like shamans.'[58] Like the shamanic female two-spirit, Agnes's call to the priesthood occurs in a dream. She claims to have been nursed back to health after the flood by a man whom she believes to be Christ: '*Be thou like as me, were His words, and I took them literally to mean that I should attend Him as a loving woman follows her soldier into the battle of life, dressed as He is dressed, suffering the same hardships*' (*Last Report*, pp. 43–4).

Significantly, this passage is as evocative of the Catholic tradition of female-to-male transvestite saints as it is of the female two-spirit that figures in certain Native cultures, echoing the words of Saint Jerome that a woman who 'wishes to serve Christ more than the world . . . will cease to be a woman and will be called man.'[59] The most celebrated of these is, of course, Saint Joan of Arc (pp. 1412–31). Indeed, it was for transvestism, not for heresy, that Joan was put on trial by the Inquisition.[60] There was even, according to legend, a ninth-century female pope. Pope Joan, whose real name is believed to have been Agnes, was exposed as a woman when she gave birth during a papal procession.[61] Thus, although such transformations were acceptable only in the sense that it was believed that the status of manhood was closer to God than womanhood, these saints are nevertheless remarkable for their 'destabilization of gender identity' in 'a tradition usually seen to cast gender in fairly fixed and dualistic terms.'[62]

Erdrich constructs Damien's mobility between his own Catholic faith and that of the Ojibway people by evoking imagery, incidents and characters that are meaningful – indeed common – to both belief systems. For instance, Agnes becomes Father Damien after a flood, one of the great apocalyptic images in the Judaeo-Christian tradition.

Swept away atop her grand piano, Agnes encounters a dead priest – killed in the flood – whom she knows to have been en route to an Indian mission. Interestingly, the dead priest is 'hanging from a branch' (*Last Report*, p. 44), which is evocative of the Ojibway custom of burying their dead in trees. Assuming his clothes and his name, Agnes is reborn as Father Damien Modeste and makes her way to Little No Horse to take his place. In the centrality of flood imagery, Erdrich echoes Ojibway folklore, in which the woodland trickster Nanabozho is credited with making the world new after a great flood.[63] Indeed, while Damien, through his female-to-male cross-dressing, is reminiscent of the shaman in Native traditions, 'the most provocative cosmological symbol in Ojibway shamanism is the character of Nanabozho.'[64] The friendship that develops between Father Damien and Nanapush – named after Nanabozho – thus highlights the complementary nature of their respective roles as spiritual leaders. The Ojibway woodland trickster, Nanabozho, 'served as the intermediary between the power spirits and the people, and, as such, had the power to transform himself at will in order to perform his tasks.'[65] A priest carries out a similar kind of intermediate role between God and the devout and in Agnes's case she actually transforms herself into a man in order to do this.

Although Erdrich never completely exonerates Damien for his early attempts to impose Christian morality on the Native population (the priest's disapproval of polygamy leads to the break-up of the Kashpaw family and the dispersal or deaths of Kashpaw and his four wives), his acknowledgement of his own complicity in 'the passing of sacred traditional knowledge' through the Christian conversion project clearly encourages the reader to think him more enlightened than Leopolda (*Last Report*, p. 239). Erdrich's disapproval of conversion is reflected in its association with theft in both novels: 'A god who enters through the rear door', according to Nanapush, 'is no better than a thief' (*Tracks*, p. 110). Father Damien, 'whose task it was to steal even the intangible about the woman beside him', is himself no better than a thief (*Last Report*, p. 100).

The association of priests with theft is suggested early in the novel when Agnes, living with Berndt Vogel at the time, is taken hostage by bank robbers. The ringleader, whom Agnes subsequently describes as the devil 'disguised in a rumpled cassock', masquerades as a priest (p. 35). A woman passing as a priest, Father Damien is 'both a robber and a priest. For what is it to entertain a daily deception? Wasn't he robbing all who looked upon him? Stealing their trust?' (p. 77). Though Damien is a thief, he is clearly not a malevolent one. Agnes 'becomes' Father Damien on the Feast of Saint Dismas, 25 March 1912 (p. 65). Saint Dismas is the Good Thief crucified with Christ, remembered as 'good' because he repents of his crimes before dying and subsequently accompanies Jesus to paradise. His last-minute conversion is echoed in *The Last Report* when the aged priest undergoes a reverse conversion to the Ojibway faith. Because there is no one he wants 'to visit except in the Ojibwe heaven', Damien decides to convert, becoming 'at long last the pagan that [he] always was at heart' (p. 310). On the contrary, Leopolda zealously pursues the ideal of conversion, with Christ's blessing, or so she reports: 'He gave me the mission to name and baptize, to gather souls' (*Tracks*, pp. 141–2). Pauline's assumption of the name Leopolda upon taking her vows is significant, likely referring to the Leopoldine Society, founded in Vienna in 1829 for the purpose of aiding Catholic missions in North America.[66] In *The Last Report*, her devotion to and success at soul-fetching is one of the reasons cited as qualifying her for sainthood.

Through Pauline's and Damien's diametrically opposed interpretations of their shared religious affiliation, Erdrich configures Catholicism as a permeable membrane through which subjects of different gender, racial/ethnic and cultural identities may 'pass.' For Pauline, the incorporation of the trappings of Catholicism leads to violence and her own profound unhappiness. However, the sympathetically drawn Father Damien suggests that Catholicism and Ojibway beliefs may be fused in a healthy, rewarding manner. The unforgiving portrait of Catholic/Ojibway syncretism that appears in *Tracks* yields, thirteen years later, to a sympathetic rendering of the same issue in *The Last Report*. DelRosso's analysis of certain women writers' attitudes towards Catholicism, 'positions from which they variously and often simultaneously view the church as vehicle of repression, of subversion, or of liberation', holds true for Pauline and Agnes.[67] Erdrich thus asserts the potential of Native/Catholic syncretism, though never quite surrenders her skepticism regarding its limitations.

Pocahontas's daughter?: authorship in *The Last Report*

If, as I argue throughout this book, passing strategies are as deeply embedded in authorial processes as they are in plot, then the cross-dressing woman in *The Last Report* may offer an insight into what authorship means for Louise Erdrich. In other words, what might Erdrich's relationship be, as storyteller and author, to the frustrated writer-of-letters in *The Last Report* and, indeed, to the narrators in *Tracks*, Pauline Puyat and Nanapush? In *Mixedblood Messages*, Louis Owens redefines the frontier, usually associated with the erasure of American Indian cultures and ways of life, as 'the zone of the trickster, a shimmering, always changing zone of multifaceted contact within which every utterance is challenged and interrogated, all referents put into question.'[68] By 'inhabiting both sides of the frontier plus the middle', the mixedblood is the ultimate embodiment of this reclaimed frontier.[69] For Owens, then, 'the frontier space of the trickster and the shifting space of mixedblood identity' are complementary.[70]

In *Tracks*, of course, the mixedblood and trickster narrators, Pauline and Nanapush, are deeply antagonistic towards one another. However, this is not to say that Erdrich does not at least flirt with identifying herself, as author, with Pauline. After all, the dedication of *Tracks* reads:

Michael,
> The story comes up different
> every time and has no ending
> but always begins with you,[71]

a passage lifted almost verbatim from one of Pauline's sections of the novel: 'It comes up different every time, and has no ending, no beginning. They get the middle wrong too. They only know they don't know anything' (p. 31). Nanapush, meanwhile, is the most obvious trickster character and is overwhelmingly associated with the oral tradition. For Nanapush, speaking denotes life and the living, boasting curative powers. When Nanapush and Fleur Pillager are discovered alive by Father Damien after the particularly harsh winter of 1912, Nanapush holds forth because: 'The sound of my own voice convinced me I was alive' (p. 7). After the deaths of his wife and child, Nanapush gets 'well by talking. Death could not get a word in edgewise, grew discouraged and traveled on' (p. 46). If, for Nanapush, talking is life-giving, for Pauline Puyat it is this property of the oral that threatens her very sanity. Having witnessed Fleur's rape in Argus, and suffered nightmares as a result, Pauline returns to the reservation, where the dreams stop 'until I made the mistake of talking aloud and bringing the whole of what had happened back to life' (p. 65).

Meanwhile, written documentation is associated with loss, death and erasure. *Tracks* opens with the juxtaposition of snow storms, 'a storm of government papers' and Ojibway deaths (p. 1). It closes with Ojibway land forever lost to lumbering, the felling of trees to generate more paper for the government, the Ojibway becoming 'a tribe of file cabinets and triplicates, a tribe of single-space documents, directives, policy. A tribe of pressed trees' (p. 225). Even the name 'Nanapush' is 'a name that loses power every time that it is written and stored in a government file' (p. 32). Damien shares the powerlessness of the Ojibway people to effect any changes in the face of such monolithic bureaucracies as the Vatican or the government – with their omni-scient, faceless, sometimes nameless figureheads. Nevertheless, he places his faith in writing. He sends letters to successive popes on various issues from the time of his arrival in March 1912 without ever receiving a reply, and by 1996 his frustration is evident:

> Apparently, one couldn't hope for a reply, oh no, that would be all too human, wouldn't it! An actual response from the Pope after a lifetime of devoted correspondence. Or could he call it that, implying as the word did some reciprocity, at least the semblance of an exchange? (*Last Report*, p. 3)

Faced with any crisis, such as the loss of Nanapush and Pillager land because of their failure to pay taxes, Damien embarks on a campaign of frenetic and ultimately futile letter-writing, targeting – among others – the mythical and powerful John James Mauser. A local tycoon who becomes wealthy by buying up land forfeited by Indians through non-payment of taxes, his 'actual person, if not identity, is mysterious' (p. 106). A disembodied presence, he appears 'not in person but in the persons of others – in the local commissioner and the tax collector general' (p. 185). Although Damien achieves corporeal transcendence, there is a sense in which this is ultimately superseded by various forms of disembodiment, especially disembodiment in the form of the textual.

The status of the text is thus ambivalent in *Tracks* and *The Last Report*. Although Damien feels disempowered by writing, an authori-tative text can, of course, wield the power to constitute one's identity in a positive or negative way. Thus, Sister Leopolda threatens to write to the bishop to inform him of Damien's sex (*Last Report*, p. 274). Nanapush is falsely named as Lulu's father on her birth certificate, but this loophole grants him the authority to remove her from the government school in which she is placed after Fleur leaves the reservation (*Tracks*, p. 225). Similarly, when the ineffectual sleuth, Jude Miller, tells Damien 'I know your secret' (*Last Report*, p. 332), Damien fears he will, after all this time, be exposed. However, Miller has merely discovered Lulu's birth certificate, on which the young priest mistakenly wrote his own name twice – as both priest and father (pp. 184, 330).

Perhaps, as in the interaction between Native and Christian beliefs, the interplay between the oral and the written is most evident in the friendship between Nanapush and Damien. Their relationship is one of reciprocity rather than coercion, mutual respect despite their differences. Nanapush, the consummate talker, finds himself snared by his own trap when Father Damien tries to convince him to take a government job: 'He used everything I'd showed him about talking, did not let me get a word in, let no thought sink into my brain. I had taught him well' (*Tracks*, p. 185). Reciprocally, Nanapush subsequently concedes that Damien is right 'in that I should have tried to grasp this new way of wielding influence, this method of leading others with a pen and piece of paper' (p. 209). Significantly, in *Four Souls* (2004), the reservation novel which succeeded *The Last Report*, Nanapush is again one of three narrators, but this time he is writing his story down. He retains his scepticism of writing, though, noting that 'this stub of a grain dealer's pencil that moves across the page of paper is not real, either, and . . . the truth lies on the other side of even these words.'[72] If both Nanapush and Damien are trickster figures grappling with the relative merits of the oral and the written, then so too is Louise Erdrich, author. As Rita Ferrari argues, her work is characterised by 'the paradox of employing and glorifying the oral tradition and its culturally cohesive function by inscribing this tradition.'[73]

Notwithstanding the ambivalence with which Erdrich treats writing versus orality, the trickster is notable for his rhetorical ability and linguistic flourishes, as several critics explicate.[74] Curiously, those same critics who note Nanapush's eloquence do not address the ways in which tricksterism might be informing the actual *production* of the work. For Mary Dearborn, adopting the persona of a trickster represents a potentially radical, though not unproblematic, device for the ethnic woman writer attempting to assert her authorship:

> the ethnic woman writer who wrote as a trickster could gain some relief
> from her feelings of anonymity or powerlessness within the dominant

culture and could wage assault against it by subverting authority within her text, passing along to alert readers messages of strategies for protest.[75]

The authority that Erdrich (playfully) subverts in *The Last Report* is her own, flanking the narrative with disavowals of her authorial authority, at times identifying with Nanapush, at times with Damien. She attributes the epigraph to Nanapush, implying that the words are unoriginal, derived from a source other than her own imagination. In her End Notes to the novel, she conspicuously distances herself from the work she has just produced. Melding fact and fiction by quoting a fax received by Damien from the Vatican, she passes Damien's letters off as 'real': 'Who is the writer? Who is the voice? Sometimes the script is familiar – the careful spidery flourish of a hand trained early in the last century. At other times – I am sure, I am positive – it is my own' (p. 358).

This slippage between fictional character (Damien) and actual author (Louise Erdrich) in this framing section raises the question of whether Erdrich ultimately identifies with this cross-dressing priest. The displacement of her own authorial authority onto the fictional character can thus be read as a kind of 'passing', a disavowal of her 'real' identity as author, for that of a fictional character. This would certainly support an analogy between cross-dresser-character and authorial berdache. Indeed, Julie Barak suggests that the close cooperation between Erdrich and her then husband, Michael Dorris, represents a type of authorial berdachism: 'Through their play with authorial gender and the gender blending of their authorial selves in their shared labor they create the exchange and transformation Erdrich sees as necessary in gendered relationships.'[76] Damien's transgression of gender boundaries may also reflect Erdrich's refusal, throughout a literary career that already spans over two decades, to submit to all sorts of behaviour expected of writers of fiction – the notion of the autonomous, individual artist and, indeed, of the coherent, stand-alone text.[77] The assumed lack of certainty – as to where Damien's letter-writing leaves off and her own fiction-creating takes over – is as close as Erdrich comes to self-consciously expressing the tensions that critics see as endemic in her work. However, she follows this section with 'The Story of Little No Horse (Told by Nanapush to Father Damien)', thus giving the last word in *The Last Report*, as she does the first, to the more conventional trickster figure.

The kind of self-conscious blurring of fictional character, authorial persona and actual author in which Erdrich engages becomes even more pronounced in the novels I examine in chapters 3 and 4. The authors of all four texts capitalise on the slipperiness of the literary categories of memoir and fiction. *Middlesex* and *The White Boy Shuffle* are novels that purport to be their first-person narrators' memoirs; *Caucasia* exploits the contemporary vogue for mixed race memoirs; *The Human Stain* is presented to the reader as a biography written by Nathan Zuckerman after his subject, Coleman Silk, has failed spectacularly with his own memoir. In each case, the authors toy with readers' assumptions regarding the autobiographical content of their work and, not coincidentally, they are all narratives of passing.

Notes

1 *The Holy Bible, containing the Old and New Testaments* (Cambridge, 1800), p. 185. *Eighteenth Century Collections Online* http://galenet. galegroup.com/servlet/ECCO (6 February 2006).

2 Mark Anthony Rolo (interview with Louise Erdrich), *The Progressive* (April 2002), www.findarticles.com/p/articles/mi_m1295/is_4_66/ai_ 84866888 (2 July 2004).

3 Walter Benn Michaels, *The Trouble with Diversity: How We Learned to Love Idenitity and Ignore Inequality* (New York: Henry Holt, 2007), pp. 5–6.

4 'American Religious Identification Survey (ARIS): Key Findings' (2001), www.gc.cuny.edu/faculty/research_briefs/aris/key_findings.htm (20 December 2005). As further evidence that the United States is far from secularised, I would point to the phenomenon of Mel Gibson's *The Passion of the Christ* (2004), which grossed $370,614,210 at the US box office and was the third highest grossing film of the year after *Shrek 2* and *Spider-Man 2*. See 'Top Grossing Movies for 2004 in the USA', www.imdb.com/Sections/Years/2004/top-grossing (1 December 2005).

5 Dennis Walsh, 'Catholicism in Louise Erdrich's *Love Medicine* and *Tracks*', *American Indian Culture and Research Journal* 25.2 (2001), 107–27.

6 Few critics state categorically that Pauline passes for white in order to become a nun. However, Nancy J. Peterson, *Against Amnesia: Contemporary Women Writers and the Crises of Historical Memory* (Philadelphia: University of Pennsylvania Press, 2001), p. 28 and Sheila Hassell Hughes, 'Tongue-Tied: Rhetoric and Relation in Louise Erdrich's *Tracks*', *MELUS* 25.3/4 (2000), 87–116 (109–10), are two that do.

7 The Dawes Act 'divided reservation lands into allotments of 160 acres and 80 acres which were assigned, respectively, to the heads of families and other individuals over the age of eighteen.' The act was designed 'to hasten the integration of Indians into American society by promoting the growth

of commercial agriculture on reservations. Allotted lands were held in trust for a period of twenty-five years, during which it was hoped that Indians would learn to become efficient farmers and acculturate to white ways through converting to Christianity and pursuing formal education at off-reservation schools.' Helena Grice, Candida Hepworth, Maria Lauret and Martin Padget, *Beginning Ethnic American Literatures* (Manchester: Manchester University Press, 2001), p. 41.

8 James McKenzie, ' "Sharing What I Know": An Interview with Francis Cree', *North Dakota Quarterly* 59.4 (1991), 98–112 (106).

9 Theresa S. Smith, 'The Church of the Immaculate Conception: Inculturation and Identity among the Anishnaabeg of Manitoulin Island', *Native American Spirituality: A Critical Reader*, ed. Lee Irwin (Lincoln: University of Nebraska Press, 2000), pp. 145–56 (p. 146).

10 Henry Goldschmidt, 'Introduction: Race, Nation, and Religion', in *Race, Nation, and Religion in the Americas*, ed. Henry Goldschmidt and Elizabeth McAlister (New York: Oxford University Press, 2004), pp. 3–31 (p. 3).

11 John A. McClure, *Partial Faiths: Postsecular Fiction in the Age of Pynchon and Morrison* (Athens: University of Georgia Press, 2007), p. 3.

12 Andrew Tate, *Contemporary Fiction and Christianity* (London: Continuum, 2008), p. 9.

13 Goldschmidt, p. 5.

14 Adam Lively, *Masks: Blackness, Race and the Imagination* (London: Vintage, 1999), p. 4.

15 Richard Dyer, *White* (London: Routledge, 1999), p. 14.

16 Dyer, pp. 16, 15.

17 Judith Halberstam, *Female Masculinity* (Durham, NC: Duke University Press, 1998), p. 21.

18 Halberstam, p. 28.

19 Wald, p. 15.

20 Judith Butler, *Bodies that Matter: On the Discursive Limits of 'Sex'* (New York: Routledge, 1993), p. 125.

21 Marjorie Garber, *Vested Interests: Cross-Dressing and Cultural Anxiety* (London: Penguin, 1993), pp. 4–5.

22 Judith Butler, *Gender Trouble: Feminism and the Subversion of Identity* (London: Routledge, 1990), p. 175.

23 Leslie Feinberg, *Trans Liberation: Beyond Pink or Blue* (Boston: Beacon, 1998), p. 27.

24 Garber, p. 17. It should be noted from the outset that although my reading of *The Last Report* is deeply indebted to Garber, I restrict my use of the term 'cross-dressing' to incidents of full gender disguise. I do not, in other words, use the term 'cross-dressing' to denote 'the synecdochic quotation of transvestism' – such as the wearing of necklaces or earrings by men – as Garber does (p. 275).

25 Feinberg, p. 27.

26 Garber, p. 11.

27 Jeana DelRosso, *Writing Catholic Women: Contemporary International Catholic Girlhood Narratives* (New York: Palgrave Macmillan, 2005), p. 75.

28 Susan M. Griffin, *Anti-Catholicism and Nineteenth-Century Fiction* (Cambridge: Cambridge University Press, 2004), p. 1.

29 Interestingly, this 'othering' of Catholicism has, in some cultural contexts outside the United States, taken the form of a preoccupation with cross-dressing nuns, priests and monks. For instance, in eighteenth- and nineteenth-century British gothic novels, and novels inspired by the gothic form, the 'notorious deployment of gender travesty in a religious context provided not only titillating shock value but also a "reading" of Catholicism as hypocritical and erotic, something to be unmasked' (Garber, p. 218). The significance of the religious transvestite figures in Matthew Lewis's *The Monk* (1796) and Charlotte Brontë's *Villette* (1853), respectively, is, according to Garber, 'as much England/France and Protestant/Catholic as it is male/female: the phantom appearance of the transvestite, once again, marks a category crisis *elsewhere*.'

30 According to the 2001 ARIS, Catholics represent almost 25 per cent of those Americans declaring a religious affiliation. Paula M. Kane notes that in 1900 there were about twelve million Catholics in America, which represented about 16 per cent of the national population. Kane further reports the projection that 'by 2020 Spanish will be the native tongue of more than 50 percent of American Catholics, a marked shift from the domination of Catholic polity by Irish and Euro-Americans.' 'American Catholic Culture in the Twentieth Century', *Perspectives on American Religion and Culture: A Reader*, ed. Peter W. Williams (Malden, MA: Blackwell, 1999), pp. 390–404 (p. 390).

31 David G. Hackett, 'Gender and Religion in American Culture', *Religion and American Culture* 5.2 (1995), 127–57 (129).

32 Hackett, p. 129.

33 Susan M. Griffin, 'Awful Disclosures: Women's Evidence in the Escaped Nun's Tale', *PMLA* 111.1 (1996), 93–107 (104).

34 Sara Maitland, *A Map of the New Country: Women and Christianity* (London: Routledge and Kegan Paul, 1983), p. 51.

35 Nancy Lusignan Schultz, 'Introduction', *Veil of Fear: Nineteenth Century Convent Tales* (West Lafayette, IN: Purdue University Press, 1999), pp. vii–xxxiii (p. xix).

36 Schultz, p. xxvii.

37 James R. Lewis, '"Mind-Forged Manacles": Anti-Catholic Convent Narratives in the Context of the American Captivity Tale Tradition', *Mid-America: An Historical Review* 72.3 (1990), 149–67 (158).

38 Louise Erdrich, *Love Medicine* (1984; New York: Bantam, 1987), p. 40. Subsequent references will be included in parentheses in the main body of the text.

39 Maria Monk, *Awful Disclosures of the Hotel Dieu Nunnery*, in Schultz, p. 47.

40 Louise Erdrich, *The Last Report on the Miracles at Little No Horse* (London: Flamingo, 2001), p. 13. Subsequent references will be contained in parentheses in the main body of the text.

41 Louise Erdrich, *Tracks* (London: Hamish Hamilton, 1988), p. 205. Subsequent references will appear in parentheses within the text.

42 David Murray, 'Spreading the Word: Missionaries, Conversion and Circulation in the Northeast', in *Spiritual Encounters: Interactions between Christianity and Native Religions in Colonial America*, ed. Nicholas Griffiths and Fernando Cervantes (Birmingham: University of Birmingham Press, 1999), pp. 43–64 (p. 50).

43 Dyer, *White*, p. 15.

44 Pope John Paul II, *The Theology of the Body: Human Love in the Divine Plan* (Boston: Pauline Books, 1997), p. 481.

45 Marie Anne Pagliarini, 'The Pure American Woman and the Wicked Catholic Priest: An Analysis of Anti-Catholic Literature in Antebellum America', *Religion and American Culture* 9.1 (1999), 97–128 (102).

46 Several critics have discussed Nanapush's affinities with the mythical trickster. For example, see Hughes, 91.

47 Jeanne Rosier Smith, *Writing Tricksters: Mythic Gambols in American Ethnic Literature* (Berkeley: University of California Press, 1997), pp. 73–4.

48 Rita Ferrari, '"Where the Maps Stopped": The Aesthetics of Borders in Louise Erdrich's *Love Medicine* and *Tracks*', *Style* 33.1 (1999) 144–65 (144). See also Peterson, p. 145.

49 Chris Weedon, *Feminist Practice and Poststructuralist Theory* (Oxford: Blackwell, 1997), p. 116.

50 DelRosso, p. 21.

51 Lulu is the daughter of Fleur, who is, one of the most visible characters in Erdrich's reservation novels, although she has not yet appeared as a narrator. She is present in: *Love Medicine* (1984), *The Beet Queen* (1986), *Tracks* (1988), *The Bingo Palace* (1994), *The Last Report on the Miracles at Little No Horse* (2001) and *Four Souls* (2004).

52 According to Pope John Paul II, suicide 'represents a rejection of God's absolute sovereignty over life and death, as proclaimed in the prayer of ancient sage of Israel: "You have power over life and death; you lead men down to the gates of Hades and back again" (Wis 16:13; cf. Tb 13:2)' (p. 545).

53 Sam D. Gill, *Native American Religions: An Introduction* (Belmont, CA: Wadsworth, 1982), p. 117.

54 Evelyn Blackwood, 'Sexuality and Gender in Certain Native American Tribes: The Case of Cross-Gender Females', *Signs* 10 (1984), 27–42 (29). Will Roscoe calls this figure a 'female berdache', which he defines as 'anatomical females occupying a named social status involving cross- or mixed-gender economic and social behavior, sometimes partial and/or occasional cross-dressing, and sometimes relationships with (non-berdache) women.' *Changing Ones: Third and Fourth Genders in Native North America* (New York: St. Martin's Press, 1998), p. 73. Because of its Arabic etymology, which connotes 'sex-slave boy', the term 'berdache' is controversial. As such, I opt for 'two-spirit' instead. Although I am only concerned with Father Damien's gender ambiguity here, Julie Barak notes these kinds of crossover in many other Erdrich characters. 'Blurs, Blends, Berdaches: Gender Mixing in the Novels of Louise Erdrich', *Studies in American Indian Literatures* 8.3 (1996), 49–62.

55 See Deirdre Keenan, 'Unrestricted Territory: Gender, Two Spirits, and Louise Erdrich's *The Last Report on the Miracles at Little No Horse*', *American Indian Culture and Research Journal* 30.2 (2006), 1–15; Pamela J. Rader, 'Dis-robing the Priest: Gender and Spiritual Conversions in Louise Erdrich's *The Last Report on the Miracles at Little No Horse*', *The Catholic Church and Unruly Women Writers: Critical Essays*, ed. Jeana DelRosso, Leigh Eicke and Ana Kothe (Basingstoke: Palgrave Macmillan, 2007), pp. 221–35 and J. James Iovannone, '"Mix-Ups, Messes, Confinements, and Double-Dealings": Transgendered Performances in Three Novels by Louise Erdrich', *Studies in American Indian Literatures* 21.1 (2009), 38–68.

56 Roscoe, p. 73; Blackwood, p. 31.

57 Roscoe, p. 73.

58 Murray, p. 52.

59 Quoted in Garber, p. 214.

60 Ibid., p. 215.

61 Ibid.

62 Elizabeth Castelli, '"I Will Make Mary Male": Pieties of the Body and Gender Transformation of Christian Women in Late Antiquity', in *Body Guards: The Cultural Politics of Gender Ambiguity*, ed. Julia Epstein and Kristina Straub (New York: Routledge, 1991), pp. 29–49 (p. 47). The most convincing of the (few) critical assessments of *The Last Report* is that of Alison A. Chapman, who argues that Erdrich 'both alludes to and revises the stories of medieval and early modern figures such as St. Cecilia, St. Agnes, St. Damian, St. Patrick, St. Dismas, St. Stanislaus Kostka, and the women known as transvestite saints' in order to investigate 'the possibility of syncretism.' 'Rewriting the Saints' Lives: Louise Erdrich's *The Last Report on the Miracles at Little No Horse*', *Critique* 48.2 (2007), 149–67 (150).

63 'Nanabozho', *Encyclopedia of North American Indians*, http://college. hmco.com/ history/readerscomp/naind/html/na_024700_nanabozho. htm (14 July 2004).

64 John A. Grim, *The Shaman: Patterns of Religious Healing Among the Ojibway Indians* (Norman: University of Oklahoma Press, 1987), p. 85.

65 Connie A. Jacobs, *The Novels of Louise Erdrich: Stories of her People* (New York: Peter Lang, 2001), p. 73.

66 'The Leopoldine Society', *Catholic Encyclopedia*, www.newadvent.org/ cathen/ 16052a.htm (2 February 2005).

67 DelRosso, p. 185.

68 Louis Owens, *Mixedblood Messages: Literature, Film, Family, Place* (Norman: University of Oklahoma Press, 1998), p. 26.

69 Ibid., p. 40.

70 Ibid., p. 39.

71 The dedication is to Erdrich's then husband, Michael Dorris. Dorris committed suicide in 1997, amid accusations of sexual and physical abuse from two of their adopted children. Erdrich and Dorris were estranged by then, having separated in 1995.

72 Louise Erdrich, *Four Souls* (New York: HarperCollins, 2004), p. 58.

73 Ferrari, p. 144.

74 Hughes notes that the trickster's doubleness of speech 'works simultaneously to undermine the power of the privileged oppressor and to appeal for his or her realignment on the side of the oppressed' (p. 87). Smith provides an exhaustive analysis of tricksterism in *Love Medicine, Tracks, The Beet Queen* and *The Bingo Palace*, pp. 71–110.

75 Mary V. Dearborn, *Pocahontas's Daughters: Gender and Ethnicity in American Culture* (New York: Oxford University Press, 1986), p. 29.

76 Barak, p. 50.

77 As Ferrari puts it, Erdrich's novels 'defy containment as they construct and transgress boundaries within discrete texts and across novels – since they deal with the same place and many of the same characters, with different emphases' (p. 160, n. 2). Furthermore, Erdrich published an expanded version of her 1984 novel, *Love Medicine*, in 1993, an act that 'challenges the primacy of first editions and questions the authenticity of all proposed "beginnings"' (Hughes, p. 113, n. 9).

4

(W)Rites-of-passing: shifting racial and gender identities in *Caucasia* and *Middlesex*

> Born theoretically white, we are permitted to pass our childhood as imaginary Indians, our adolescence as imaginary Negroes, and only then are we expected to settle down to being what we really are: white once more.
>
> Leslie Fiedler, *Waiting for the End* (1964)[1]

Despite his problematic assumption of a uniformly white 'we', Leslie Fiedler's hypothesis is relevant because it yokes together the notion of racial mobility and the process of a child's journey towards maturity. This chapter examines contemporary first-person fictions of adolescence in which the protagonists' adolescence, as an in-between stage that is *not* childhood and *not* adulthood, is inextricably bound up with other indeterminacies mapped upon their bodies, especially those of race and gender. Danzy Senna's *Caucasia* (1998) and Jeffrey Eugenides's *Middlesex* (2002) invoke the alienating experience of adolescence as a lens through which to refract their protagonists' 'othered' bodies. As Brenda Boudreau notes of *Caucasia*:

> [the] adolescent girl's body becomes a perfect stage on which to illustrate the tenuousness of both whiteness and blackness because so much of the girl's identity is intricately linked to her physical body, and it is on the physical body that we expect racial identity to make itself visible.[2]

Crucially, in both novels, the protagonists also engage, with varying degrees of commitment and success, in the act of creative writing, which serves to reflect back inevitably upon the authorship of the novels themselves. If the novel of adolescence, like the *Bildungsroman*, tends to be heavily autobiographical, *Caucasia* and *Middlesex* toy with this convention.[3] *Middlesex* purports to be its protagonist's 'memoirs' while *Caucasia* plays into the contemporaneous publishing phenomenon that is the mixed race memoir.[4] The two works discussed in this chapter thus challenge the reader to (re)consider boundaries of genre and of form – memoir, after all, exists in the interstices between fiction and autobiography – as well as those of the race and/or gender of their protagonists.

Before beginning the analysis, it is necessary first to outline briefly what I understand by the term 'fictions of adolescence.' As Barbara White observes, critics 'usually associate the novel of adolescence with either the *Bildungsroman* or the initiation story.'[5] Although the novel of adolescence is heavily indebted to the *Bildungsroman*, it may introduce some key variations on this traditional form. According to White, in the novel of adolescence:

> Plot elements from the *Bildungsroman* may be put to a different use; for instance, the journey, which in the *Bildungsroman* is a vehicle for vertical development, may become in the novel of adolescence an oscillation from side to side. Instead of progressing from *A* to *B*, the hero vacillates between *A* and *A'* and never gets to *B* or, perhaps, rejects the idea of *B*.[6]

A similar point is made by Gina Hausknecht in the distinction she elucidates between what she calls 'the Girls' story' and 'the Girl's own story.' For Hausknecht, 'the Girls' story' features such staple elements as 'triumph over the various adversities associated with adolescence; acquisition of self-knowledge; assertion of control over character defects (often having to do with not being socially graceful, popular, or feminine enough); and getting the boy' whereas the 'the Girl's own story' relates 'how it feels to encounter such imperatives and definitions. The latter reveals the former as a bewildering script that a Girl cannot enact without the surrender of her own self-image and self-imaginings.'[7]

The novel of adolescence, then, rejects the linear progression that is typical of the *Bildungsroman*. This makes it particularly receptive to the introduction of a passing plot, which is also non-linear, frequently involving multiple journeys back and forth across the color line, and sometimes featuring multivalent typologies of passing (racial, gender, sexual), all of which impinge upon and intersect one another.[8] In *Caucasia* non-normative gender and sexual identities accompany the subject's racial in-betweenness, while in *Middlesex* indeterminacy of sexual orientation and ethnicity go hand-in-hand with the protagonist's ambiguously gendered body.

Caucasia is a contemporary novel of racial passing while Middlesex is not 'about' gender passing in the strictest sense for its protagonist is intersexed. However, comparing the two novels foregrounds the constructedness of the one-drop rule, for just as Calliope Stephanides in Middlesex is neither/nor and both male and female, according to conventional definitions of these terms, Birdie Lee in Caucasia is neither/nor and both black and white. In other words, the very term 'passing' accepts and reinforces the racial hierarchy instituted by the one-drop rule. One can only be passing for something (white) if one is 'really' something else (black). According to the one-drop rule, the child of one white and one African American parent is 'really' black. For this reason, Birdie – and indeed, this is true of any story of racial passing – can no more accurately be described as passing than can Calliope, an intersexed individual – a chromosomal male with 5-alpha-reductase deficiency – raised as a girl until the age of fourteen.[9]

Covering the years 1975 to 1982, Caucasia juxtaposes the incendiary political situation of the desegregation of Boston's public schools with the simultaneous disintegration of an interracial family. White-skinned Birdie Lee and her older sister, darker-complexioned Cole, are the children of a white activist mother and a black academic father, whose marriage crumbles shortly after the novel opens. When their mother, Sandy, is suspected of storing guns in the basement of their house, the children – who have heretofore been living with their mother – are separated according to their skin colour. Deck takes Cole to Brazil; Sandy and Birdie go on the run for four years.[10] Finally settling in New Hampshire, Sandy and Birdie change their names and pose as the widow and daughter of an invented Jewish academic called David Goldman. Two years later, Birdie flees New Hampshire in search of her father and sister, and finds them, at last, in California. Middlesex has a much broader geographical and temporal scope. From a contemporary (2001) vantage point, forty-one-year-old Cal, currently living in Berlin, narrates his life story.[11] Books 1 and 2 cover 1922 to 1960, describing Cal's grandparents' (who are brother and sister) escape from Smyrna in Asia Minor in 1922 amid Graeco-Turkish conflict, their successful emigration to Detroit, Michigan and the marriage of their American-born son, Milton, to a fellow Greek American and distant cousin, Tessie Zizmo. Books 3 and 4 span Calliope's birth in 1960 to her discovery, in 1974, that she is intersexed, to her running away when faced with the prospect of 'corrective' surgery, to his eventual return – as Cal rather than Callie – some months later upon learning of the death of his father.

'Running a thousand miles for freedom': geographies of body and nation

As is the case with several passing narratives, the act of passing in *Caucasia*, which was historically undertaken to achieve social mobility, is metaphorically conceived in terms of geographical mobility. In practical terms, it is much easier to reinvent oneself as 'white' in a place which affords the passer a degree of anonymity. As Samira Kawash observes, 'the metaphor of the color line itself is not biological, but spatial.'[12] Consequently, in passing narratives, the symbolic 'crossing of the color line' is often accompanied by geographical displacement.[13] By extension, in *Caucasia*, whiteness and blackness, racial and interracial relationships are imagined as actual places. Accordingly, both Sandy and Deck make reference to 'the land of miscegenation'.[14] Even during the heyday of their marriage, they never say 'I love you' to each other, but instead 'I miss you', incongruously registering their affection in terms of geographical distance (p. 19). As the section, and indeed the British title of the novel, *From Caucasia, with Love* implies, whiteness itself is configured as a geographical location. Equally, the section entitled 'Negritude for Beginners' – evocative of a language-learning tutorial or textbook – constructs blackness as a geographical space with its own unique tongue. Cole and Birdie even invent their own language which they use to communicate between themselves. Elemeno, Cole tells Birdie, isn't 'just a language, but a place and a people as well' (p. 7). After Birdie reinvents herself at school, she proclaims, 'There was no way I was going back to the never-never land of my old self' (p. 65).

Given that racial passing is bound up with geographical mobility, it is unsurprising that modes of transport, and their relationship to Birdie's body in particular, assume great significance in *Caucasia*. After Birdie and Sandy go on the run, they change cars several times over the course of four years in order to cover their tracks. However, their last vehicle before settling in New Hampshire they have had for two years: 'It had once been yellow. I could tell because some of the paint was left on the interior, a nice buttery chrome yellow. Now it was no color at all; the color of something stripped clean for the sake of starting over' (pp. 142–3). The van's fadedness reflects Birdie's own situation as she and her mother are on the threshold of settling in New Hampshire. Yellow is, of course, the symbolic 'colour' of racial ambiguity, or mixedness, a situation that derives from the custom of describing light-skinned African Americans as 'yellow' or 'high yellow.' (Significantly, Cole's car is a 'butter-yellow Karmann Ghia' (p. 403)). Whiteness, on the other hand, derives its representational power from the fact that 'white is not anything really, not an identity, not a particularising quality, because it is everything – white is no colour because it is all colours.'[15] The description of the van anticipates Birdie's fear that geographical stasis will fix her into a white identity that she does not want. Whereas four years of constant flux is a comfort to Birdie, allowing her the 'sense that as long as we kept moving, we could go back to what we had left behind' (p. 137), the prospect of settling provokes the anxiety that once 'we had stopped moving, allowing our new selves to bloom, it seemed the old had to disintegrate' (p. 188).

For Birdie's father, the MBTA subway lines in Boston are 'racial codes', each one leading to areas inhabited by different racial and ethnic groups – Jews, Italians, Irish, African Americans (p. 296). Significantly, Birdie has 'a thick blue vein like a subway line etched in [her] forehead' (p. 297). Boston's racially segregated neighbourhoods are thus mapped upon Birdie's mixed race body, where black and white are irrevocably united.[16] Predictably enough, given the importance of school desegregation within the narrative, the school bus becomes, arguably, the most symbolically charged mode of transport. In her new home in New Hampshire, Birdie first encounters Samantha, another mixed race girl, while staring at her through a school bus window: 'The girl was black like me – half, that is. I could spot another one immediately' (p. 223). Identifying with her, Birdie senses that the facts about Samantha – which she learns from her classmates – may 'hold clues to my own disappearance' (p. 225). Through Samantha, Birdie feels a renewed connection with her sister Cole: Samantha is 'the color of cinnamon' (p. 226), Cole 'cinnamon-skinned' (p. 5), and like Cole, Samantha has 'ashy' knees (pp. 49, 226). Samantha's presence reminds Birdie of Cole's absence, and spurs Birdie in her quest to find her lost sister. In exercising her agency, Birdie registers her refusal 'to be black like Samantha. A doomed, tragic shade of black. I wanted to be black like somebody else' (p. 321). This is an important reversal of the conventional trajectory in most passing narratives – and indeed, that of *Caucasia* prior to Birdie's

decision to run away and find her sister – in which the passing mulatta
is sought out and relentlessly pursued. Unlike those literary mulattas
who are unmasked and demystified when they are finally pinned
down, Birdie takes control of her own self-definition, choosing to out
herself in the process.

At the close of the novel, after Birdie and Cole are reunited in
California, she spots another 'cinnamon-skinned girl' through another
school bus window:

> For a second I thought I was somewhere familiar and she was a girl I
> already knew. I began to lift my hand, but stopped, remembering where
> I was and what I had already found. Then the bus lurched forward,
> and the face was gone with it, just a blur of yellow and black in motion.
> (p. 413)

The 'yellow and black' of the *moving* school bus contrasts with the
yellow-faded-to-'no color' of the (symbolically, at least) *stationary* van
that 'served as our home' before Sandy decides to settle indefinitely in
New Hampshire (p. 143). Although Birdie has 'found' what she sought,
the literary mulatta, Senna seems to suggest, will perpetually be in a
state of reinvention and reinterpretation. After all, when Birdie flees
New Hampshire she takes a bus to Boston and reflects 'that this was
where I felt most safe – on a moving vehicle, rolling toward some
destination but not quite there' (p. 293).

Similarly, in *Middlesex*, the potential to remake oneself endlessly is
bound up with geographical mobility. Just as Cal's grandparents'
passing as French enables them to gain passage aboard a ship and
hence escape smouldering Smyrna in 1922 (p. 61), Callie refuses the
surgery recommended by Dr. Luce by running away from her parents
and transforming herself into the boy she now believes herself to be:
'Every jolt in the road dropped my Adam's apple another notch in my
neck' (p. 449). Geographical movement, it would seem, offers Cal the
opportunity of, if not transcending, at least mastering his own body.
He starts living as male, he and his mother move from Michigan and
he has 'been moving ever since', his job in the Foreign Service
enabling this constant motion (p. 106). The forty-one-year-old narrator
of the novel, describing the trip around the world he takes after college,
observes that he 'tried to forget my body by keeping it in motion'
(p. 320).

Significantly, although Cal, the adolescent, eventually returns to the
bosom of his family after several months' absence on the road and in

California, Cal, the forty-one-year-old adult, is permanently exiled in
Germany. The symbolic choice of Germany – which was divided after
World War II only to be reunified in 1990 – is reinforced by the fact
that Cal lives in Berlin. Although the city was, geographically, located
in East Germany, it was itself split into East and West. As Cal notes,
'This once-divided city reminds me of myself. My struggle for
unification, for *Einheit.* Coming from a city still cut in half by racial
hatred, I feel hopeful here in Berlin' (p. 106). The symbolism of a
unified east and west is compounded by Cal's somewhat awkward
courtship of Julie Kikuchi, whom he meets in Berlin. Julie bridges the
apparent polar opposites of east and west. She is 'Asian, at least
genetically', and therefore 'eastern' (p. 41), but American, and thus
'western.' Raised in northern California, on the western seaboard, she
is a graduate of the Rhode Island School of design, on the east coast of
the United States (p. 107).

In *Caucasia* and *Middlesex* the protagonists' flights terminate in
California. In Oakland and Berkeley, Birdie is reunited with her father
and sister. In San Francisco, Cal lives rough for a while with
Deadheads, subsequently taking a job performing in an erotic show.
California emerges in both novels as a place of possibility for infinite
shapeshifting. In other words, these destinations are not really 'ends'
because California holds the potential (paradoxically, given its location
at the end of the continent) for permanent mobility. After all, as Sandy
tells Birdie, in California 'even the ground moves' (*Caucasia*, p. 383).
Indeed, the deferral of identity evoked by Birdie on the bus could,
arguably, be applied to California for many have claimed, following
Theodore Roosevelt, that California is 'west of the west.'[17] California
offers both Birdie and Cal the opportunity to come to terms finally
with their bodies. For Birdie, California is 'not so whitewashed' as
New England (p. 332). Meanwhile, Cal – en route to California – evokes
the mythology of the Gold Rush as he masturbates: 'Half-paying
attention, while I watched Johnny Carson, my hand prospected'
(*Middlesex*, p. 453).

Although Birdie and Cal travel to California, they end up in places
that are conspicuously *not* Los Angeles. Perhaps for Eugenides, San
Francisco is an appropriate destination for Cal not only because it is a
mecca for queer people, but because its very topography supports an
analogy with Cal's body, which only becomes problematic when s/he
begins to grow up. Built on a peninsula, as David Fine and Paul
Skenazy observe, 'San Francisco did not have much space to grow. Los

Angeles, by contrast, could, and did, spread across a vast basin.'[18]
According to Fine and Skenazy, because California 'is populated still
for the most part by people from elsewhere who bring with them their
pasts as they seek new futures', much writing about San Francisco
'features a past-future dialectic that takes a pronounced geographical
form, a turning in two directions. The past is somewhere else, the
future is at the edge of water.'[19] San Francisco thus provides a
geographical complement to the novel's, and the protagonist's, Janus
face. Cal is at once a product of what has gone before, the victim of a
recessive gene, and also undeniably representative of the future. As
Zora, a fellow hermaphrodite performer in San Francisco, tells Cal:
'we're what's next' (*Middlesex*, p. 490).

By establishing their narrators' bodies as mobile entities between
various spaces and places, both Senna and Eugenides effectively yoke
the public to the private, the political to the personal, the national to the
domestic. In *Caucasia*, amid the turbulence of the Boston busing
crisis, in which public schools became highly contested territories
along racial lines, Senna creates a corresponding familial war zone.
Thus, the racial politics of the busing crisis encroach both literally *and*
metaphorically on the Lee family. For example, while the *attic* of their
Columbus Avenue house is the space in which Cole and Birdie while
away their carefree days, playing children's games and speaking their
own private language, the *basement* of the family home, where Sandy
and her activist friends store guns, becomes the site in which such
domestic tranquillity is disrupted. Cocooned in their attic haven,
Birdie, who is eight in 1975, as yet registers no differences in skin tone
between herself and her older sister, Cole. The basement, on the other
hand, is 'grown-up land' (*Caucasia*, p. 8). Downstairs, the racial
violence of the outside world is rapidly invading their home. The
conjunction of domestic space and nation is explicitly invoked when
Lucas, one of the political fugitives to whom Sandy offers sanctuary, is
arrested and taken away. Lucas's reaction is surprise, 'as if he had
expected more from our country, as if he had expected more from our
house' (p. 39).

Throughout *Middlesex*, the history of Callie's recessive gene –
which is responsible for her conflicted body – is juxtaposed with
contested local, national and international spaces. Her grandparents
flee an area over which Greeks and Turks have been vying for control
for centuries. Detroit, where they end up, was 'a fort fought over by
the British and French until, wearing them out, it fell into the hands

of the Americans' (p. 79). While the Stephanides family initially settle in Detroit's east side, they move to the west side, and eventually, out of the city altogether. The midwestern location of Michigan lies between the continental poles of New York and California, in which Cal also spends time. As in *Caucasia*, the occupation of domestic spaces is inextricably bound up with the segregation of bodies within public space, which in turn reflects back inevitably upon the body of the protagonist as a site of conflict. When Milton Stephanides's restaurant on the east side of the city is destroyed in a fire at the height of the Detroit race riots in 1967, the resulting insurance payout enables Milton to move the family from their home in the increasingly racially mixed city to the mostly white suburb of Grosse Pointe. This episode demonstrates the extent to which Calliope is in-between in terms of her ethnic background as well as her gender. For while black–white racial tensions facilitate the Stephanideses' 'white flight', the estate agent who sells them their new home evidently does not consider them quite white enough for Grosse Pointe: '*Let's see. Southern Mediterranean. One point. Not in one of the professions. One point. Religion? Greek church. That's some kind of Catholic, isn't it? So there's another point there*' (p. 255). She sells them their unusual Hudson Clark-designed house because she realises that only an '*Italian or a Greek*' (p. 256) will buy it and because Milton, like the one Jewish family who live in the neighbourhood, pays for it in cash (p. 262). Its location on Middlesex Boulevard is, of course, deeply symbolic. As Cal subsequently realises, the house is 'a place designed for a new type of human being, who would inhabit a new world. I couldn't help feeling, of course, that that person was me, me and all the others like me' (p. 529).

In 1971 domestic space and the cityscape, familial and political disputes are again linked. As Callie and her brother bicker (over Chapter Eleven's acne and Callie's wish for a bra), they assume their father's roar of 'Goddamn it!' is his attempt to quieten them (p. 290). In fact, he is responding to a television news item reporting Judge Roth's decision to desegregate Detroit's public schools and introduce the busing of white students from the suburbs to the city. The siblings' quarrel over their adolescent bodies and the segregation of white and black bodies are thus conjoined. Callie's parents react to Roth's order by removing her from the public school system and enrolling her in an all-girls' private institution. As such, Callie's adolescent body is segregated within the public space of the school by gender as well as by race. In this way, the problematic bodies of the protagonists become localised sites upon which national conflicts are played out.

By the same token, political subversives – dangers to national security – are conceived in terms of sexual dangers to the bodies of Callie and Birdie as children. In *Middlesex*, for instance, when seven-year-old Callie befriends Marius, a member of the Black Panthers and a customer at her father's restaurant, Milton orders him to 'stay away from her' and tells Callie to 'stay away from people like that' (p. 231). As Milton perceives it, the threat of black nationalism and the imagined sexual menace posed to his daughter by an older, black man are fundamentally the same. Similarly, in *Caucasia*, black activism and sexual menace are united in the figure of Redbone, a light-skinned, red-haired associate of Birdie's mother who eventually betrays her cohort and 'sold [them] down river' (p. 175). It is never clear whether the threat posed by Redbone is sexual or political, as is borne out when he shows eight-year-old Birdie two rifles. The phallic connotations of the guns are laid bare when Deck comes upon them and demands 'What the fuck do you think you're doing holding my daughter over those guns?' (p. 16). Sandy warns Birdie not 'to talk to anyone except your school friends. You understand? There are perverts, crazies, dirty old men, and they want little girls like you' (p. 66), but the only man who approaches Birdie at school is Redbone, who asks if he may take her photograph (p. 109). The link is made most explicit when Birdie returns to Boston as a teenager and 'imagined red-haired rapists dressed like Feds, waiting for me in the bushes' (p. 359). What Redbone's character illustrates, and the entire novel confirms, therefore, is that the sexual is inextricable from the political, the protagonist's body ineluctably bound up with the nation.

'Passing' from childhood to adulthood

Like the protagonist of *The Autobiography of an Ex-Colored Man*, who is first educated at home and subsequently attends public school, Birdie is alternately home-schooled by her mother and educated at a mainstream school. However, unlike in Johnson's novella, in which the shift from home to public school precipitates a confrontation with his racial identity and his concomitant 'otherness', Birdie and Cole are othered even in their home-school environment. Their mother specialises in teaching 'special children' who are 'dyslexic, retarded, or simply bad-natured' (*Caucasia*, p. 137). A slippage is thus introduced between the 'otherness' of her regular pupils and that of her own children. As Birdie observes, 'When my mother wasn't teaching those disturbed and delayed children, she taught me' (p. 137). Sandy's own mother, who disapproves of the girls' being home-schooled, tells Sandy that she is 'wonderful with those mongoloids' but 'normal children are simply not [her] specialty' (p. 105). The term 'mongoloid' in this case functions as a pejorative description of a person with learning difficulties. However, 'Mongoloid', with a capital 'm', also bears racial connotations. Specifically, it recalls Deck Lee's view of his own marriage as an experiment in miscegenation. A photo of his wedding day marks a page in his encyclopaedia delineating 'the three racial phenotypes of the world – Mongoloid, Negroid, and Caucasoid' (p. 30). The labels 'Mongoloid' – as neither 'Negroid' nor 'Caucasoid', like Cole and Birdie – and 'mongoloid' thus serve to reinforce the association between Sandra's overlapping roles as teacher and mother to children who are 'different.'

Ironically, given what occurs in the basement of their Boston home, Sandra favours home-schooling her children 'to keep [them] safe from the racism and violence of the world' (p. 26). Although the girls are 'othered' even through their home-schooling, the school functions as the space in which they are initiated into their racial difference. However, unlike the narrator of Johnson's *Autobiography of an Ex-Colored Man*, who learns of his mixedness when he is designated as 'nonwhite' or 'other' by a schoolteacher, white-looking Birdie attends an all-black school and as such, her fellow students ask: 'What you doin' in this school? You white?' (p. 43).[20] In a scene reminiscent of William Wells Brown's *Clotel* (1853), Birdie is cornered in the school toilets by a girl who threatens to cut her hair. In *Clotel* the mixed race heroine is ordered to cut off her long hair by her mistress, Mrs. French, who is jealous of her beauty.[21] Because 'the glossy ringlets of her raven hair' are what Phillip Brian Harper calls 'a prime signifier of European beauty', the actual and threatened cutting of Clotel's – and Birdie's – hair represents an attempt by Mrs. French and Maria, respectively, 'to "Africanize" their appearance' and thus render them less alluring to both white and black men.[22] For, as Maria asks Birdie, 'You think Ali's gonna like you when you don't got no hair?' (*Caucasia*, p. 47)[23]

In *Middlesex*, Calliope is alerted to her own difference by the pubescent changes taking place in her peers' bodies. Shortly before her twelfth birthday, on the first day of sixth grade, a classmate arrives at school 'wearing a slight but unmistakably self-satisfied smile. Below this smile, as if displayed on a trophy shelf, were the new breasts she had gotten over the summer' (p. 282). As Jane Blunt's thighs 'get a little bit longer every week' and a 'patch of light brown hair' appears when Beverly Maas raises her hand (p. 285); as Peter Quail's voice deepens by two octaves over the course of a month (p. 286), Calliope 'in the second row, is *motionless*, her desk *stalled* somehow, so that she's the only one who takes in the true extent of the metamorphoses around her' (p. 286, emphasis added). Thus, in *Middlesex*, metaphors of statis and fixity in time and place evoke Callie's *pubescent* body just as metaphors of travel and movement reflect the possibility of her mobility between genders. In other words, Birdie's and Cal's journeys, and their bodies' relationships to spaces and places, cannot be viewed independently of their status as adolescents. Their bodies are ambiguous not only because they are in-between in terms of race and gender, respectively, but also because of their age. Both *Caucasia* and *Middlesex* are, essentially, novels of adolescence, structured by tropes such as stealing and running away that appear in the majority of such works.[24] Birdie takes various items belonging to her mother and Jim, her mother's new boyfriend, notably a postcard on which her aunt Dot's address in Boston is written (*Caucasia*, p. 241). This clue will become the starting point for Birdie's search for her father and sister. Callie steals three hundred dollars from her father to help her on her journey away from New York and Dr. Luce (*Middlesex*, p. 438). In other words, the conventions of the adolescent novel are particularly receptive to the stories of Birdie and Cal, except that the peculiarities of these protagonists' bodies multiply the adolescent experience of alienation one-hundredfold.

For example, as Barbara White observes, the adolescent heroine often 'feels torn between her mother and her father.'[25] This is certainly true of Birdie Lee, but her experience is complicated and compounded by the fact that her mother is white, her father black, and she, mixed race. In the same way, if 'in novels of female adolescence conflict over gender identity is the major theme', Calliope's dramatic confrontation with the 'truth' about *her* gender far surpasses the average adolescent's experience.[26] According to White, 'many adolescent protagonists clash with society over their reluctance to undergo a lengthy period of low status wherein they are separated from children and adults and denied the privileges of either.'[27] Because of their problematic bodies, Birdie and Cal will encounter great difficulty *ever* overcoming the 'low status'

– the status of Other – to which all adolescents are relegated for a period in their lives.

Poised in an intermediate zone between childhood and adulthood, the protagonists' quests for selfhood are complicated even further by their indeterminate bodies. Because of her nomadic lifestyle, Birdie feels herself 'to be incomplete – a gray blur, a body in motion, forever galloping toward completion – half a girl, half-caste, half-mast, and half-baked, not quite ready for consumption', which refers as much to the process of growing up as it does to her ambiguous racial identity (*Caucasia*, p. 137). Reflecting on the nomadic life that she leads for four years, Birdie recalls waking up in a new place and having no idea

> which city we were in, which day of the week it was, even where we had been just the day before. I felt somehow more lucid in that half-waking state, as if that place of *timelessness* and placelessness and forgetfulness was the only space one could possibly inhabit. (p. 155, emphasis added)

Evidently, Birdie appreciates the suspension of time and age – and, by extension, the postponement of 'growing up' – as much as she does her racial liminality. The inextricability of Birdie's pubescent body from her mixed raceness is also reflected in her friends' efforts to make her over. Just as Maria, Birdie's best friend at Nkrumah, turns Birdie's 'straight hair . . . curly', thus symbolically 'blackening' her (p. 69), so Mona, her best friend in New Hampshire, teaches her 'how to be a girl . . . how to apply lipstick properly, how to stick in a tampon, how to stuff your bra with shoulder pads ripped right off a department store mannequin' (p. 227).

Meanwhile, Cal's escape from an unambiguously female identity – his refusal to undergo surgery to align his genitalia with his upbringing as a girl – is inextricable from his experience as a typical adolescent longing for the somewhat mundane privileges of adult life: 'I was free now to let my teeth rot or to put my feet up on the backs of seats' (*Middlesex*, p. 450). However, these benefits are, naturally, accompanied by adult worries: 'Suddenly I had to pay attention to things I'd never paid any attention to. To bus schedules and bus fares, to budgeting money, to *worrying* about money, to scanning a menu for the absolutely cheapest thing that would fill me up' (p. 445). While Cal could never accurately be described as passing as a male or female, he does 'pass for older' (p. 445), informing the people who pick him up as a hitchhiker that he is on his way to California to commence his undergraduate studies at Stanford. Cal's status as the classic adolescent runaway – rather than the particular circumstances of his flight – are emphasised when the narrator notes: 'Long before my naked body appeared in medical textbooks, my face appeared on bulletin boards and in windows across the nation' (p. 467). He subsequently claims – again conflating bodily change and geographical travel – that his 'change from girl to boy was far less dramatic than the *distance* anybody travels from infancy to girlhood' (p. 520, emphasis added). Back in Detroit he is eventually reunited with his ageing grandmother, Desdemona, who asks her granddaughter-turned-grandson: 'What happened to you?' to which he responds: 'I grew up' (p. 520).

In both *Caucasia* and *Middlesex* the milestones of female adolescent experience take on a deeper political significance because of the ways in which the protagonists' bodies are closely bound up with US history and politics. Consequently, when Birdie sexually experiments with Nicholas Marsh, the son of her New Hampshire landlord and landlady, Senna explicitly evokes the history of the systematic rape of black women that occurred during slavery. Nicholas boasts of his encounter with a black prostitute in Amsterdam in terms which inevitably recall the sexual relations that existed between white men and black women at that time: 'I heard that black girls were supposed to be good, anyway, so we *bought* this one' (p. 199, emphasis added). After deciding not to engage in sexual intercourse with Nicholas, Birdie leaves the Marshes house, 'racing through the woods, as if there were dogs at my heels' (*Caucasia*, p. 208), an image that is evocative of a runaway slave chased by bloodhounds. The impression is reinforced by the fact that Sandy and Birdie live in a cottage – as distinct from 'the big house' – on the Marshes land (p. 147). Furthermore, the rite of passage that is the adolescent's first sexual experience represents an irrevocable break with childhood. Thus, after her sexual encounter with Nicholas, Birdie avoids the Marshes for several weeks, instead reverting 'to childish games' (p. 209). For Birdie, sex with Nicholas would involve making a transition not simply from childhood to adulthood, but from an indefinite racial identity to a *white* one (p. 274).

In *Middlesex*, Calliope's sexual encounter with the Obscure Object's brother precipitates her confrontation with the complexity of her adolescent, gender and sexual identities. As Callie engages in intercourse with Jerome, she watches the Object and Rex Reese fumble on the other cot in the same room. She then realises that she 'wasn't a girl but something in between. I knew this from how natural it felt to enter Rex Reese's body, *how right it felt* (p. 375). Quite apart from the fact that not being a girl, and being 'something in between', can just as easily refer to the state of adolescence and the transition from childhood to adulthood, the mature narrator of *Middlesex* makes Callie's self-realisation about her gender contingent upon her sexual desire for the Object. Obviously, it does not follow that because Callie is sexually attracted to women she is necessarily male. Accordingly, both *Caucasia* and *Middlesex* play out the slipperiness of identity by multiplying the simplistic terms in which it is typically conceived, and revealing the contingency of these terms – race, ethnicity, gender, sexuality, age – upon one another.

The 'hardest adjustment' which Cal undergoes in his transition from adolescent girl to boy is switching from the use of women's restrooms to men's rooms (*Middlesex*, p. 451). As both Garber and Halberstam observe, the 'bathroom problem' is a recurring trope in tales of ambiguously gendered subjects because 'it so directly posits the binarism of gender (choose either one door or the other) in apparently inflexible terms, and also (what is really the same point) because it marks a place of taboo.'[28] For Halberstam, 'men's rest rooms tend to operate as a highly charged sexual space in which sexual interactions are both encouraged and punished' whereas 'women's rest rooms tend to operate as an arena for the enforcement of gender conformity.'[29] Interestingly, Cal's experience is the direct reverse of this. The women's toilet stall at his old school had once 'been a haven for [him]! That was all over now' (p. 451). In the basement bathroom, the stalls are covered with graffiti: 'Sketched in blue ink were little men with gigantic sexual parts. And women with enormous breasts. Also various permutations: men with dinky penises; and women with penises, too. It was an education both in what was and what might be' (p. 329). The 'subterranean realm' is thus a space in which 'people wrote down what they couldn't say' (p. 329). Rather than acknowledge 'their most shameful longings' as the women do (p. 329), in the men's room, the men at urinals look 'straight ahead like horses with blinders' (p. 451).

In texts that interrogate gender, sexuality automatically and inevitably becomes an issue. The risk of too closely correlating indeterminate gender with fluid sexuality is discussed in Chapter 2 and is confirmed in *Middlesex*, in which Calliope's sexual orientation remains stable while his/her gender changes. As Zachary Sifuentes puts it, 'No matter how sexuality is defined, Calliope's decision to maintain an "uncorrected" body but change her gender exposes the degree to which sex and gender assumptions are embedded in sexuality as the fictional conditions for sexuality to emerge.'[30] Julie Kikuchi fears that Cal is a closet gay for whom an Asian woman is his 'last stop' before coming out, as female Asian bodies are perceived as being boyish (*Middlesex*, p. 184). Cal reassures her, however, that he has 'always liked girls. I liked girls when I *was* a girl' (p. 513). In *Caucasia*, Birdie's adolescent experimentation with her burgeoning sexuality is at times same-sex-oriented. In fact, her first sexual experiences are with Alexis, a girl whom she meets while she and her mother are living at Aurora, a women's commune in upstate New York. While she is experimenting sexually with Nicholas Marsh, Birdie recalls having done 'some strange things' with Alexis at Aurora: 'Some nights, on the mattress we shared, I had straddled her in a game we called "honeymoon." She would say, "You be the guy, and I'll be the girl. Pretend you have to hold me down. Pretend you're the boss"' (p. 199). By conjuring the spectre of lesbianism, Senna continues the long tradition of passing narratives in which miscegenation is simultaneously evoked (by the protagonist's mixed race body) and, curiously, contained by displacing the phantom of miscegenation onto other sexual practices considered deviant or illicit, such as homosexuality, prostitution and incest.[31]

It is no coincidence, then, that Birdie's 'coming out' – her flight from New Hampshire to Boston and, thus, from the white identity into which she has been passing – is juxtaposed with a homosexual coming-out: that of Ronnie Parkman, a former friend of Deck's and the father of Birdie's childhood boyfriend, Ali. When she returns to Boston, she seeks out Ali, hoping that, through his father, she will be able to acquire information as to the whereabouts of Deck and Cole. But Ali tells Birdie that his own father is 'missing too' and thinks he 'might be dead' (p. 327). Ali employs euphemisms historically invoked by the African American community when describing a family member who had passed as white to avoid telling her that, since he last saw Birdie, his father has come out as gay. The link is reinforced when Ronnie, whom Birdie subsequently meets and who provides her with Deck's address in Oakland, describes Ali's shame about his father's homosexuality in terms that are explicitly reminiscent of the seminal moment in racial passing narratives, in which the passer denies a close member of his or her family in order not to give away his/her 'true' racial identity: 'He ignored me. He looked right past me as if he didn't know me from Adam' (p. 350).[32] Interestingly, though, Senna reverses the usual dynamic of this scenario. Here, it is *Ali* who is cast in the role conventionally occupied by the passer: the character who feels his own selfhood threatened by a relative who openly and obviously belongs to a subjugated group. By extension, it could be inferred that Ali is the one concealing something about his past. Meanwhile, Ronnie – who for many years passed as straight – and Birdie – who for a couple of years passed as white – are both out.

Birdie's and Cal's ambiguously raced or gendered bodies foreground a concomitant concern not only with sexuality, but also with other identity categories. Accordingly, Cal's problematic gender identity is intimately bound up with her Greek American identity. In describing her transformation from a girl into a teenage boy, Cal feels 'like an immigrant, putting on airs, who runs into someone from the old country' (*Middlesex*, p. 471). Indeed, Cal's ethnicity is deeply implicated in the specific form of pseudohermaphroditism which he is experiencing. According to Doctor Luce, Cal's 'rare genetic condition' is known to express itself in the populations of 'the Dominican Republic, Papua New Guinea, and southeastern Turkey. Not that far from the village [Milton's] parents came from. About three hundred miles, in fact' (p. 428).[33] Cal's grandmother, Desdemona, corroborates this link when, confronted with her granddaughter-turned-grandson, she recalls her mother telling her: 'In the village, long time ago, they use to have sometimes babies who were looking like girls. Then – fifteen, sixteen, they are looking like boys!' (p. 526). Just as Cal's hermaphroditic body and his Greek ancestry are inseparable, Birdie's racial liminality is reinforced by her gender ambiguity. Staring at the bathroom mirror, Birdie sees 'a twelve-year-old girl who might be a boy if it weren't for the scraggly ponytail falling down her back' (*Caucasia*, p. 180). To escape the notice of pursuing Federal agents, Birdie aims for an identity that is not only white – and thus, inconspicuous – but also gender-ambiguous so that agents will have to ask themselves: '*Was the child a boy or a girl? They can't quite remember*' (p. 177). Furthermore, when Nicholas Marsh tells Birdie she has a moustache that 'makes [her] look dirty, like [he] could lick [her] clean' (p. 200), there is a clear association between her (racial) darkness ('dirty') and masculinity ('mustache').

American fictions of adolescence have often been interpreted as state-of-the-nation novels and the ways in which Eugenides and Senna interweave their adolescent protagonists' bodies with US history and politics certainly supports this view.[34] However, the historical setting of the novels – at some twenty-five or thirty years' remove from the time of their composition – begs the question whether the authors are, in fact, drawing parallels between the 1970s and present-day concerns. Significantly, the appearance of *Caucasia* in 1998 and *Middlesex* in 2002 coincided with the increasingly politicised multiracial and intersex movements in the late 1990s and at the turn of the twenty-first century. Characters in both *Caucasia* and *Middlesex* express a kind of optimism that their protagonists' ambiguous bodies will not be considered 'abnormal' in a future beyond the 1970s. Deck Lee tells Birdie of her maternal grandmother: 'She'll be gone soon. She's a dying breed. You're the future' (*Caucasia*, p. 365). Meanwhile, Cal's friend Zora predicts: 'we're what's next' (*Middlesex*, p. 490).

From the vantage point of the beginning of the twenty-first century, however, these predictions do not ring true. Eugenides admits to perceiving a shift from when he grew up in 'the unisex 1970s, when everyone was sure that gender role was just environmentally conditioned' and now, when this situation is 'completely reversed.' *Middlesex*, he claims, 'tries to open up a space for free will again in human nature.'[35] Senna, meanwhile, worries that in the new millennium, 'people will assume that we've somehow got distance on the past, and on what happened in the twentieth century' and warns of 'the proximity of the past.'[36] Thus, when she writes of the 'Mulatto Millennium' – referring to the contemporary celebration of multiracial identities – she jokes that her new driver's licence now reads 'quadroon' instead of 'black.'[37] She thus suggests that the multiracial movement risks reverting not only to the essentialist definitions of blackness prevalent during the height of the Black Power era – the setting for her novel – but might also precipitate a resurgence of the racial classifications associated with slavery. There is a fine line, Senna implies, between *reclaiming* terms previously applied pejoratively by the dominant group and merely reviving them in reverse.

Ex- marks the spot

In this final section, I want to consider the issue of authorship in *Caucasia* and *Middlesex*. As in Erdrich's novels, this is best elucidated through the complex and often contradictory power relations that exist between seeing and not seeing, the simultaneous *hyper*visibility and *in*visibility of the body that is indeterminate in terms of race or gender.

Caucasia and *Middlesex* foreground the paradox that the hybrid body can, at once, be objectified and thus lack agency and, at the same time, function as a radical, *invisible* disruption to the status quo. In these two novels the paradoxical nature of seeing/not seeing, hypervisibility and invisibility are inextricably bound up with writing as an act symbolic of both agency and powerlessness.

In *Middlesex* the paradox of power(lessness) and seeing is, appropriately enough, evoked through the narrator's identification with the Greek mythological figure of Tiresias. Calliope even assumes the role in a school production of Sophocles's *Antigone*: 'My wild hair suggested clairvoyance. My stoop made me appear brittle with age. My half-changed voice had a disembodied, inspired quality. Tiresias had also been a woman, of course' (p. 331). In the most famous account of Tiresias, as is the case with Cal's ambiguous body, sex-changing is intimately bound up with Tiresias's subsequent blindness *and* powers of prophecy.[38] Tiresias's loss of sight is counterbalanced by his ability to 'see' into the future. The 'sightseeing suggestions' offered by two visiting doctors while Cal is undergoing assessment by a specialist in New York are ironic because, of course, by observing Cal's unconventional body, it is the doctors who are really 'sightseeing' (p. 420). As a pseudohermaphrodite, Cal's photograph has appeared in a medical textbook 'standing naked beside a height chart with a black box covering my eyes' (p. 3). Although the black box is superimposed over Cal's eyes presumably to protect his anonymity, it also functions as a blindfold, symbolically preventing Cal from returning the gaze directed upon him by curious readers of *Genetics and Heredity*. Cal's looked-*at*-ness points to his objectification in scientific writing. The opening lines of *Middlesex* challenge the 'specialized reader' to recall having 'come across me in Dr. Peter Luce's study, "Gender Identity in 5-Alpha-Reductase Pseudohermaphrodites", published in the *Journal of Pediatric Endocrinology* in 1975' (p. 3). 'Guinea-pigged' (p. 3) by the medical profession, Cal is 'a living experiment' (p. 408) for them, 'a body of research material' (p. 412).

However, the impotence implied by Cal's being the object of the gaze of the medical profession and, by extension, his figurative blindness is, at times, challenged by the protagonist's own assumption of narrative authority. Dr. Luce, who carries out the assessment of Callie in New York, requests that she write what the doctor calls a 'Psychological Narrative.' Luce uses this document to judge the extent to which Callie has been socialised as a girl in order to determine what should be done about her genitalia. But what the doctor does not know is that Callie discovers that 'telling the truth wasn't nearly so much fun as making things up' and so she fabricates most of what she writes, 'pretending to be the all-American daughter my parents wanted me to be' (p. 418). Having read Callie's narrative, Luce concludes that Callie's genitalia should be 'normalized' to complement her feminine upbringing. By making Luce's decision on Callie's condition contingent upon her 'Psychological Narrative' – which is fiction – Eugenides demonstrates that medical discourse is not objective, as it purports to be, but is itself a discourse that borrows from and relies heavily upon pre-existing narratives.[39]

The invented 'Psychological Narrative', which is embedded in the text of *Middlesex* (pp. 435–7), represents the micro-level at which Cal's narrative agency exists. For Cal, as the narrator of his own memoirs, claims an omniscience that is close to Tiresias's soothsaying. Recounting his father's death – which occurred when Cal was thousands of miles away in California – Cal's voice intervenes in the narrative, self-reflexively penetrating the consciousnesses of the individuals involved: 'And now I have to enter Father Mike's head, I'm afraid' (p. 509). Of his father's dying thoughts, he claims: 'I have to be honest and record Milton's thoughts as they occurred to him' (p. 511). By writing his memoirs, Calliope – whose emblems are, significantly, a stylus and wax tablets – interweaves knowledge and supposition, honesty and pure invention. According to William Gass, an 'honest autobiography is as amazing a miracle as a doubled sex, and every bit as big a freak of nature.'[40] Eugenides literalises Gass's analogy by passing *Middlesex* off as the autobiography of a hermaphrodite.

The notions of (prophe-)seeing, writing and monstrousness thus become intimately bound up in the form of the novel, which is a novel passing for a memoir. Indeed, it took Jeffrey Eugenides nine years to write the fictional memoir that is *Middlesex*, a period that witnessed 'the triumph of the memoir' as a publishing phenomenon.[41] Having read the memoirs of a 'real' intersexed individual, *Herculine Barbin: Being the Recently Discovered Memoirs of a Nineteenth-Century French Hermaphrodite*, Eugenides admits to feeling frustrated by the '19th century convent-school prose – very melodramatic, evasive about the anatomical details and really unable to render the emotional situation in any regard' and thinking: 'I'd like to write the story I'm not getting from this book.'[42] Interestingly, Eugenides makes Cal, his fictional narrator, the mouthpiece for words to this effect. Of

Herculine Barbin, Cal observes that her memoirs, 'which end shortly before her suicide, make unsatisfactory reading, and it was after I finished them years ago that I first got the idea to write my own' (*Middlesex*, p. 19). In this passage Eugenides introduces a slippage between author-protagonist and actual author. Just as supposition, speculation and invention inform Cal's memoir, a fictional framework – or mantle – offers Eugenides the opportunity to evade the constraints of (auto)biography and to transcend its demands of veracity. *Middlesex* thus toys with generic boundaries that are perhaps imaginary, but nevertheless, rigidly policed.[43]

Ultimately, however, authorship emerges – like passing and seeing – as an ambivalent form of agency. Significantly, Cal remains an outsider, though a self-exiled one, to the agenda of the increasingly politicised US intersex movement. He does not participate in the activities of the Intersex Society of North America (ISNA), although he is a member (pp. 106, 319). Cal thus finds that:

> Writing my story isn't the courageous act of liberation I had hoped it would be. Writing is solitary, furtive, and I know all about those things. I'm an expert in the underground life. Is it really my apolitical temperament that makes me keep my distance from the intersexual rights movement? Couldn't it also be fear? Of standing up. Of becoming one of them. (p. 319)

For Cal, then, the act of writing is a way of 'passing' unnoticed by his fellow hermaphrodites, even when associating with them might result in political gain for all.

According to Alice Dreger, there is 'significant value in listening to intersexuals' autobiographies. As in the personal histories of "interracial" people, in intersexuals' stories we can hear first-hand what it is like to live on one of the great cultural divides.'[44] That Dreger explicitly infuses intersexual and multiracial testimony is significant because *Caucasia*, too, is deeply embedded in the 1990s vogue for memoirs. It appeared at a time during which mixed race memoirs and edited collections of mixed race testimony were proliferating. Senna herself contributed an autobiographical piece to one of these collections.[45] *Caucasia* is a work of fiction but the interviews that Danzy Senna gave, coupled with the novel's first-person narrator and the obvious biographical parallels between Birdie and Senna (Senna was a biracial girl growing up in Boston during the desegregation crisis of the mid-1970s) suggest that its success may have been due, in part, to what Paul Spickard calls the '1990s boom in biracial biography.'[46] Many of the scholarly explorations of *Caucasia* would appear to support this link between the novel and mixed race memoirs. Senna's novel has been discussed alongside roughly contemporaneous memoirs – Shirlee Taylor Haizlip's *The Sweeter the Juice* (1993), James McBride's *The Color of Water* (1996) and Rebecca Walker's *Black, White, and Jewish: Autobiography of a Shifting Self* (2001).[47] Senna provides a book jacket blurb in praise of *Black, White, and Jewish*, just as James McBride offers a blurb in praise of *Caucasia*. All three are published by Riverhead Books.

In *Caucasia*, as in *Middlesex*, the tropes of seeing versus blindness, writing versus reading (or being read) are inextricably interconnected. When Birdie and Cole join the Black Power school in Roxbury, Birdie's new classmates speculate as to her racial and/or ethnic identity. As they try to read her race ('She a Rican or something?' (p. 43)), Birdie attempts to read the graffiti on her desk. Feeling lumps of dried bubblegum underneath, she moves her fingertips over them 'as if I were trying to read Braille' (p. 44). This scene is crucial because it can be read in two ways which illustrate powerfully the paradoxical relationship between power(lessness), seeing and writing. Birdie's objectification under the gaze of her classmates precipitates her own metaphorical blindness and/or tracing the dried bubblegum underneath her desk is a means of combating the stares of her classmates in the form of covert writing.

To her black classmates, Birdie is hypervisible because of her white skin. However, Birdie also feels invisible on several occasions, and such invisibility is accompanied by 'the thrill of anonymity' (p. 13), the potential to be 'a spy in enemy territory' (p. 269). The condition of the literary mulatta – simultaneous *hyper*visibility and *in*visibility – is most evident in the relationship between Birdie and her father. After the breakdown of his marriage, when he meets his daughters on Saturday mornings, 'he never seemed to see [Birdie] at all' (p. 55). When Deck does 'see' Birdie, it is from the vantage point of an academic, watching her 'the way a scientist looks at an amoeba through a telescope' (p. 388). To Birdie, Deck is a kind of Frankenstein, and she, his monster: 'He was the same father who had started me, who had begun but never finished me' (p. 393). This image of Birdie as Frankenstein's monster recalls the blue vein on her forehead: 'Alexis had told me once that it made me look like Frankenstein. I had liked that image of myself as a monster, an unfinished creation turned against its maker' (p. 297).[48] Deck uses both his daughters as research material, having them take a racial IQ test for his book *Wonders of the Invisible World* (p. 27). Ronnie Parkman calls Deck and Sandy 'great mad scientists' whose interracial marriage is a 'marvellous, ambitious experiment' (p. 349). In support of his theories of race, Deck creates a chart of famous 'tragic' mulattoes throughout history. In the last column he includes photographs of his daughters and their birthdates but 'where the others had their fates written, there was a blank space' (p. 393). In her critique of *Caucasia*, Habiba Ibrahim objects to what she interprets as Senna's discrediting of Deck's 'over intellectualized' views on race in favour of Sandy's 'pre-political' valorisation of 'food, love, shelter, and a good education.' For Ibrahim, this points to the novel's privileging of the personal over the political.[49] On the contrary, it seems clear to me that Senna not only demonstrates the intimate connections between the personal and the political but with Deck, she comments on the seemingly unbridgeable gap between scholars' commitment to social constructionism and *actual* subjects' lived experiences as raced subjects.

For Birdie to assert herself in that blank space by depicting herself would involve her in a double bind, for the mulatta has been over-determined, for a century and a half, by both whites and African Americans in US print media. Thus, to rewrite such narratives is, ineluctably, to perpetuate the mythology that they have instituted. For Senna, as for Eugenides, authorship is an ambivalent form of agency. On the one hand, producing a text is undoubtedly preferable to having one's body constitute a text. After all, Birdie's determination not to end up like Samantha is based upon what Birdie perceives as Samantha's inability to transcend her body-as-text. Samantha's eyes are 'a dark charcoal gray, the color of slate, of dirty blackboards' (*Caucasia*, p. 225), which recalls Birdie's earlier feeling 'like such a blank slate' when her mother confers upon her a Jewish identity and decides to settle in New Hampshire (p. 130).

On the other hand, in Birdie's own efforts at authorship, her narrative choices further entrench her in the ethno-racial essentialism she detests. When Birdie, as part of her home-schooling, is required to write a novel, her mother provides her with 'a black-and-white marbled composition book' and tells her the novel can be 'anything I chose' (p. 171). Birdie, too, with her 'black-and-white' but ostensibly 'white' body, can choose to identify herself, ethno-racially speaking, in any number of possible ways.[50] Interestingly, in the characterisation of her story, Birdie subscribes to the very kinds of stereotype to which one would imagine she would be sensitive, given her own experiences. Her narrative describes a Mexican family, featuring 'a religious, perpetually pregnant mother; a banjo-playing, sombrero-donning papa; and their teenage son, the main character, Richie Rodriguez, who is a bad seed looking for a way out' (pp. 171–2).

Birdie's dilemma – how to write oneself into the 'tragic mulatta' tradition without collaborating with such depictions – is thus the writer's own, for Senna is herself a writer of mixed racial ancestry with an avowed 'obsession with passing.'[51] Senna offers only a symbolic resolution to this double bind. When Birdie finally reaches her father's home in Oakland, she notices that: 'A page sat in the typewriter, blank and ready. I typed in the name "Birdie" and sat staring at the word for a moment' (p. 385). Birdie attempts to counterbalance textual over-determination and silence by registering her resistance on the page with one written word only. Rather than continue to have her 'body fill in the blanks', Birdie prefers to fill in the blanks with a written word, by becoming an author (p. 1). This contrasts with Samantha's anonymity and, by extension, lack of authorial agency, which is presented in terms of the unidentified 'X.' Birdie once catches Samantha 'wetting a finger, drawing a wet line in the dust that coated her, drawing what turned out to be an X there on her gray knee, the way you sign your name through the steam of fog in a car window' (p. 226).

However, the ambivalence of authorship, as a paradoxical act of what Linda Hutcheon calls 'complicitous critique',[52] ghosts the word that Birdie types on to the blank sheet of paper: her first name. As in *Erasure*, the fact that Birdie has been subjected to relentless naming and unnaming all her short life reflects the dual creative and destructive aspects of authorship. At birth, her mother wishes to call her 'Jesse' after her Suffragette grandmother. Her father prefers Patrice, for Patrice Lumumba, the Congolese liberator (*Caucasia*, p. 19). As a consequence her birth certificate reads only 'Baby Lee', suggesting that, paradoxically, such a profusion of names (or identities) can ultimately signify no name (or identity). She is christened Birdie by her sister, Cole, and this is the name to which her parents finally acquiesce. Carmen, her father's girlfriend, registers her profound disinterest in Birdie by getting her name wrong and calling her 'Bernie' (p. 112). As a member of the 'Brown Sugars' at Nkrumah, she is called 'Le Chic' (p. 65). As the daughter of a deceased Jewish academic, she becomes Jesse Goldman (p. 128). Most interestingly, Nicholas Marsh calls her, alternately, Pocahontas (pp. 192, 203, 214) and Jesse James (pp. 170, 205), thereby conjoining the earliest narrative of miscegenation in American history and an infamous outlaw, a coexistence echoed in one of Birdie's subsequent inner musings: '*you are against the law, Birdie Lee. Your body is a federal offense*' (p. 303).

In Chapter 4 I turn to two novels of passing in which authorship is also configured as simultaneously radical *and* complicit; both as revelatory *and* obfuscatory; as creative *and* degenerative. Discussing Paul Beatty's *The White Boy Shuffle* (1996) and Philip Roth's *The Human Stain* (2000) together enables me to demonstrate that these novels have as much in common with the others discussed in this book as they do with each other. In other words, the chapter progression of this book need not and must not be considered linear. Instead, I reveal that the narratives under discussion throughout interlock and intersect in endlessly fascinating ways. What unites all the novels most emphatically, of course, is the ways in which they engage with the notion of authorship. Both *The White Boy Shuffle* and *The Human Stain* – like all the novels discussed in this book, to one degree or another – feature author-protagonists.

Notes

1 Leslie Fiedler, *Waiting for the End* (New York: Stain and Day, 1964), p. 134.
2 Brenda Boudreau, 'Letting the Body Speak: "Becoming" White in *Caucasia*', *Modern Language Studies* 32.1 (2002), 59–70 (60).
3 Barbara E. White, *Growing up Female: Adolescent Girlhood in American Fiction* (Westport, CT: Greenwood, 1985), p. 3; Martin Japtok, *Growing Up Ethnic: Nationalism and the Bildungsroman in African American and Jewish American Fiction* (Iowa City: University of Iowa Press, 2005), p. 22; Geta Leseur, *Ten is the Age of Darkness: The Black Bildungsroman* (Columbia: University of Missouri Press, 1995), p. 26.
4 Jeffrey Eugenides, *Middlesex* (2002; London: Bloomsbury, 2003), p. 19. Subsequent references will be included in parentheses in the main body of the text.
5 White, p. 3. Geta Leseur provides a useful definition of the *Bildungsroman* form: 'The bildungsroman is a novelistic form of German origin. Goethe's *Wilhelm Meisters Lehrjahre*, published in 1795, served as a model for the form as it was later seen in France, England, other parts of the European continent and the United States. The form has been defined in various ways: the novel of development, novel of education (the literal translation

of *Bildungsroman*), "apprenticeship" novel, autobiographical novel, novel of childhood and adolescence, and the novel of initiation. The word came into use in the late nineteenth century outside Germany and became popular in England in the early Victorian era' (pp. 2–3, n. 1).

6 White, p. 13.

7 Gina Hausknecht, 'Self-Possession, Dolls, Beatlemania, Loss: Telling the Girl's Own Story', *The Girl: Constructions of the Girl in Contemporary Fiction by Women*, ed. Ruth O. Saxton (London: Macmillan, 1998), pp. 21–42 (p. 22).

8 Interestingly, in Japtok's study of African American and Jewish American *Bildungsromane*, two of the three African American novels discussed – *The Autobiography of an Ex-Colored Man* (1912) and *Plum Bun* (1928) – are also narratives of racial passing.

9 According to Alice Dreger, 5-alpha-reductase (5-AR) deficiency is 'one of the most striking forms of hermaphroditism because it results in an apparent female-to-male transformation at puberty. During fetal development the "male" child's testes produce testosterone. But in order for the developmental "message" of the testosterone to be "heard" in the child, the tissues must have the enzyme 5-alpha-reductase, which converts the testosterone "readable" dihydrotestosterone. If it is lacking, as it is in cases of 5-AR deficiency, the fetus will develop female-like genitalia. Therefore 5-AR individuals are born with feminine-looking genitalia, including generally a short vagina and apparent labia and clitoris. At puberty, however, the testes of these individuals produce more testosterone, and for the pubertal changes to occur the body doesn't need the converting work of the 5-AR enzyme. So now the testosterone messages *are* read, and "masculinizing" puberty occurs. The body grows taller, stronger, more muscular, usually with the addition of significant body and facial hair but with no breast development, and the voice drops. Often at this time the testes descend into the assumed-labia, and the penis/clitoris grows to look and act more like a penis.' Alice Domurat Dreger, *Hermaphrodites and the Medical Invention of Sex* (Cambridge, MA: Harvard University Press, 1998), p. 39.

10 It is significant that Deck Lee chooses Brazil as the destination for himself, Carmen and Cole. As Ronnie Parkman subsequently tells Birdie, Deck thinks of Brazil as a 'Xanadu, this grand Mulatto Nation' (*Caucasia*, p. 355). Deck's choice recalls Brian Redfield's desire to move his family to Brazil in Nella Larsen's *Passing* (1929), in order to escape the rigid racial order with which they have to contend in New York. As it turns out, Brazil does not fulfil Deck's expectations and he returns to the United States, settling in California.

11 Faced with what Jeffrey Eugenides calls 'the pronominal problem with he/she', throughout this chapter I will refer to Calliope Stephanides as Callie and use feminine pronouns to denote the narrator's experiences up

to the age of fourteen. From that point forward, I will call the protagonist Cal and use masculine pronouns. Laura Miller, 'Sex, Fate, and Zeus and Hera's Kinkiest Argument' (interview with Jeffrey Eugenides), *Salon.com* (8 October 2002) www.archive.salon.com/books/int/2002/10/08/eugenides/ print.html (14 September 2005).

12 Samira Kawash, 'Haunted Houses, Sinking Ships: Race, Architecture, and Identity in *Beloved* and *Middle Passage*', *New Centennial Review* 1.3 (2001), 67–86 (67).

13 Examples of this are virtually endless, but two of them are John Warwick in Charles Chesnutt's *House Behind the Cedars* (1900), who discovers he is legally black in North Carolina but can be legally white if he moves to South Carolina, and Angela Murray in Jessie Fauset's *Plum Bun* (1928), who passes after moving from Philadelphia to New York.

14 Danzy Senna, *From Caucasia, with Love* (London: Bloomsbury, 2001), pp. 111, 114. Subsequent page references are to this edition and will be given in parentheses in the body of the text. The novel was first published in the USA, under the title *Caucasia* (New York: Riverhead Books, 1998).

15 Richard Dyer, 'White', *Screen: The Last Special Issue on Race* 29.4 (1988), 44–64 (p. 45).

16 The blue vein on Birdie's head also recalls Charles Chesnutt's story 'The Wife of His Youth', which features a Blue Vein Society for light-complexioned African Americans, whose membership is determined according to the visibility of blue veins through translucent, pale skin. Charles Waddell Chesnutt, 'The Wife of His Youth', *Tales of Conjure and the Color Line: Ten Stories* (New York: Dover, 1998), pp. 47–56.

17 Quoted in Krista Comer, *Landscapes of the New West: Gender and Geography in Contemporary Women's Writing* (Chapel Hill: University of North Carolina Press, 1999), p. 59.

18 David Fine and Paul Skenazy, 'Introduction', *San Francisco in Fiction: Essays in a Regional Literature* (Albuquerque: University of New Mexico Press, 1995), pp. 1–20 (p. 5).

19 Ibid., p. 12.

20 Johnson, *Autobiography of an Ex-Colored Man*, p. 7.

21 William Wells Brown, *Clotel; or, the President's Daughter* (1853). *Three Classic African-American Novels*, ed. and intro. Henry Louis Gates, Jr. (New York: Random House, 1990), p. 129.

22 Brown, p. 93; Phillip Brian Harper, *Are We Not Men? Masculine Anxiety and the Problem of African-American Identity* (New York: Oxford University Press, 1996), p. 107.

23 Hair as a metonym for Europeanised beauty – along with light skin colour – is a recurring trope in African American fiction after Brown. In *Our Nig* (1859), Mrs. B shaves Frado's 'glossy ringlets', which may be viewed as a corollary to her insistence that Frado never 'shield her skin from the sun.' Harriet E. Wilson, *Our Nig; or, Sketches from the Life of a Free Black*,

In a Two-Story White House, North. Showing that Slavery's Shadows Fall Even There. By 'Our Nig', introd. R. J. Ellis (1859; Nottingham: Nottingham Trent University Press, 1998), pp. 36, 19. In *Their Eyes Were Watching God* (1937), Mrs. Turner, who has internalised white standards of beauty, seeks Janie Crawford out for a friend because she has a 'coffee-and-cream complexion' and 'luxurious hair' (1937; New York: Harper Perennial, 1990), p. 134.

24 White, p. 14.

25 Ibid., p. 157.

26 Ibid., p. 20.

27 Ibid., p. 14.

28 The term 'bathroom problem' is Halberstam's, p. 22; see also Garber, p. 14. The bathroom dilemma is foregrounded in the promotional poster for the award-winning film *Transamerica* (2005), which features Stanley/ Sabrina (Felicity Huffman) facing two public restrooms, one marked 'male' and the other marked 'female.' The tagline is 'Life is more than the sum of its parts.'

29 Halberstam, p. 24.

30 Zachary Sifuentes, 'Strange Anatomy, Strange Sexuality: The Queer Body in Jeffrey Eugenides' *Middlesex*', in *Straight Writ Queer: Non-Normative Expressions of Heterosexuality in Literature*, ed. Richard Fantina (Jefferson, NC: McFarland, 2006), pp. 145–57 (p. 149).

31 For a discussion of incest and homosexuality in Johnson's *Autobiography of an Ex-Colored Man*, see Siobhan Somerville, *Queering the Color Line: Race and the Invention of Homosexuality in American Culture* (Durham, NC: Duke University Press, 2000), p. 122. In Nella Larsen's *Passing* (1929), Irene warns Clare that if she attends a Negro dance unaccompanied, she might be mistaken for one of the 'ladies of easy virtue looking for trade' (p. 199). See also McDowell. Miscegenation has always provoked fears of incest, perhaps because one of the effects of male slaveholder–female slave relationships was the existence of children who never knew who their fathers were, and thus who their half-siblings were. Literary juxtapositions of actual or potential or suggested incest as a direct result of miscegenation are present in Richard Hildreth's *The Slave; or Memoirs of Archy Moore* (1836; the affianced Archy and Cassy have the same father), Lydia Maria Child's *A Romance of the Republic* (1868), Pauline Hopkins's *Hagar's Daughter* (1901–2) and *Of One Blood* (1902–3), William Faulkner's *Absalom, Absalom!* (1936) and Willa Cather's *Sapphira and the Slave Girl* (1940). See also Sollors's *Neither Black Nor White* for a discussion of the intersection of incest and miscegenation, pp. 285–335.

32 See, for example, Fauset's *Plum Bun* (pp. 158–9) and Langston Hughes's 'Passing', in *The Ways of White Folks* (1933; London: Vintage, 1990), pp. 51–5 (p. 51).

33　Dreger notes the greater frequency of the occurrence of 5-ARD among populations in which intermarriage is practised, and specifically cites the rural area of the Dominican Republic and the Sambia people of Papua New Guinea as examples of such populations. She does not, however, mention the population of southeastern Turkey (pp. 40–1).

34　Neil Campbell, 'Introduction: On Youth Cultural Studies', *American Youth Cultures* (Edinburgh: Edinburgh University Press, 2004), pp. 1–30 (p. 2).

35　Eugenides in Miller, 'Sex, Fate, and Zeus and Hera's Kinkiest Argument.'

36　Danzy Senna, 'Novel Companions: Books for the 21st Century' (interview with Amy Aronson), *Ms. Magazine* (December 1999) www.msmagazine. com/dec99/books-senna.html (10 January 2005).

37　Danzy Senna, 'Mulatto Millennium', *Salon.com* (24 July 1998) http://archive.salon.com/mwt/feature/1998/07/24feature.html (3 July 2004).

38　Eugenides recounts this story as follows: 'He [Tiresias] was walking one day and saw two snakes copulating, threw his staff at them, and he was turned into a female. Then seven years later he saw the same snakes, threw the same staff at them, and was turned back into a man. The story you're recalling is an argument between Zeus and Hera over which sex has a better time in bed. Strangely, I think, Zeus thinks women have a better time and Hera thinks men do. [. . .] So they get Tiresius [sic] and he says women have more fun, and she loses. Because she's angry at Tiresius [sic], Hera makes him blind, but then she or another god gives him foresight, prophecy.' Miller, 'Sex, Fate, and Zeus and Hera's Kinkiest Argument.' Eugenides's Tiresias story is likely drawn from the version told in Ovid's *Metamorphoses* (1. 327–35).

39　See Venla Oikonnen, ' "The Final Clause in a Periodic Sentence": Sexing Difference in *Middlesex*', in *Masculinities, Femininities and the Power of the Hybrid in U.S. Narratives: Essays on Gender Borders*, ed. Nieves Pascual, Laura Alonso-Gallo and Francisco Collado-Rodríguez (Heidelberg: Universitätsverlag, 2007), pp. 245–59.

40　William Gass, 'The Art of Self: Autobiography in an Age of Narcissism', *Harper's Magazine* (May 1994), 43–52 (45).

41　James Atlas, 'Confessing for Voyeurs: The Age of the Literary Memoir is Now', *New York Times Magazine* (12 May 1996), 25.

42　Eugenides in Miller, 'Sex, Fate, and Zeus and Hera's Kinkiest Argument.'

43　In reviews of *Middlesex*, the novel is described as one or more of: a 'comic epic', 'road novel', 'coming-of-age story', 'love story', 'autobiography', 'fictional memoir' and 'family saga.' See Geraldine Bedell, 'He's Not Like Other Girls', *Observer* (6 October 2002) http://books.guardian.co.uk/impac/story/0,14959,1285050,00.html (15 September 2005) and Laura Miller, ' "Middlesex": My Big Fat Greek Gender Identity Crisis', *New York Times* (15 September 2002) www.nytimes.com/2002/09/15/books/my-big-fat-greek-gender-identity-crisis.html (15 September 2005).

44 Dreger, p. 168.

45 'The Mulatto Millennium' appeared in *Half and Half: Writers on Growing Up Biracial and Bicultural*, ed. Claudine Chiawei O'Hearn (New York: Pantheon, 1998), pp. 12–27.

46 Paul R. Spickard, 'The Subject is Mixed Race: The Boom in Biracial Biography', *Rethinking 'Mixed Race'*, ed. David Parker and Miri Song (London: Pluto, 2001), pp. 76–98 (p. 77). A mixed race memoir that made only a modest impression upon its publication in 1995 but has since, and for obvious reasons, enjoyed phenomenal sales worldwide is Barack Obama's *Dreams from My Father*.

47 See Bost, pp. 185–9, Reginald Watson, 'The Changing Face of Biraciality: The White/Jewish Mother as Tragic Mulatto Figure in James McBride's *The Color of Water* and Danzy Senna's *Caucasia*', *Obsidian III: Literature in the African Diaspora* 4.1 (2002), 101–13 and Lori Harrison-Kahan, 'Passing for White, Passing for Jewish: Mixed Race Identity in Danzy Senna and Rebecca Walker', *MELUS* 30.1 (2005), 19–48.

48 The mulatta-as-monstrous recalls mixed race Lisa Jones's reporting her experience of watching the 1934 film version of *Imitation of Life*, thinking she will see in Peola 'a big-screen version of myself.' Instead, she finds that 'this Peola isn't me at all, she's a remake of Frankenmulatta, that character from *The Octoroon Concubine of Frankenstein*, one of Mary Shelley's lost sequels.' *Bulletproof Diva: Tales of Race, Sex, and Hair* (London: Penguin, 1995), p. 1.

49 Habiba Ibrahim, 'Canary in a Coal Mine: Performing Biracial Difference in *Caucasia*', *Literature Interpretation Theory* 18.2 (2007), 155–72 (168–9).

50 Birdie's ethnicity is alternately taken to be, or described as, Sicilian (pp. 27–28, 130), Puerto Rican (p. 43), Italian (pp. 107, 194), French (p. 107), Greek (p. 130), Pakistani (p. 130) and Indian (p. 378). While on the lam, her mother tells her she can choose her new identity from a range of ethnic options but eventually decides to reinvent her daughter as Jewish.

51 Danzy Senna (interview with Amy Aronson). The writer of passing stories with whom Senna is most often compared is Nella Larsen. Like Larsen, whose entire novelistic oeuvre consists of *Quicksand* (1928) and *Passing* (1929), Senna has, to date, written just two novels, both of which are concerned with passing and mixed race identities. See Claudia M. Milian Arias, 'An Interview with Danzy Senna', *Callaloo* 25.2 (2002), 447–52 (447) and Michele Hunter, 'Revisiting the Third Space: Reading Danzy Senna's *Caucasia*', in *Literature and Racial Ambiguity*, ed. Teresa Hubel and Neil Brooks (Amsterdam: Rodopi, 2002), pp. 297–316 (p. 310) for comparisons of Senna with Larsen. In an interview with Bill Vourvoulias, Senna herself cites Larsen's *Passing* and Ellison's *Invisible Man* as influences on *Caucasia*. 'Talking with Danzy Senna: Invisible Woman', *Newsday* (29 July 1998), B11.

52 Hutcheon, *Politics of Postmodernism*, p. 2.

5

Bodies/texts: passing and writing in *The White Boy Shuffle* and *The Human Stain*

Years ago, in the middle of the Whitewater investigation, one heard the first murmurs: white skin notwithstanding, this is our first black President. Blacker than any actual black person who could ever be elected in our children's lifetime. After all, Clinton displays almost every trope of blackness: single-parent household, born poor, working-class, saxophone-playing, McDonald's-and-junk-food-loving boy from Arkansas.

Toni Morrison, *The New Yorker* (1998)[1]

In her famous defence of Bill Clinton, Toni Morrison articulated succinctly the question with which all standard racial passing narratives wrestle: if blackness is not physically manifest, then what is it? A form of behaviour? A state of mind? A set of cultural affiliations? Conversely, if blackness *is* physically apparent but the behaviour/state of mind/cultural affiliations do not accompany this, is the subject still 'black'? In this chapter I analyse Paul Beatty's *The White Boy Shuffle* (1996) and Philip Roth's *The Human Stain* (2000), neither of which fits easily within the 'standard racial pass' (black-to-white) and 'reverse racial pass' (white-to-black) schema that Phillip Brian Harper elucidates: the first, like Everett's *Erasure*, because it features an African American protagonist who passes to become black(er); the second, like Senna's *Caucasia*, because it foregrounds black-for-Jewish passing. Both Gunnar Kaufman from *The White Boy Shuffle* and Coleman Silk from *The Human Stain* grapple with the weight of their genealogy and ancestors. Both rely on their bodies as a key site of self-definition through their commitment to their respective sports (basketball; boxing). Both are, moreover, committed writers: Gunnar becomes a celebrated poet and the novel, like *Middlesex*, passes as his 'memoirs' (p. 2); Coleman fails to publish his own *magnum opus*, memoirs entitled *Spooks*.

Beatty's *The White Boy Shuffle*, a first-person narrative, traces Gunnar's late childhood, adolescence and early adulthood in Santa Monica, Los Angeles and Boston as he struggles to become a published poet. In contrast with the novels of adolescence discussed in Chapter 4, in which the ambiguities of race and gender are mapped upon the *bodies* of the protagonists, in *The White Boy Shuffle*, the protagonist's racial indeterminacy is cultural rather than physical. When thirteen-year-old Gunnar and his younger sisters, raised in predominantly white Santa Monica, tell their mother that they do not wish to attend an all-black summer camp because 'they're different from us' (p. 41), Brenda Kaufman moves the entire family to a West Los Angeles ghetto called Hillside in an attempt to furnish them with 'her vaunted "traditional black experience."'[2] Gunnar's adolescent rite of passage, therefore, is to pass – to become 'black.' In Hillside, Gunnar befriends a jazz aficionado called Nicholas Scoby, comes to excel at basketball and poetry-writing and, against the backdrop of the Rodney King riots of 1992, helps local gangster Psycho Loco to open a safe looted from a department store. While *Caucasia* and *Middlesex* are fictions of adolescence, *The White Boy Shuffle* is a mock *Bildungsroman*, more obviously setting up the conventions of the genre in order to subvert and parody them. It also operates as a *Künstlerroman*. A published poet himself, Beatty treats Gunnar's artistic coming-of-age in a way that begs the question whether the discourse of black authenticity to which his protagonist is subjected is something which he himself must also negotiate in his literary career.

If Morrison's configuration of Bill Clinton as America's 'first black President' emphasises socio-cultural rather than epidermal blackness, it is significant that Roth creates imaginative parallels between his passing protagonist, Coleman Silk, and the forty-second president.[3] The action of *The Human Stain* is played out against the backdrop of the media circus surrounding the Clinton–Monica Lewinsky affair in the summer of 1998. Narrated by one of Roth's fictional *alter egos*, Nathan Zuckerman, it focuses on the parallel transgressions of disgraced college professor Coleman Silk, forced to resign two years previous to the novel's opening for employing what was construed as a racial epithet ('spooks') when referring to two of his African American students. Coleman's latest peccadillo is the relationship he has begun with Faunia Farley, half his age and an apparently illiterate janitor at his former place of employ, Athena College. Coleman and Faunia are eventually murdered by Faunia's psychotic ex-husband,

Vietnam veteran Lester Farley. It is only when his darker-skinned sister Ernestine attends Coleman's funeral that Zuckerman discovers his friend was born into an African American family and has been passing since the 1940s. He enters the navy as a white man in October 1944, but after meeting his future wife, Jewish American Iris Gittelman, in the early 1950s, he decides to pass permanently, and as Jewish.

Inauthentic Negroes/inauthentic Jews

Some might claim that *The White Boy Shuffle* ought not to be considered a passing narrative at all. As Baz Dreisinger remarks of the resurgence of passing in contemporary American culture, 'How can we refer to passing at a time when "creolization" and "cross-cultural borrowing" seem more appropriate terms, and when "multiracialism" has become the catchword of the day?'[4] We can continue to use passing as an interpretive framework for novels such as *The White Boy Shuffle*, I would argue, because the narrative alludes so self-consciously to the conventions of such stories that it must, at the very least, be read as a playful engagement with the subject. For instance, when Gunnar first meets Scoby, his new friend assesses Gunnar's speech patterns and general behaviour and tells him, 'You dark as fuck for someone with Teutonic blood' (p. 73). Here, Beatty invokes the blood quantum of racial discourse common to narratives of standard racial passing. That Scoby 'sees through' Gunnar's darkness to his supposed 'whiteness' – and thus, by implication, accuses Gunnar of passing as black – is significant, because Gunnar observes elsewhere that Scoby has a particular aptitude for spotting 'passers', if the other way around. His friend has 'the power to tell if someone had a drop of Negro blood in his gene pool. Nicholas claimed he could smell a passing octoroon from a block away' (p. 132). Gunnar's supposed possession of 'Teutonic blood' is reinforced by the names that Beatty attributes to his protagonist and to his forebears, most of them (Swen, Franz von, Wolfgang, Ludwig, Rölf) stereotypically Germanic or Nordic.[5]

The White Boy Shuffle's engagement with the notion of racial passing is reinforced by its several intertextual references, first, to W.E.B. DuBois's *The Souls of Black Folk* (1903) and second, to famous narratives of black-to-white passing. In the novel's opening, Gunnar claims that he is not the typical protagonist of the African American novel because 'fate shorted me by six brothers and two uncles.' Gunnar is most decidedly *not* 'the seventh son of a seventh son of a seventh son' (p. 5). This phraseology recalls DuBois's assertion in *The Souls of Black Folk* that 'After the Egyptian and Indian, the Greek and Roman, the Teuton and Mongolian, the Negro is a sort of seventh son, born with a veil, and gifted with second-sight in this American world.'[6] Through the first intertextual reference to DuBois, Beatty inevitably invokes the better-known and oft-quoted second: 'The problem of the twentieth century is the problem of the color-line – the relation of the darker to the lighter races of men in Asia and Africa, in America and the islands of the sea' (*Souls of Black Folk*, p. 9). Passing narratives are explicitly concerned with DuBois's claim. As Gayle Wald puts it, the fiction of DuBois's 'color line' has been 'of urgent concern to racially defined subjects throughout the twentieth century (and into the twenty-first), exploiting the notion of their visible, corporeal "difference" from a "white" norm to sustain and enforce social relations of white supremacy.'[7] The appearance of *The White Boy Shuffle* at the end of the twentieth century confirms the accuracy of DuBois's foresight: 'the color-line' is indeed still a 'problem', though, in *The White Boy Shuffle*, perhaps differently to the way in which DuBois imagined it in 1903.

Equally, the novel makes important allusions to Mark Twain's *Pudd'nhead Wilson* (1894). An ancestor of Gunnar's, Franz von Kaufman, is the pet slave of Compton Benjamin Quentin Tannenberry. Like Tom Driscoll and Chambers in *Puddn'head Wilson*, who are born on the same day, Compton and Franz von are born within days of each other and share 'the same crib and nipples' (p. 17). The reference to *Pudd'nhead Wilson* functions to set up Beatty's intervention in the infamous nature-nurture debate staged in Twain's novella, but the character of this intervention remains as obscure as it does in *Pudd'nhead Wilson*. Gunnar claims that '[e]ven in infancy Franz von's subservience was evident' (p. 17). In Twain's novella, the often frustrating ambiguity with which the author treats the nature-nurture debate is predicated on the fact that Chambers's slave mother, Roxy, has switched the almost identical slave and aristocrat babies. In *The White Boy Shuffle*, however, no mention is made of Compton and Franz von having been switched, which serves to render the deferred resolution to the issue in *Pudd'nhead Wilson* even more elusive in Beatty's novel. The Franz von Compton anecdote is also, of course, a clever reference to William Faulkner's interest in genealogy, the interrelated issue of fate versus free will and, in *Light in August* (1932) and *Absalom, Absalom!* (1936), racial passing, whether by accident or design. Quentin Compson, who features in *Absalom, Absalom!*, is also a key character in *The Sound and the Fury* (1929). In *The White Boy Shuffle* his given name is amalgamated with that of his 'idiot' brother, Benjy, and Compson becomes Compton, the name of a predominantly black area of East Los Angeles.

The trope of racial passing, which is here black-to-black rather than black-to-white or white-to-black, offers Beatty the perfect framework for a satirical investigation of the discourse of black authenticity in *The White Boy Shuffle*, for the arbitrariness of the color line in Beatty's novel pivots not upon legal or medical definitions of race, but upon this problematic and powerful discourse. After all, for Gunnar to be considered black demands that he, literally, 'pass' certain tests to prove his legitimacy. He is overjoyed, for example, the first time Scoby calls him 'nigger' (p. 73). At first, his attempts are unsuccessful. His inability 'to walk the walk or talk the talk' leads to a series of almost daily drubbings (p. 57). Made to feel inadequate by his largely black contemporaries, Gunnar, like Birdie in *Caucasia* and Cal in *Middlesex*, experiences his own body as freakish: 'If I had walked up the streets with a carnival barker to promote my one-by sideshow, I could have made some money' (p. 57). Because of his inability to 'saunter or bojangle my limbs with rubbery nonchalance', he feels as if he has 'Frankenstein's autonomic nervous system' (p. 57). Initiation into his new environment and a 'black' identity is akin to an adolescent rite of passage: 'If I wanted to come correct, I'd have to complete some unspecified warrior vision quest. The gods of blackness would let me know when I was black enough to be trusted' (p. 58). Gunnar's faith in the existence of 'gods of blackness', implying omnipotence but invisibility, reveals the paradoxical power that inheres in the very vagueness of the discourse of black authenticity.

The grafting of Gunnar's coming-of-age onto his narrative of 'becoming black' confirms the importance of adolescence as a struc- turing trope in contemporary novels of passing. Indeed, even in *The Human Stain*, not strictly a coming-of-age story, the cultivation of Coleman's secret (his passing as white) is made analogous to 'growing up.' After he introduces his white girlfriend, Steena Palsson, to his mother and sister – thereby revealing himself to be black – Steena terminates the relationship. Coleman subsequently starts dating an African American woman called Ellie Magee, who, through carefully framed questions, divines that he has been passing: 'Losing the secret, he feels like a boy again. The boy he'd been before he had the secret.'[8] Knowing that Ellie knows allows him to regain his 'innocence' (p. 136).

After Gunnar leaves Santa Monica for Hillside, he concedes that '[o]f all my laidback Santa Monican friends, I miss David Joshua Schoenfeld the most. He was off-white and closest to me in hue and temperament (*White Boy Shuffle*, p. 42). Similarly, Sandy in Danzy Senna's *Caucasia* tells Birdie that she isn't 'really passing because Jews weren't really white, more like an off-white. She said they were the closest I was going to get to black and still stay white.'[9] Birdie and Gunnar both conceive of Jewishness as a *viable* intermediate identity – in a way that being light-skinned or of mixed race simply is not – between blackness and whiteness. For Gunnar, mixed race is inadequate because, quite simply, it is a synonym for 'white', as evidenced in his description of his Santa Monica school as 'Mestizo Mulatto Mongrel Elementary, Santa Monica's all-white multicultural school' (*White Boy Shuffle*, p. 31). When Birdie removes the Star of David that she has worn since becoming Jesse Goldman, after suffering anti-Semitic taunts from her New Hampshire peers, this act symbolises the inevitable – though involuntary – end of her shapeshifting, of the 'comfort' she derives from being in a 'state of incompletion' and the beginning of her final transformation into a white girl.[10] In *The Human Stain*, once Coleman decides to pass permanently, he also self-identifies as Jewish.

As I note in the introduction, two recent scholarly works, Stephen J. Belluscio's *To Be Suddenly White* (2006) and Catherine Rottenberg's *Performing Americanness* (2008) make a convincing case for considering African American narratives of passing of the late nineteenth and early twentieth centuries alongside contemporaneous narratives of Jewish assimilation. Indeed, in an earlier essay, Daniel Itzkovitz notes that the 'association of Jews with race-shifting' is 'indicated by the number of Jewish characters surfacing in modern novels that were ostensibly about African Americans passing for white.'[11] Perhaps more striking, however, is the degree to which Jewishness surfaces in *contemporary* narratives of passing. For Marjorie Garber, as I argue in Chapter 3, the cross-dresser represents a 'third term' which 'questions binary thinking and introduces crisis.' Three 'puts in question the idea of one: of identity, self-sufficiency, self-knowledge.'[12] In *Caucasia* and *The Human Stain*, Jewishness is the 'third term' that the authors introduce in order to challenge binary thinking. As Lori Harrison-Kahan puts it:

> Adding a third term to the typically black-and-white schema of US race relations, these contemporary texts deploy Jewishness to expose the social construction and plurality of whiteness as well as to challenge existing theories of mixed race identity that rely on binary configurations.[13]

Similarly, as Dean J. Franco observes, the fundamental tension regarding race in Roth's work is between 'the wash of non-identity found in terms like "Caucasian" and "American"' and 'those specifically noted by racial designations like black, white, or Semite on the other.' Poised at the centre of that tension is 'Jew.'[14] The question is whether, as Judith Halberstam contends of Garber's work, the 'third space tends to stabilize the other two.'[15] This certainly seems to be the case for Gunnar, whose friendship with the 'tanned Jewish kid' David Schoenfeld is the means by which he 'learned [he] was black and that being black meant something, though [he's] never learned exactly what' (*White Boy Shuffle*, pp. 42, 44). Equally, in her discussion of Rebecca Walker's memoir *Black, White and Jewish* (2000), Harrison-Kahan argues that '[i]n affirming her own multiplicity, Walker ends up overlooking the multiplicity of Jewishness itself.'[16] In *The Human Stain*, however, Coleman's black-for-Jewish passing provides Roth with the means of setting up and then reversing ubiquitous stereotypes of both American blacks *and* Jews.

Like Beatty in *The White Boy Shuffle*, Roth emphasises *cultural* interplay and exchange as the primary indicator of racial and/or ethnic interrelationships. In one important episode, while Coleman is dating Steena in New York in the 1940s, his lover dances for him:

> She was getting undressed, and the radio was on – Symphony Sid – and first, to get her moving and in the mood, there was Count Basie and a bunch of jazz musicians jamming on 'Lady Be Good', a wild live recording, and following that, more Gershwin, the Artie Shaw rendition of 'The Man I Love' that featured Roy Eldridge steaming everything up. [. . .] All at once, with no prompting from him – seemingly prompted only by Eldridge's trumpet – she began what Coleman liked to describe as the single most slithery dance ever performed by a Fergus Falls girl after little more than a year in New York City. She could have raised Gershwin himself from the grave with that dance, and with the way she sang the song. Prompted by a colored trumpet player playing it like a black torch song, there to see, plain as day, was all the power of her whiteness. (*Human Stain*, p. 115)

Steena's dance evokes the endlessly interrelated forms of cultural exchange and appropriation that have taken place between black, white and Jewish Americans. Steena, with Icelandic and Danish ancestry (pp. 113, 123), is an exaggerated Nordic, dancing and singing along to an African American soloist, accompanied by an orchestra led by Jewish American Artie Shaw, playing music composed by Jewish American George Gershwin, and watched by her boyfriend, Coleman, a black man passing for white. It is no coincidence that musical performance is the terrain on which this racial and cultural mixing is played out, since the assumption of blackness by Jewish performers has a long history in the USA. At least since blackface minstrelsy became a ubiquitous popular culture form, Jewish and other ethnic Americans have blacked up, Michael Rogin argues, in order to emphasise their *difference* from African Americans and thereby claim their right to assimilate to the American mainstream. According to Rogin, minstrelsy 'passed immigrants into Americans by differentiating them from the black Americans through whom they spoke, who were not permitted to speak for themselves.'[17] Coleman's birth circa 1927 coincides with a late example of this in Al Jolson's Jakie Rabinowitz, of *The Jazz Singer*, the movies' first talkie.

Given this history, *The Human Stain* could be read as an attempt to address some of the recurring, oscillating tropes of identification, repudiation, appropriation and displacement that have historically characterised black–Jewish relations, especially from the 1940s (when Coleman first passes as white) to the late 1990s (the contemporary setting of the novel).[18] According to Eric Sundquist:

> Whatever remained of the structural similarity between blacks and Jews at the end of World War II – and despite the evident devotion of many Jews to the cause of black rights in years to come – started to dissipate as Jews embarked on a rapid ascent of the social and economic ladder, while African Americans, however much their lives were improved by the downfall of segregation, began an ascent destined to be far slower and more erratic.[19]

Coleman's assumption of a Jewish identity might also represent an ironic reversal of the often problematic nature of Jewish identification with African Americans, which, as Roth is acutely aware, easily collapses into appropriation of the Other's oppression. This is evident in the proposition of Jewish Dr. Fensterman, who approaches Mr. and

Mrs. Silk when Coleman is a senior in high school to ask them to arrange for their son to underperform academically so that his own son, Bertram, will become class valedictorian, and thereby enjoy an easier passage to medical school. He offers the Silks 3,000 dollars in exchange for their cooperation. In Fensterman's rhetoric, there is a profound emphasis on the affinities he sees between his own and the Silks' situations in terms of their common struggle against quotas in academic institutions and prejudice in the wider society (p. 86). When Coleman remembers Dr. Fensterman's offer, his decision to pass as Jewish strikes him as 'spectacularly comical . . . a colossal sui generis score-settling joke' (p. 131).

His decision to marry Iris and pass permanently as Jewish is based on somewhat similar superficial affinities, which he, like Dr. Fensterman, exploits to his own ends. On a purely physical level, Coleman realises that Iris's 'Negroid hair', 'a labyrinthine, billowing wreath of spirals and ringlets, fuzzy as twine and large enough for use as Christmas ornamentation' (pp. 136, 129) will provide a plausible explanation should their children ever manifest 'Negroid' physical attributes. A further happy coincidence for Coleman is the fact that his mother, a nurse convinced of the hygienic benefits of circumcision – a traditional rite among Jews – chose to have him circumcised at birth (p. 130). The absence of Coleman's antecedents is reasonably explained by the fact that the changing of Eastern European surnames at Ellis Island and other ports resulted in the irrevocable obscurity of many Jewish immigrants' genealogy once they reached the United States. Coleman tells Iris that the name 'Silk' is an Ellis Island corruption of 'Silberzweig' (p. 130).

The character of Coleman Silk is reputedly based on Anatole Broyard, a celebrated book reviewer for the *New York Times* from the 1960s until his death in 1990, who was born into a self-identifying black family from New Orleans but subsequently passed as white (though not Jewish). In an article written for *Commentary* in July 1950, Broyard himself trades on perceived affinities between African and Jewish Americans when he employs Jean-Paul Sartre's 'Portrait of the Inauthentic Jew' as a model for exploring what he calls 'The Inauthentic Negro.' *Commentary* prefaces Broyard's article with some biographical details, noting enigmatically that 'the situation of the American Negro' is one which Broyard knows 'at first hand.'[20] In his article, published in the same periodical in May 1948, Sartre argues that in fleeing from his Jewishness, the inauthentic Jew actually reinforces anti-Semitic mythology rather than subverting it, as he sets out to do. As I note in my introduction, the same critique is often applied to narratives of racial passing. As Amy Robinson puts it, 'the social practice of passing is thoroughly invested in the logic of the system it attempts to subvert.'[21] Indeed, Sartre's rhetoric recalls many of the tropes one associates with African Americans passing for white – 'running away', 'flight', denial, a sense of duality and alienation from self, inner conflict, divided selfhood and so on.[22]

Just as Coleman Silk's assumption of a Jewish identity challenges readers to consider Jewish appropriations of African American culture, his black-for-Jewish passing protagonist enables Roth to undercut the traditional passing narrative itself. As Harper argues, one of the limitations of such narratives is that 'for an instance of passing to register as a challenge to the logic of racial identification, it must disclose itself as an instance of passing in the first place, which disclosure typically would also constitute the failure of the act.'[23] However, in *The Human Stain* the act is self-consciously and *prematurely* disclosed so as to defy the conventions of the passing narrative and, thus, its limitations. Early in the novel, Zuckerman appraises Coleman Silk as follows:

> All in all, he remained a neat, attractive package of a man even at his age, the small-nosed Jew type with the facial heft in the jaw, one of those crimped-haired Jews of a light yellowish pigmentation who possess something of the ambiguous aura of the pale blacks who are sometimes taken for white. (pp. 15–16)

Predicated on the speculation and suspense generated by the ambiguously raced protagonist, Zuckerman and Roth effectively give the game away scarcely a fifth of the way through the first chapter. The chapter's title – 'Everyone Knows' – thus refers as much to readers of *The Human Stain* as it does to the letter Delphine Roux has sent to Coleman.

Ancestor worship?

In *The White Boy Shuffle*, Gunnar's new ghetto home emerges as the site of an 'authentic' black identity which, as a location, is distinguished by its implication in the related oppositions between nature/nurture and fate/free will. In the ghetto, as Scoby points out, 'Fate picks your friends, and you choose your family. Everybody starts out an orphan in this hole' (p. 96). As Gunnar subsequently confirms, 'living out there was like being in a never-ending log-rolling context. You never asked why the log was rolling or who was rolling the log. You just spread your arms and kept moving, doing your best not to fall off' (p. 113). The narrative of racial passing has always engaged with the notion of fate versus free will on ambivalent terms. To choose to pass – to refuse to allow one's African American ancestry to determine one's economic and social status – is, ostensibly, an act of free will. However, to paraphrase Gayle Wald, since the decision to pass may be due to fundamental inequalities in the law and society, passing can only ever, at best, be considered a choice among very few available options.[24] Meanwhile, a recurring fear in passing narratives is that of 'atavism', literally, 'great-grandfather-ism', a descendant's 'surprising resemblance to grand-parents or more remote ancestors rather than to parents', an occurrence over which the passer has no control.[25] Even when the passer wilfully decides to pass, therefore, his or her actions may yet be circumscribed by external forces. *The White Boy Shuffle*, like *Middlesex*, toys with the contemporary fascination with the scientific discourse of genetics and struggles to find a middle ground between destiny and free will. The fact that the novel passes itself off as Gunnar's 'memoirs' reflects this quest. For if, as novelist William Gass claims, (auto)biographers 'are almost always desperate determinists', the literary form of the memoir – somewhere between autobiography and fiction – blurs the straightforward determinism of autobiography.[26]

By outlining at the outset Gunnar's genealogy, comprised of ancestors who are each inauthentically 'black' in some way, Beatty intimates provocatively that Gunnar's own black inauthenticity is *inherited*. As Gunnar puts it, he has been '[p]reordained by a set of weak-kneed DNA to shuffle in the footsteps of a long cowardly queue of coons, Uncle Toms, and faithful boogedy-boogedy retainers' (*White Boy Shuffle*, p. 5). For example, Gunnar describes the ambitions of one of his forebears, a free man called Swen Kaufman, to become a serious dancer. In pursuit of this dream, he migrates from Boston to antebellum North Carolina. Watching slaves at work in the fields of a tobacco farm, 'the rise-and-fall rhythms of the hoes and pickaxes and the austere urgency of the work songs' inspire him to compose a 'groundbreaking dance opera' (p. 14). 'Entranced with the possibilities', Swen joins the slaves at work and thus becomes 'the first person ever to run away into slavery' (p. 13). For Beatty, then, the quest for authenticity is itself a kind of bondage, for in his desire to gain access to 'real' African American experience, Swen quite literally jumps over 'the wooden fence that separated the slave from the free' (p. 14). Interestingly, when Gunnar asks his mother for money to buy some basketball shoes, she suggests he 'buy some tap-dancing shoes instead' because 'no one would shoot you for your tap-dancing shoes', implying a link between Gunnar's pursuit of black authenticity in playing basketball and his dancer-ancestor Swen's attempts to create a dance-opera based on 'real' slave experience. A further link with Swen is established via Gunnar's own inability to dance in an authentically 'black' way, his steps configured as 'the white boy shuffle' of the novel's title (p. 136).

Not surprisingly, black authenticity is, at times, metaphorically linked to skin tone. Gunnar's 'shameful history' continues with the story of his great-uncle, Wolfgang Kaufman, which he recounts to his fellow classmates 'to the rustle of brown paper bags' (p. 20). This recalls subtly the 'brown paper bag test' which decreed that if one's skin was darker than a brown paper bag, one was 'black.' Wolfgang Kaufman provides suggestions for Amos 'n' Andy to improve their show. Wolfgang's son, Ludwig, manages white bands such as Gladys White and the Waitress Tips who rip off the success of Motown. So inauthentically black and anti-heroic are Gunnar's ancestors that they actually live out some of the most deeply held racist myths in American history and culture. At high school, for instance, Gunnar's own father emulates Noah in a real-life re-enactment of the Curse of Ham: 'My father drank so much he passed out. He came to naked, his entire body spray-painted white, his face drool-glued against the trunk of the swing-low tree. He ran home under the sinking Mississippi moon, his white skin tingling with assimilation' (p. 25). According to the racist myth, the genealogy of the African race owes itself to the curse of black skin placed by Noah on his son, Ham, as punishment for mocking him in his naked, drunken state. In Gunnar's retelling of the story, Gunnar is equally 'cursed' by his (fore)father(s), but with a legacy of black inauthenticity rather than with a physical transformation from white to black.

At every stage of Gunnar's story, the role of fate is emphasised. It even infuses Gunnar's view of the marriage that his friend, Psycho Loco, arranges for him. Gunnar is initially angry with Psycho Loco for committing him to wedding a Japanese mail-order bride, but his friend tells him: 'you don't even have an alarm clock, so don't give me no bullshit that I've altered your destiny' (p. 182). After meeting Yoshiko, Gunnar decides to go through with the wedding because 'Sometimes the inevitable just seems right' (p. 184). When Gunnar considers which college to attend on basketball scholarship, he is impressed with the representative from Boston University. His mother likes the idea of Gunnar going to university in Boston because he will be 'following in the footsteps of your great-great-great-great-great-great-great-grandfather Euripides. It's as if the Kaufman legacy has come full circle' (p. 179). Thus, even Gunnar's *choice* of university is infused with an air of destiny.

In ostensible contradistinction to this preoccupation with fate, Gunnar's ability alternately to perform blackness and whiteness as different situations demand seems to imply that race is *learned* and performed through the exercise of free will, a notion which is supported by the emphasis on Gunnar's schooling throughout the novel. His adolescence is, he claims, 'like going to clown college' (p. 57). The pedagogic metaphor is significant because, as in several other narratives of racial passing, notably James Weldon Johnson's *Autobiography of an Ex-Colored Man*, the protagonist finds that his various educational environments are spaces in which he is initiated into his racial difference. Similarly, in *The White Boy Shuffle*, when Gunnar's third-grade Santa Monica teacher, Ms. Cegeny, wears a t-shirt celebrating the common humanity of all races, 'she seemed to pay special attention' to Gunnar and to the two other nonwhite students in the class (p. 32). In homeroom on his first day at Manischewitz Junior High, his first school in Hillside, the raucous atmosphere is the catalyst for Gunnar's discovery that he is 'a cultural alloy, tin-hearted whiteness wrapped in blackened copper plating' (p. 69), a realisation borne out by Scoby's judgment on Gunnar's 'fusion' musical tastes as a 'little black style with weepy bland white sedative sensibilities' (p. 73).

After Gunnar becomes involved in stealing a safe during the LA riots that ensued after the Rodney King decision, his parents insist on his switching schools to attend El Campesino Real High, 'an elite public school in the San Fernando Valley' (p. 169). They hope that 'the reinfusion of white upper-class values' will discourage him from committing further felonies (p. 169). At El Campesino, Gunnar employs his skills at performing, alternately, 'whiteness' – or 'ethnic obfuscation' (p. 170) – *and* 'blackness' – or 'rubbing burnt cork over our already dusky features and taking the stage as the blackest niggers in captivity' (p. 170). At this predominantly white school, Gunnar imitates his peers' way of speaking: 'you never forget how to raise your voice a couple of octaves, harden your r's, and diphthong the vowels: "Deeeewwuuuude. Maaaaiin. No waaaaaeey"' (p. 169). Interestingly, whiteness appears to be easier to simulate than blackness, for even after living for more than a year in Hillside, Gunnar's failure to completely assimilate is evident in his speech: 'I still said "ant" instead of "awwwnt" and "you guys" rather than "y'all"' (p. 105). At El Campasino, at times, it is of strategic value to perform 'blackness' as an excuse for non-completion of homework: 'Mistah Boss, sir. I'z couldenst dues my homework 'cause welfare came and took my baby brother to the home and he had all the crayons' (p. 170). By exploiting white assumptions about blackness, Gunnar succeeds in manipulating his teachers. At Boston University, on sports scholarship, Gunnar experiences the drawbacks of his ability to sashay back and forth across the color line – the alienation that inheres from belonging to neither group. In his creative writing class, confronted with classmates who discover he is *the* Gunnar Kaufman, originator of their favourite poetry, he feels 'like I'd been outed and exposed by my worst enemies, white kids who were embarrassingly like myself but with whom somehow I had nothing in common' (p. 197).

Echoing Jeffrey Eugenides, Gunnar observes that although the saying goes that 'the fruit never falls far from the tree', he has 'tried to roll down the hill at least a little bit' (p. 27). Beatty thereby hints that destiny and free will need not be conceived in completely oppositional terms. The ambivalence with which the fate versus free will debate is treated is exemplified in Gunnar's relationship with his father, who works for the LAPD, which, in *The White Boy Shuffle*, functions to symbolise the racism of white society.[27] When two LAPD officers pay Gunnar, newly arrived in West Los Angeles from Santa Monica, a visit in the spirit of 'preventative police enforcement' (p. 53), Gunnar notes that they are 'dressed to oppress' (p. 50). His father works as a sketch artist for the LAPD rather than as a cop. He is thus both *part of* but not *of* the LAPD Gunnar's father himself features as something of an absent presence, for his parents are divorced and Gunnar sees little of him. This simultaneous absence and presence reflects the ambivalent way in which ancestry is treated in the novel more generally, as both oppressive and irrelevant.

In *The Human Stain*, too, racial passing is bound up with the tensions between fate and free will. Coleman's objective in passing is 'for his fate to be determined not by the ignorant, hate-filled intentions of a hostile world but, to whatever degree humanly possible, by his own resolve' (p. 121). As in *The White Boy Shuffle*, however, the assertion of the supremacy of one over the other is decidedly equivocal. As David Brauner argues of the protagonists of Roth's 'American Trilogy' – *American Pastoral* (1997), *I Married a Communist* (1998) and *The Human Stain* – their

> self-mythologising nicknames demonstrate a shared conviction that they are masters of their own destinies, with the power to make of their lives – and themselves – what they will, but the allegorical elements of their first names suggest, on the contrary, that their fate is predetermined: Coleman an be read as 'coal man', a reference to the racial identity that he tries to efface.[28]

The ambivalence of Roth's position on fate versus free will is similarly wrought in terms of a discourse of ancestry and genealogy.

Coleman's first opportunity to pass arises when, as a student at Howard University in Washington DC, he learns of his father's death. He promptly leaves university, enlists in the army and, in so doing, passes as white. The death of his father brings with it 'Silky's freedom. The raw I. All the subtlety of being Silky Silk' (*Human Stain*, p. 108). This, and his brother Walter's absence at war, deprives Coleman of both his 'bulwarks' and he finds himself 'repowered and free to be whatever he wants, free to pursue the hugest aim, the confidence right in his bones to be his particular I' (p. 109). For Coleman, the decision to pass is equivalent to choosing individualism over group identity:

> You can't let the big they impose its bigotry on you any more than you can let the little they become a we and impose its ethics on you. Not the tyranny of the we and its we-talk and everything that the we wants to pile on your head. (p. 108)[29]

When, some years later, Coleman visits his mother to inform her of his decision to pass as white permanently and to explain that he will no longer see her or the rest of his family, she tells him 'You think like a prisoner. You do, Coleman Brutus. You're white as snow and you think like a slave' (p. 139). On the contrary, Coleman conceives of passing as rebellion against 'the idolatry that is ancestor worship', itself a form of 'imprisonment' (p. 144).

Like Beatty, moreover, Roth deploys metaphors of performance to reinforce the notion of self-making over determinism. Coleman sneers at those people of his acquaintance who fail to recognise that one's

invented self is as much a fiction as that which it replaces, that all
identity is performance. A former colleague of his, Smoky Hollenbeck,
he describes as 'Mr. Athena Square squared, performing in every
single way he's supposed to perform. Appears to have bought into the
story of himself one hundred percent' (p. 30). What distinguishes
Coleman from Smoky is that Coleman possesses '[s]elf-knowledge but
concealed. What is as powerful as that?' (p. 108). Meanwhile, Coleman
and Delphine Roux, his personal and professional adversary, are
engaged in a common struggle: that of emerging from the shadow of
overbearing parents to forge their own identities unencumbered
by issues of class, race or nationality. Delphine flees her homeland
of France:

> Because I could not make a French success, a real success, not with my
> mother and her shadow over everything – the shadow of her
> accomplishments but, even worse, of her family, the shadow of the
> Walincourts, named for the place given to them in the thirteenth century
> by the king Saint Louis and conforming still to the family ideals as they
> were *set* in the thirteenth century. (p. 274)

However, while Delphine is merely a 'bit player in the long-running
drama – entitled *Etc.* – that was the almost criminally successful life
of her mother' (p. 199), the relationship between Coleman and Faunia
Farley is described as a 'theatrical performance' by 'two leading actors'
which is 'flawlessly performed' (p. 51). Like Delphine and Coleman,
Faunia is remaking herself – as wife, mother, janitor, dairy worker –
in direct opposition to the way in which she was raised, as 'a rich,
privileged kid. Brought up in a big sprawling house south of Boston'
(p. 28). Equally, Coleman's former lover, Steena, from a small
Minnesota town, flees to New York at the age of eighteen because of
her overbearing father: 'Hard to be a daughter to that kind of feistiness.
He kind of submerges you' (p. 119).

At first glance, Roth's engagement with ancestors appears to be less
conflicted than Beatty's, his emphasis on 'the raw I' and performativity
seemingly at odds with *The White Boy Shuffle*'s balancing act of
inheritance *and* self-making, destiny *and* free will. However, the
novel's preoccupation with ancestry and genealogy is not exclusively
concerned with Coleman's rejection of his father and brother, for
Coleman is himself the father to four grown-up children. The 'human
stain' of the novel's title is configured as one's leaving 'a trail', an
'imprint' that is 'so intrinsic it doesn't require a mark' (p. 242). By

focusing on a member of Coleman's biological trail, his youngest son, significantly called Mark, Roth's ambivalence regarding fate/free will emerges. Although Mark spends his entire life attempting to go against the grain of his father and family, it is through this very rebellion that he, in fact, finds it impossible to do anything but *emulate* his father. Soon after he goes to kindergarten, Mark begins a lifelong 'protest against his family and their sense of things' (p. 61), recalling Coleman's mother's conviction that her son's detachment from his family was so severe that as a baby, Coleman was 'seriously disinclined even to take the breast' (p. 139). At twenty Mark enrages his father – as no doubt Coleman would have enraged his own, had he lived to see it – by dropping out of university (p. 61). Now 'a narrative poet' who spends his time writing 'biblically inspired poems that not even the Jewish magazines would publish', his literary incompetence parallels his father's own failure with *Spooks* (p. 61). There are further parallels at paternal funerals. Coleman's fraught relationship with his father does not prevent him from weeping copiously at the funeral, his 'manly effort at sober, stoical self-control' stripped away (p. 107). Similarly, Coleman's funeral ends with Mark's being 'overcome' with a 'hysteria' that sees him 'helplessly flailing his arms in the air and, through a wide-open mouth, wailing away' (p. 314).

Sporting/writing/passing

In both *The White Boy Shuffle* and *The Human Stain*, the protagonists are accomplished writers and thinkers (Gunnar as poet; Coleman as a Classics scholar) *and* talented sports people. If passing has the potential to explode racial categories, it is significant that these passing protagonists are adept at both intellectual *and* physical pursuits, for African Americans have historically been defined under 'body' in the mind/body dichotomy. It is of no small consequence, moreover, that Beatty and Roth choose sports that are popularly associated with African American practitioners. Some 83 per cent of NBA players are African American, and in the period during which Coleman is involved in boxing, African Americans had supplanted the Irish and Jews as the dominant ethnic group in the professional sport.[30] Coleman's decision to take up boxing at the age of fourteen (circa 1941) coincides with twelve years of Joe Louis's domination of the world heavyweight boxing scene, from 1937 to 1949. Gunnar's and Coleman's abilities at both cerebral and sporting activities reveal the

failure of such binary oppositions to do justice to the complementar-
ities of the mind and body, rather than their supposed incompatibility.

Arguably, the only school at which Gunnar is truly comfortable with
his racial identity is Phillis Wheatley High, where he distinguishes
himself as both a basketball star and a budding poet. The school, of
course, is named after the first African American to publish a
collection of poetry. Significantly, Gunnar's coach is Motome Chijiiwa
Shimimoto, who acts as a mentor to Gunnar not only on the basketball
court but also, as his art teacher, by nurturing his aesthetic sensibility
(*White Boy Shuffle*, p. 127). Thus, Gunnar's abilities at basketball are
juxtaposed throughout with his growing artistic sensibility. When he
confesses on his début that he has never played a game of basketball
in his life and that he 'ain't no ballplayer', Scoby responds: 'I know you
ain't. I seen you looking at those sonnets, drool dripping out of your
mouth' (p. 79). In contrast to Scoby, who, according to Tracy Curtis,
'has no public persona outside basketball', Gunnar 'cultivates two
public personae at once' – basketball star and poet – affording him an
'alternative to basketball that serves his neighbours' needs.'[31] On the
surface, then, the basketball-poetry combination seems to offer a
potentially positive answer to Gunnar's self-proclaimed status as
'cultural alloy', the sport dominated by African American practitioners,
the realm of poetry more readily associated with an Anglo-European
tradition.[32]

However, Gunnar's role as neighbourhood bard is ultimately as
externally circumscribed and regulated as his status as basketball star.
Gunnar's task is to compose poems lauding neighbourhood gang
leaders, which demands he 'say enough scholarly bullshit to keep from
getting my head chopped off' (p. 116). Furthermore, just as Gunnar's
basketball performances transform him into a 'commodity',[32] so he
becomes 'a human Hallmark card' through his composition of epithalamia and panegyrics (p. 116). He is pursued to his home by adoring
Creative Writing classmates at Boston University, and his teacher asks
if they can keep the clothes Gunnar has discarded 'as mementos'
because 'they might be worth something some day' (p. 199). Professor
Edelstein arranges for Gunnar's poetry to be published in a collection
entitled *Watermelanin*, which sells 126 million copies (p. 1).[34] Thus,
Gunnar's sporting prowess and creative writing are both commodified,
which is foreshadowed early in the novel when, in a bid to locate his
('black') soul, he starts 'playing Thoreau in the Montgomery Ward

department store', turning its 'desolate sporting goods department into a makeshift Walden' (p. 59).

The distinction between basketball-playing, ostensibly focused on the body, and poetry-writing, seemingly associated with the mind, is blurred even further by the specific poetic context in which Beatty is writing the novel. Beatty is himself a poet, having published two collections of poetry – *Big Bank Take Little Bank* (1991) and *Joker, Joker, Deuce* (1994) – prior to the appearance of *The White Boy Shuffle*, his first novel, in 1996. Beatty's verse is associated with the spoken word urban poetry scene of the 1990s, which became the subject of both a documentary, *Slam Nation* (1998), and a fictional film, *Slam* (1998).[35] In 1990 Beatty won the first annual Grand Slam contest at the Nuyorican Poets' Café.[36] The spoken word poetry of the slams is itself a hybrid form, which borrows liberally from the Beats (one of Beatty's creative writing tutors was Allen Ginsberg),[37] Amiri Baraka's signifyin' thereupon, black stand-up comedians such as Richard Pryor and Eddie Murphy and hip-hop music. Bryan Dexter Davis's claim that 'Slam is rather like an Olympics of poetry' is interesting for its sporting metaphor: the *performance* is equally as important as the content of the slam poem.[38] Thus, although Gunnar's poetry would seem to represent a more solitary, writerly pursuit than basketball, once again, it is the *performance* that is essential. Although he does not participate in any poetry slams, Gunnar certainly performs his poetry, most notably at the funeral for Gun Totin' Hooligans' gang leader, Pumpkin. The opposition between basketball and poetry collapses completely when the intimate connection between spoken word poetry and hip hop music is taken into account. As Jeffrey Lane observes, hip-hop, basketball and drug culture enjoy an 'incestuous relationship.'[39] Noting that all three have 'co-opted each other's vocabularies', Lane continues with a basketball/hip hop analogy: 'Like the pompous, confrontational basketball played today, most rap music is about one-upmanship and black male machismo.'[40]

If basketball and poetry are, for better or worse, complementary rather than oppositional pursuits in *The White Boy Shuffle*, in *The Human Stain* Coleman's athletic talent (first in track, then in boxing) and his scholarship/writing are both inextricable from passing. Just as the death of his father provides Coleman with his first opportunity to pass as white over a sustained period of time, so his boxing career starts out as an act of 'filial defiance' that he attempts to conceal from his family (p. 118). He begins to 'sneak' down to the Newark Boys Club, where all the other boys are 'colored,' and 'secretly' trains to be a fighter (p. 89). When his father discovers the truth, he forbids him from training at the Newark Boys Club and instead places him in the hands of Doc Chizner, a Jewish dentist with a passion for boxing. Through Coleman's relationship with Chizner, both boxing and Jewish identity become connected to camouflage, self-concealment and a discourse of secrecy, all of which Coleman subsequently cultivates in passing as white.

The first time Coleman passes on a temporary basis, it is upon the advice of his coach, while boxing at West Point against competition from the University of Pittsburgh. Chizner does not suggest that Coleman lie about his racial identity, just that he need not mention the fact that he is black: 'You're Silky Silk', Chizner tells him, 'that's enough' (p. 98). Chizner's recommendation that he be 'counter-confessional' corresponds with Coleman's boxing tactics of being a 'counterpuncher' (p. 100): 'All the answers that you came up with in the ring, you kept to yourself, and when you let the secret out, you let it out through everything *but* your mouth' (p. 200). Indeed, Coleman's subsequent decision to pass over permanently, to repudiate his mother and to keep his family antecedents a lifelong secret, is portrayed in terms of boxing strategy: 'Throw the punch, do the damage, and forever lock the door' (p. 139). For Coleman, the refusal to be defined and circumscribed according to his race, his assertion of the right to self-discovery is 'the punch to the labonz' (p. 108), a term he acquires from Chizner (p. 101).

The boxing metaphors continue to proliferate throughout the novel. When he meets his future wife, Iris, he is still dating Ellie, an African American girl who knows he is passing. Iris's appeal lies in the fact that she doesn't know his secret: 'Along comes Iris and he's back in the ring. His father had said to him, "Now you can retire undefeated. You're retired." But here he comes roaring out of his corner – he has the secret again' (p. 135). Ultimately, the connection Roth suggests between boxing and passing may best be explained by Gerald Early's articulation of the black intellectual's reluctance to celebrate the sport unequivocally: 'boxing, finally, for the black fighter is an apolitical, amoral experience of individual esteem, which the black fighter purchases at the expense of both his rival's health (and often his own) and his own dignity.'[41] The same could be applied to the way racial passing has historically been conceived: as a forsaking of family and community in one's own ruthless self-interest, a decision that inevitably proves to be psychically and emotionally impoverishing. For Walter, Coleman is 'a traitor to his race' (p. 342). As James Weldon Johnson's narrator famously puts it, he has 'sold [his] birthright for a mess of pottage.'[42]

Boxing and writing are linked in the novel via their common associations with passing. A further way in which the relationship between passing and writing may be discerned in *The Human Stain* is by unpacking the relationship between Coleman and his supposed real-life antecedent, Anatole Broyard. Henry Louis Gates's profile of Broyard in the *New Yorker* in 1996 suggests that one of the key motivating factors in Broyard's decision to pass as white was in order that 'he could be a writer, rather than a Negro writer.'[43] According to Ellen Schwamm, a friend of Broyard's, 'He felt that once he said, "I'm a Negro writer," he would have to write about black issues, and Anatole was such an aesthete.'[44] For Broyard to be a Negro writer would expose him to the kind of criticism levelled at Ralph Ellison and James Baldwin by Irving Howe in the 1960s. Gates intimates that the reason for Broyard's inability to produce a novel 'was that he was living it – that race loomed larger in his life because it was unacknowledged, that he couldn't put it behind him because he had put it beneath him.'[45] He concludes that the final irony in Broyard's life – and there were many – was that 'the man wanted to be appreciated not for being black but for being a writer, even though his pretending not to be black was stopping him from writing.'[46]

Zuckerman appears to engage with Gates's observations when he addresses the reasons for the dismal failure of Coleman's attempt at writing a memoir based upon his witch-hunt at the hands of the Athena College political correctness brigade: 'Of course you could not write the book. You'd written the book – the book was your life . . . Your book was your life – and your art? Once you set the thing in motion, your art was being a white man' (*Human Stain*, pp. 344–5). Gates and Zuckerman rightly identify the inextricability of passing and writing, but Zuckerman's view is subtly different from Gates's.[47] As Paul Spickard observes, Gates 'implies – without offering any evidence – that Broyard's failure to complete a novel was caused by his denial of his Black authenticity', seeing the connection between passing and writing in oppositional terms. By contrast, Zuckerman's understanding of Coleman's passing places it in a complementary relationship to writing.[48] For Zuckerman, Coleman's passing is *equivalent* to an act of writing because it is, in itself, a valid act of (self-)invention and creativity. But Broyard's passing, as Gates would have it, *prohibits* Broyard from producing a work of (literary) art.

In *The White Boy Shuffle* and *The Human Stain*, the issue of authorship may be considered at both a narrative and meta-narrative level, for while both protagonists are authors, so the novels' authors have themselves been subject to criticism regarding the appropriateness of their subject matter and/or literary techniques. In his *New York Times* review of Beatty's novel, Richard Bernstein argues that:

> when Mr. Beatty draws on his actual experience growing up sharp-eyed and black in Los Angeles, his novel reaches its heights. When he attempts a kind of inner-city magical realism, the less successful product falls somewhere in the vague zone between the Swiftian absurd and kvetchy political posturing.[49]

For Bernstein, the deployment of what he sees as a 'magical realist' mode represents a transgression into literary territory unsuited to the African American novelist (although commentators on Toni Morrison's work might disagree). The best passages in *The White Boy Shuffle* are, for Bernstein, those 'that sound genuinely experiential.'[50] Beatty's work is, at least in Bernstein's review, appreciated only for those aspects that are deemed appropriately 'black.'

Although it is difficult to believe given his now canonical status, Roth was not immune, early in his career, to similar pigeon-holing and critical indictment. Like Ralph Ellison, Roth found himself the object of a scathing critique by Irving Howe.[51] Initially laudatory in his assessment of Roth's *Goodbye, Columbus* (1959), Howe revised his good opinion in a 1972 article written for *Commentary*. What prompted Howe's originally positive reaction was that the story 'Defender of the Faith' led him, mistakenly as he subsequently claimed, 'to assume that this gifted new writer was working in the tradition of Jewish self-criticism and satire' when Roth 'has chosen to tear himself away from that tradition.'[52] Insisting once again on the contingency of 'the imagination' and 'a bruising involvement with social existence',[53] Howe accused Roth of not being 'Jewish' enough in his writing, just as, some nine years previously, he saw Ralph Ellison's assertion of 'esthetic distance' from 'Negro experience' as disingenuous. Such distance was, for Howe, 'a moral and psychological impossibility.'[54]

In both *The White Boy Shuffle* and *The Human Stain*, as in the other contemporary novels discussed in this book, the response to this double bind emerges in the depiction of the act of writing as profoundly ambivalent: as radical *and* complicit; as revelatory *and* obfuscatory; as creative *and* degenerative. For instance, Gunnar, like *Middlesex*'s Cal, grapples with the seeming futility of literary endeavour, the paradox that although writing is a creative act, it is ultimately passive. Both suspect that, politically, it achieves nothing. In *The White Boy Shuffle*, the LA riots provide Gunnar with a key lesson regarding his art: 'The day of the L.A. riots I learned that it meant nothing to be a poet' (p. 146). Unlike Psycho Loco, Gunnar's gang-leader friend, whose violence has a 'semblance of closure and accomplishment', Gunnar realises that the American poet is 'a tattletale, a whiner, at best an instigator' (p. 146). This is a significant moment in the novel because it provides one of the few occasions during which Beatty's own views on authorship may be speculated upon. In *The White Boy Shuffle*, Beatty's satire 'instigates' debates and, arguably, 'whines' about a number of issues without offering any suggestions for their resolution. Certainly, this is Bernstein's view when he observes that whenever the novel 'seems about to adopt a position, Mr. Beatty pulls it into parody.'[55]

In both *The White Boy Shuffle* and *The Human Stain*, the act of writing is configured as a form of physical debilitation which, in its most extreme form, results in metaphorical or actual death or suicide. For Gunnar, poems 'are like colds.' Feeling a poem coming on, his 'chest would grow heavier, [his] eyes watery; [his] body temperature would fluctuate, and a ringing in [his] ears would herald the coming of a timeless verse' (*White Boy Shuffle*, p. 87). Threatened with violence if he does not write the 'right' words about his gang member subjects, Gunnar's poetry becomes a matter of life and death, quite literally. Eventually, Gunnar's status as bestselling poet affords him a platform from which to speak to the African American masses. Hailed as a new black leader at a Boston University rally, Gunnar's speech endorses self-murder as the definitive form of racial protest, or 'the ultimate sit-in' (p. 2), spurring a number of African Americans across the country to commit suicide, but not before forwarding their suicide notes – or 'death poems' (p. 222) – to Gunnar. The act of writing thus becomes bound up with self-murder, erasure, the annihilation of the self.

In *The Human Stain*, Coleman and Zuckerman first become acquainted when Coleman approaches the local author shortly after the death of his wife, Iris, with the request that he write the story of his victimisation and vilification in the aftermath of the 'spooks' controversy. By 'creating their false image of him, calling him everything that he wasn't and could never be', his enemies at Athena, according to Coleman, 'had killed his wife of forty years' (p. 11). From the outset, therefore, writing and death are intertwined. When Zuckerman refuses to write the story, Coleman determines to go to work on the book himself. Two years later, during which he finds himself 'knee-deep in [his] own blood' in completing the first draft of *Spooks*, Coleman has given up on the idea of publishing it. But Zuckerman is surprised to note that Coleman feels no 'suicidal despair' when he realises that the book is 'shit' (pp. 19–20). Without the book, 'he appeared now to be without the slightest craving to set the record straight; shed of the passion to clear his name and criminalize as murderers his opponents, he was *embalmed* no longer in injustice' (p. 20, my emphasis). From this early passage, it is clear that in *The Human Stain*, the relationship of writing to death is twofold. One aspect of a text's association with fatality is that the act of writing can produce such extreme physical and psychical debility that, as a process, it may itself lead to 'suicidal despair' (p. 20). However, a written document – as evidence or testimony – can function as a means of exposing and avenging foul play which has led to death (the murder of Iris Silk, as Coleman perceives it). By the end of the novel, ironically, it is Zuckerman who seeks, through the act of writing, to 'clear [Coleman's] name' and 'criminalize' his murderer.

The most poignant juxtaposition of text and death in the novel is the Vietnam War Memorial. Unlike other memorials on Washington DC's Mall and surrounding areas – such as the Korean War Veterans Memorial and the Marine Corps War Memorial in Arlington, Virginia – the Vietnam War Memorial is not a representational sculpture.[56] It does not depict soldiers in battle, but is simply a V-shaped granite wall inscribed with the names of fifty-eight thousand soldiers who perished in Vietnam. The goal of Lester Farley's support group is to guide him through a process which will eventually lead to his confronting either the actual memorial in Washington DC or the Moving Wall:

> The name of each of the dead was about a quarter of the length of a man's little finger. That's what it took to get them all in there, 58,209 people who no longer take walks or go to the movies but who manage to exist, for whatever it is worth, as inscriptions on a portable black aluminum wall. (p. 252)

Fellow veteran Louie Borrero counsels countless former soldiers through the traumatic pilgrimage, taking care of 'the guys terrified they were going to cry too hard or feel too sick or have a heart attack and die' (p. 214). The memorial thus generates intense anxiety among those faced with the prospect of reading the names of deceased comrades.

However, while the Wall represents war fatalities, it can also have a therapeutic, restorative effect on those who lost friends or relatives in Vietnam. A sign in front of the Ramada Inn, in the parking lot of which the Moving Wall is temporarily installed, reads 'The Wall That Heals' (p. 253). Louie claims that the Wall 'changed [his] life', enabling him to make 'peace with Mikey' (p. 248). The Wall is thus an apt symbol of a text's capacity to signify simultaneously death (erasure) and life (regeneration). Indeed, several articles written about the Memorial compare it, alternately, with bodies and texts. For Vietnam veteran Tom Carhart, who opposed Maya Lin's design, the Wall is 'a black gash of shame.'[57] For Norman B. Hannah of the *National Review*, the memorial is 'clearly an "open book" in which Americans can not only honor their dead but see the Vietnam War in the stream of our history.'[58] Similarly, for Gordon O. Taylor, the memorial's black granite panels are like 'pages' that are bound, 'booklike.'[59] Of course, perhaps more than any other war in American historical memory, the Vietnam War is associated with multiple cover-ups, such as the My Lai massacre of 1968. For, after all, what will replace the 'true' account of what happened except a replacement story, an alternative story? Wiping the facts from written record – erasure – is an act of regeneration. For Taylor, the Wall is 'a text both sacred and profane, perhaps in both aspects the nearest we have to a communally agreed-upon writing and reading of the Vietnam War.'[60] However, that Lester's encounter is with the Moving Wall reminds us that the memorial is not a definitive text. The actual memorial stands on Washington DC's Mall, but is supplemented by a mobile version that travels the country. In 1998, moreover, a Virtual Wall was launched which enables visitors 'to scan all the names and click on the name of the person they are searching for.' Visitors can 'get a virtual name rubbing, or leave text, audio, and photographic remembrances online.'[61] The multiplication of the versions of the Vietnam Wall testifies to the permeability of texts, and the possibility of reproducing and/or of faking them.

At the end of *The Human Stain*, Zuckerman finally meets Lester Farley ice-fishing in the wilderness of the Berkshires, describing him as 'the only human marker in all of nature, like the X of an illiterate's signature on a sheet of paper. There it was, if not the whole story, the whole picture' (p. 361). This 'X', the novel's last image, yokes together disavowed authorship (not attributing one's writing to oneself) and illiteracy (not being able to acknowledge one's authorship), both recurring conceits throughout the novel. Like the passer, whose body defies the assumption that blackness must be visibly evident, documents and texts of all kinds that purport to comprise one's identity, many self-penned – emails, letters, diaries, internet postings, *curricula vitae*, personal adverts, poems – prove slippery. The most significant of these is Delphine Roux's 'Everyone knows' letter, the centrality of which is underscored by its appearance, scroll-like with 'Everyone knows' partially visible and partially obscured, on the book jacket of the novel. When she learns of Coleman's affair with Faunia Farley, she sends him an anonymous letter informing him that 'Everyone knows' he is 'sexually exploiting an abused, illiterate woman' half his age (p. 38). As she composes it, writing 'in big block letters', she deludes herself momentarily 'that no one would recognize [the handwriting] as her own' (p. 196). But as soon as she mails the letter, she realises that 'Even after her having left it unsigned, even after her having employed a vulgar rhetoric not her own, the letter's origins are going to be no mystery to someone as fixated on her as Coleman Silk' (p. 201). Delphine's decision to leave the letter unsigned – her doomed endeavour at 'passing' through the act of writing – contrasts with Coleman's successful racial passing, which is configured as his refusal 'to accept automatically the contract drawn up for your signature at birth' (p. 155). In other words, Delphine's and Coleman's common struggle is symbolically wrought in terms of the signature: to sign or not to sign. What differs is their *execution* of this endeavour. Delphine's manifesto is to 'go to America and be the author of my own life' (p. 273). However, her 'authorship' – her effort at dissembling on paper and in life – is not convincing and she 'winds up as the author of nothing' (p. 273).[62]

Coleman realises immediately that the 'Everyone knows' letter has come from his former colleague who led the campaign against him in the aftermath of the 'spooks' incident. As confirmation, he carefully compares the handwriting on the letter with samples of Roux's handwriting in documents pertaining to the 'spooks' affair. When he subsequently shows the evidence to Zuckerman, it is indisputable that Coleman has 'nailed the culprit who'd set out to nail him' (p. 39). Like Henry Louis Gates, in his efforts to authenticate the manuscript of

The Bondwoman's Narrative, Coleman even travels to Boston to have a handwriting expert substantiate his claims (p. 55). Similarly, when Coleman reads the *curriculum vitae* and autobiographical essay Delphine submits as a candidate for an academic job at Athena, he observes that, like Rousseau, she hides herself only for her rhetoric to give her away (pp. 189–90). Consequently, despite what she writes, Coleman can *read* through the artifice. His derisive attitude towards Delphine thus springs not from the fact that she is pretending to be something she is not, but from the fact that she fails to pretend in a credible way. Like Delphine and Coleman, Faunia's reinvention, and others' perception of her, is depicted through the symbolism of writing and reading – or rather, *not* reading and *not* writing, for she feigns illiteracy. Taking 'willingly upon herself this crippling shortcoming all the better to impersonate a member of a subspecies to which she does not belong and need not belong' (p. 164), Faunia is, like Coleman, posthumously 'outed' when Zuckerman overhears her father and his nurse discuss the diary she left behind (p. 297).

After the deaths of Coleman and Faunia, those directly implicated in the case or involved in some way with the victims – Delphine Roux, Lester Farley, Coleman's family, Faunia's father – are concerned to impose their own narrative interpretation on the events. The writing of *The Human Stain* thus represents Zuckerman's contribution to the proliferation of stories that emerge in the aftermath of the car wreck that kills Coleman and Faunia. To avoid 'a scandalous trial that would be written up sensationally in the local papers and lodged indelibly in local memory', Coleman's children request that Zuckerman refrain from 'urging any further investigation by the police' (p. 308). At Coleman's funeral, Herb Keble is, according to Zuckerman, 'another one out trying to kosher the record' (p. 312). Sylvia, nurse to Faunia's father, announces that she will burn the diary – the 'record . . . of filth' (p. 301) – that Faunia left behind. Zuckerman begins the book that the reader is expected to believe is *The Human Stain* as part-investigative act, part-biography of an extraordinary man. When Coleman's daughter asks Zuckerman 'how could all this happen?' Zuckerman can offer her no answer 'other than by beginning to write this book' (p. 304). If his efforts at acting as an 'amateur detective' to aid the investigation into the deaths are repeatedly foiled (p. 295), his novel becomes a kind of detective story, what Lester Farley subsequently calls a 'whodunit' (p. 359). Zuckerman's overlapping roles as detective, biographer and fiction-writer recall Monk Ellison's description of himself as a 'hermeneutic sleuth' (*Erasure*, p. 31) and Henry Louis Gates's 'meticulous research and detective work' in identifying the author of *The Bondwoman's Narrative*.[63]

However, what Michael Gilmore describes as Zuckerman's 'mild genuflection to the detective form'[64] itself fails, for if the trajectory of the detective story is 'from chaos to solution',[65] then Zuckerman's graveside encounter with Coleman's sister, Ernestine, only serves to make Coleman 'more of a mystery' to him: 'Now that I knew everything, it was as though I knew nothing' (p. 333). His conversation with Ernestine also highlights that biography as 'posthumous sleuthing'[66] can only, like the 'human biography' that is Coleman's tattoo, be 'a tiny symbol to remind me why our understanding of people must always be at best slightly wrong' (p. 22). Coleman acquires the tattoo when, during his stint in the US Navy during World War II, he is slung out of a white brothel in Norfolk, Virginia after being recognised as black (p. 183). The 'blue pigment' of the tattoo serves to remind Coleman that his 'black' pigmentation almost gave him away and could have led to a court martial and a dishonourable discharge. Not only is the tattoo inscribed upon Coleman's body, but it also contains: '[t]he ineradicable biography ... the prototype of the ineradicable, a tattoo being the very emblem of what can never be removed' (p. 184).

This slippage between bodily inscribed signs (Coleman's tattoo) as biography and textual output (*The Human Stain*) as biography (of Coleman by Zuckerman; of Broyard by Roth) dovetails neatly with the final chapter of this book. There I examine recent controversies of authorship in which the *analogy* between passing and writing explored throughout this book becomes actualised. In producing embellished or 'fake' memoirs, itself a form of (auto)biography, the authors in question also engage in acts of racial and gender passing.

Notes

1 Toni Morrison, 'Talk of the Town', *New Yorker* (6 October 1998), 31–2.
2 Paul Beatty, *The White Boy Shuffle* (London: Minerva, 1996). Subsequent references will be given in parentheses in the body of the text.
3 For sustained discussions of the Clinton/Silk parallels, see Anthony Hutchison, *Writing the Republic: Liberalism and Morality in American Political Fiction* (New York: Columbia University Press, 2007) and Dean J. Franco, 'Being Black, Being Jewish, and Knowing the Difference', *Studies in American Jewish Literature* 23 (2004), 88–103.

4 Dreisinger, p. 124.
5 The name 'Gunnar' is likely an allusion to Swedish sociologist Gunnar Myrdal, who in 1944 published *An American Dilemma: The Negro Problem and Modern Democracy*. For Myrdal, racial inequality in the USA was attributable to the conflict between the general American Creed of rights to equality and liberty and the particularities, especially in the US South, of white supremacist thought, the tension between the universalist and the regionalist producing the dilemma of the title. Myrdal fully subscribed to the (then) emergent discourse of race-as-culture, rather than race-as-biology. See Richard H. King, *Race, Culture, and the Intellectuals, 1940–1970* (Baltimore: Johns Hopkins University Press, 2004), pp. 21–48. However, Gunnar Kaufman's 'American Dilemma' is that he feels just as circumscribed by the discourse of race-as-culture as by race-as-biology.
6 W.E.B. DuBois, *The Souls of Black Folk* (1903; New York: Dover, 1994), p. 2. Subsequent references will be included in parentheses in the main body of the text.
7 Wald, p. 5.
8 Philip Roth, *The Human Stain* (London: Vintage, 2001). Subsequent references will be given in parentheses in the body of the text.
9 Senna, *Caucasia*, p. 140.
10 Ibid., p. 137.
11 Daniel Itzkovitz, 'Passing Like Me: Jewish Chameleonism and the Politics of Race', in Sánchez and Schlossberg, pp. 38–63 (pp. 44–5).
12 Garber, p. 11.
13 Harrison-Kahan, p. 22.
14 Franco, p. 88.
15 Halberstam, p. 26.
16 Harrison-Kahan, p. 38.
17 Rogin, p. 56.
18 See Hasia R. Diner, *In the Almost Promised Land: American Jews and Blacks, 1915–1935* (Baltimore: Johns Hopkins University Press, 1995); Ethan Goffman, *Imagining Each Other: Blacks and Jews in Contemporary American Literature* (New York: State University of New York Press, 2000) and Jeffrey Melnick, *A Right to Sing the Blues: African Americans, Jews, and American Popular Song* (Cambridge, MA: Harvard University Press, 2001).
19 Eric J. Sundquist, *Strangers in the Land: Blacks, Jews, Post-Holocaust America* (Cambridge, MA: Harvard University Press, 2005), p. 4.
20 Anatole Broyard, 'Portrait of the Inauthentic Negro: How Prejudice Distorts the Victim's Personality', *Commentary* 10.4 (1950), 56–64 (56).
21 Robinson, 'Forms of Appearance', p. 237.
22 Jean-Paul Sartre, 'Portrait of the Inauthentic Negro', *Commentary* 5.5 (1948), 389–97.

23 Harper, 'Passing for What?', p. 382.

24 Wald, p. 187.

25 The definition of atavism is from Sollors's *Neither Black Nor White*, p. 49. The notion of atavism is explored in, to give just two examples, Kate Chopin's short story 'Desirée's Baby' (1893) and Nella Larsen's *Passing* (1929).

26 Gass, p. 46.

27 Richard Bernstein, 'Books of the Times: Black Poet's First Novel Aims the Jokes Both Ways', *New York Times* (31 May 1996), 25.

28 Brauner, p. 149.

29 In fact, as Mark Maslan argues convincingly, *The Human Stain* is 'only nominally about an individualist's struggle against the group; it is essentially about an American's struggle to realize his nationality', a point borne out by the fact that 'Coleman's experiment in whiteness, which begins at West Point and ends, as the novel untiringly reminds us, in the former surroundings of Herman Melville and Hawthorne, sometimes reads like an overheated Smithsonian tour book of historical American places.' In other words, for Roth, the rejection of African American (group) identity is 'merely the precondition for embodying [another group identity,] a national one.' 'The Faking of the Americans: Passing, Trauma, and National Identity in Philip Roth's *The Human Stain*', *Modern Language Quarterly* 66.3 (2005), 365–89 (379–81).

30 Aaron Baker, *Contesting Identities: Sports in American Film* (Urbana: University of Illinois Press, 2003), p. 100.

31 Curtis, p. 67.

32 In the basketball-poetry combination, Beatty is echoing Trey Ellis, who in 1989 explicated a 'New Black Aesthetic.' According to Ellis, young black artists of his generation share a feeling of being 'misunderstood by both the black worlds and the white', which manifests itself in art that 'shamelessly borrows and reassembles across both race and class lines.' Ellis calls this 'NBA' for short, initials that bring the National Basketball Association more readily to mind. 'The New Black Aesthetic', *Callaloo* 38 (1989), 233–43 (234). Although Beatty has explicitly disavowed his association with the New Black (or 'Post-Soul') Aesthetic, Bertram D. Ashe finds that his work nonetheless 'places him solidly within that aesthetic.' 'Paul Beatty's White Boy Shuffle Blues: Jazz, Poetry, John Coltrane, and the Post-Soul Aesthetic', in *Thriving on a Riff: Jazz and Blues Influences in African American Literature and Film*, ed. Graham Lock and David Murray (Oxford: Oxford University Press, 2008), pp. 106–23 (p. 107).

33 Curtis, p. 64.

34 The title of Gunnar's poetry collection is likely a nod to the film *Watermelon Man* (1970) in which white racist Jeff Gerber awakens one morning to find he has been transformed into a black man.

35 Bryan Dexter Davis provides a useful and concise explanation of what is involved in a poetry slam: 'Slamming poets perform a "set" of two or three of their own poems. Randomly selected members of the audience judge the poetry spontaneously with a score of 1–10 immediately following each "reading." Slam poems are judged as much on content as on dramatic delivery.' Heather E. Bruce and Bryan Dexter Davis, 'Slam: Hip-Hop Meets Poetry – A Strategy for Violence Intervention', *English Journal* 8.5 (2000), 119–27 (121).

36 Jabari Asim, 'Grand Slam Champ', *Washington Post* (13 June 1999), X12.

37 According to Graham Caveney, Ginsberg 'likened Beatty's work to the music of Miles Davis', suggesting yet another form of hybridity between poem/music. 'The Books Interview: Paul Beatty; Sweet Talk and Fighting Words', *Independent* (22 July 2000), 9.

38 Bruce and Davis, 121.

39 Jeffrey Lane, *Under the Boards: The Cultural Revolution in Basketball* (Lincoln: University of Nebraska Press, 2007), p. 3.

40 Ibid. pp. 6, 12.

41 Gerald Early, *The Culture of Bruising: Essays on Prizefighting, Literature, and Modern American Culture* (Hopewell, NJ: Ecco, 1997), p. 28.

42 Johnson, *Autobiography of an Ex-Colored Man*, p. 100.

43 Henry Louis Gates's article on Broyard first appeared under the title 'White Like Me' in the *New Yorker* on 17 June 1996. I quote from the version reprinted in Henry Louis Gates, Jr., 'The Passing of Anatole Broyard', *Thirteen Ways of Looking at a Black Man* (New York: Random House, 1997), pp. 180–214 (p. 184). For reviews of and articles about *The Human Stain* citing Anatole Broyard as Roth's inspiration for Coleman Silk, see Kakutani, Kaplan, Moore, Posnock and Safer.

44 Gates, 'The Passing of Anatole Broyard', p. 203.

45 Ibid., p. 198.

46 Ibid., p. 203.

47 The difficulty of identifying this distinction is evident in Brett Ashley Kaplan's otherwise fascinating article, in which she unpicks the mesh of allusions to Broyard's life and writings in Roth's novel. She echoes Gates in claiming that Broyard 'paid for his vision of a world beyond race by his inability to formulate his longed-for novel. Were racial categories more openly fluid, Broyard would presumably have been equipped to write beyond the limiting confines of the designation *black writer*.' Yet, her position is closer to that of Zuckerman when she asserts that 'when Roth writes Coleman, he literalizes Broyard's self-understanding as a fiction.' Brett Ashley Kaplan, 'Anatole Broyard's Human Stain: Performing Postracial Consciousness', *Philip Roth Studies* 1.2 (2005), 125–144, 190 (129, 136).

48 Spickard, p. 81.

49 Bernstein, 25.

50 Ibid., 25.

51 Timothy Parrish, Michael T. Gilmore and Ross Posnock (in *Philip Roth's Rude Truth*), convincingly, I think, read *The Human Stain* in relation to Ellison's *Invisible Man*. All three emphasise certain structural similarities between the two novels – the importance of the words 'spooks' and 'invisible', and the centrality of boxing in both books. This discussion of Howe and Roth is particularly indebted to Parrish.

52 Irving Howe, 'Philip Roth Reconsidered', in *Philip Roth*, ed. Harold Bloom (New York: Chelsea, 1986), pp. 71–88 (pp. 79, 80).

53 Ibid., p. 75.

54 Howe, *A World*, p. 114.

55 Bernstein, 25.

56 This is one of the reasons for which the design for the Vietnam War Memorial was so controversial at the time. As a compromise, a sculpture of three servicemen and an American flag, a few feet's distance from the Wall, was added a year after the Wall was dedicated in 1982. A decade later the Women's Memorial, honouring the nurses who served in Vietnam, was also added. Other sources of controversy included the V-shape of the memorial, which some felt immortalised 'the antiwar signal, the V protest made with the fingers', and the fact that the memorial is in black granite, 'not the white marble of Washington.' 'The Week: Stop that Monument', *National Review* (18 September 1981), 1064.

57 Quoted in Wolf Von Eckhardt, 'Storm over a Viet Nam Memorial: An Eloquently Simple Design for Washington's Mall Draws Fire', *Time* (9 November 1981), 103.

58 Norman B. Hannah, 'The Open Book Memorial', *National Review* (11 December 1981), 1476.

59 Gordon O. Taylor, 'Past as Prologue', *Genre* 21.4 (1998), 579–84 (579).

60 Ibid., 581.

61 Valerie Lewis, 'Build the Virtual Wall', *America's Network* (November 2000), 38–9 (39).

62 In his non-fiction Roth overtly links letter-writing and fiction-writing. In a discussion of Norman Mailer's *Advertisements for Myself* (1959), Roth observes that 'times are tough for a fiction writer when he takes to writing letters to his newspaper rather than those complicated, disguised letters to himself, which are stories.' Philip Roth, 'Writing American Fiction', in *The Novel Today: Contemporary Writers on Modern Fiction*, ed. Malcolm Bradbury (London: Fontana, 1977), pp. 32–47 (p. 37). Incidentally, Mailer's infamous essay, 'The White Negro', is collected in *Advertisements for Myself*. In his analysis of *The Human Stain*, Ross Posnock distinguishes between the 'racial primitivism' of a Mailer-esque Jewish appropriation of a black identity, and Coleman's black-for-Jewish passing, which is 'a

practical solution to his quest for self-invention.' 'Purity and Danger: On Philip Roth', *Raritan* 21.2 (2001), 85–101 (95).

63 Time Warner press release, *The Bondwoman's Narrative* by Hannah Crafts (2 April 2002) www.twbookmark.com/books/48/0446530085/ press_release.html (22 November 2004).

64 Gilmore, p. 176.

65 Catherine Nickerson, *The Web of Iniquity: Early Detective Fiction by Women* (Durham, NC: Duke University Press, 1998), p. 57.

66 G. Thomas Couser, 'Genome and Genre: DNA and Life Writing', *Biography* 24.1 (2001), 185–96 (187).

6

Conclusion: 'passing' fads?: recent controversies of authenticity and authorship

I feel that none of the slight liberties I took in writing my memoir really affect the overall work, but nonetheless, you should know a few things: I am not, in fact, black.

Nor am I, to the best of my knowledge, a woman. Anything in my book that suggests otherwise is the result of a typographical error. That this error was compounded by my decision to pose for my author photo and bookstore appearances in drag and blackface is, I will acknowledge, unfortunate.

The portions of my book dealing with Depression-era Ireland are, I have been reliably informed, copied verbatim from Frank McCourt's *Angela's Ashes*. I can only conclude that I accidentally confused my manuscript with my notes for my memoir in which I copied large portions of other writers' works, just to see how they were structured. In hindsight, the fact that I was born 40 years after the Depression should have been a tip-off.

Tim Carvell, *New York Times* (2006)[1]

I quote extensively from Tim Carvell's satirical response to the controversies involving J.T. LeRoy and James Frey because it reiterates in comic fashion the key issues which I identify and unpack throughout this book. Here, he makes explicit the connections between the acts of passing and writing. This is due in no small part to the fact that the visual economies of race and gender are transliterated onto the book jacket he describes in the form of an author photograph, just as, in *Erasure*, Monk Ellison's readership expects him to treat certain themes in his writing because, as they can see from his photograph, he is African American. I began this book by questioning why the metaphors of concealment, subterfuge and deception that have historically characterised passing are still pervasive in US culture. In this concluding section I interrogate three recent controversies of authorship in which the connection between the contemporary fascination with the theme of passing and *authorial* concealment, subterfuge and deception becomes glaringly evident.

The first is the exposure of the author J.T. LeRoy as a 'fake', the second, the 'embellishments' James Frey added to his memoir of drug and alcohol addiction, *A Million Little Pieces* (2005) and the third, the passing of a middle-class white woman, Margaret Seltzer, as Margaret B. Jones, a working-class 'mixedblood', in authoring a ghetto memoir entitled *Love and Consequences: A Memoir of Hope and Survival* (2008). In the preceding chapters I begin with the *theme* of passing and describe the ways in which the treatment of passing *within* the text often reflects the writers' engagement with issues of authorship *beyond* the text. In this concluding section, I reverse this methodology, beginning with the issue of authorship and working my way back to the content of the texts in question. Whichever way the narratives are read, the symmetry is not coincidental, though it may or may not be deliberate on the part of the authors in question.

When the memoir was in vogue

It is no accident that the contemporary American novels discussed in chapters 4 and 5 either 'pass' as memoirs or toy self-consciously with this form, for the last ten years has witnessed an explosion of memoirs in the United States and elsewhere, a publishing phenomenon which shows no signs of abating. At the end of his March 2005 article in the *New York Times*, William Grimes lists no fewer than twenty-eight recently published memoirs.[2] Meanwhile, the British-based *Bookseller* magazine reported that of the top one hundred bestselling paperbacks in 2006, eleven were 'misery memoirs.'[3] Indeed *Bookseller* is credited with coining the term 'misery memoir' or 'misery lit' – though this descriptor is not yet used as widely in the USA – to describe the genre: memoirs that trace the author-protagonist's triumph over a history of physical/psychological/sexual abuse, addiction, poverty or racism (or a combination thereof). From the outset, the trend has been greeted with a great deal of debate. For instance, Frank McCourt's bestselling, Pulitzer-Prize-winning memoir, *Angela's Ashes* (1996), met with hostility in Irish and Irish-American circles over McCourt's alleged exaggeration of poverty in Limerick and his cruel treatment by the Christian Brothers of the city.[4] That the objections to *Angela's Ashes* as a memoir are inextricable from more recent sagas involving LeRoy,

Frey and Jones is evident in the frequency with which McCourt's comment has been sought in reports about these cases.[5]

Even the deployment of the term 'memoir' or 'memoirs' can prove contentious. In 2001 Mineko Iwasaki filed suit against Arthur Golden, author of the bestseller *Memoirs of a Geisha* (1997), for breach of contract. Iwasaki, a former geisha, claimed that Golden promised to protect her anonymity, which, in naming her in the book's acknowledgements, Golden failed to do. According to the *New York Times*, 'many in the geisha community said they found the novel troubling because it is written so convincingly in the first person that many readers have come to regard it as fact.'[6] In the cases of McCourt and Golden, the criticism of their books arises from the perceived blurring of boundaries between fact and fiction. The one, a 'real' memoir, deploys too much fiction at the expense of fact; the other, a novel passing as a memoir, too much fact at the expense of fiction. By 'exaggerating' his autobiography, McCourt 'fictionalised' aspects of *Angela's Ashes*. By using the description 'memoirs' in the title of his novel, Golden 'passed' fiction off as autobiography.

The memoir, with its permeable boundaries which allow fiction and (auto)biography to overlap and coexist, would appear to qualify as the quintessential postmodern literary form. Linda Hutcheon argues, for example, that in postmodern literature, '[t]he borders between literary genres have become fluid' and that 'the most radical boundaries crossed' have been 'those between fiction and non-fiction and, by extension, between art and life.'[7] Dave Eggers, in his memoir *A Heartbreaking Work of Staggering Genius* (2000), both identifies and exploits memoir's postmodernist potential when he includes self-consciously a preface and acknowledgments replete with caveats and disclaimers regarding the book's veracity. 'For all the author's bluster elsewhere', Eggers announces in the preface, 'this is not, actually, a work of pure nonfiction. Many parts have been fictionalized in varying degrees, for various purposes.'[8] I would argue, however, that the principal reason for which the memoir has become contested literary territory is not so much that is a paradigmatic postmodern genre, but because, like passing, it embodies, and thus foregrounds, some of the most tendentious aspects of literary postmodernism. Most intriguingly, the popularity of memoirs, and the debates that arise when they veer into 'fiction', reveal the ever-widening gap between the academy and the general public, for whom postmodernist principles persist only in their apparent irrelevancy.

That memoir exists in the interstices of fiction and autobiography, and is exceedingly difficult to pin down, is borne out by the seeming impossibility of defining the category. Memoirist Mary Karr's attempted distinction between 'novelist' and 'memoirist' – 'the novelist creates events for truthful interpretation, whereas the memoirist tries to honestly interpret events plagiarized from reality' – is poetic but unhelpful.[9] What is particularly striking about Karr's formulation, however, is her use of the term 'plagiarized', implying, intentionally or not, that the memoirist is always already engaged in fraudulent authorial behaviour. Novelist William Gass observes:

> [a] memoir is usually the recollection of another place or personality, and its primary focus is outward bound . . . Even when the main attention of the memoir is inward, the scope of the memory tends to be limited (how I felt at the first fainting of the queen), and not wide enough to take in a life.[10]

This does shed more light on the issue, but only in distinguishing the memoir from other forms of life writing – diary, notebook, journal – rather than from fiction. Intriguingly, in true poststructuralist fashion, both Karr and Gass only classify memoir in relation to *other* literary genres. Memoir, it seems, does not have any intrinsic characteristics but only acquires meaning when placed next to other kinds of writing with which it can be compared.

It is, as James Atlas insists, 'a democratic genre', which embraces indiscriminately the voices of the old and the young, the famous and the obscure, the crazy and the sane.[11] Brent Staples concurs, noting in 1997 that 'the market is teeming with tenderfoot memoirs by ordinary Janes and Joes, many of them scarcely out of their 30's.'[12] William Grimes, writing almost a decade later, describes the memoir phenomenon as 'more a plain than a mountain, a level playing field crowded with absolutely equal voices, each asserting its democratic claim on the reader's attention.'[13] Such polyphony is consistent with postmodernist claims both to pluralism and to the effacement of boundaries, what Fredric Jameson calls 'the erosion of the older distinction between high culture and so-called mass or popular culture.'[14] On the other hand, far from confirming the 'death of the author', the memoir is a literary genre that restores the 'unstable authorial "I" that came under assault in English departments across the land during the 70's and 80's to center stage.'[15] Instead of 'the death of the subject', memoirs tend to affirm rather than challenge the notion of a coherent, stable self, albeit a self whose unity may have been achieved only after undergoing and writing about a series of traumatic experiences from the author's past.[16]

Memoir, it would appear, tests the limits of postmodernism. Paradigmatically postmodern in some respects, it is hopelessly un-postmodern in others. What happens, then, when the author *is* revealed to be literally dead or, at least, non-existent? But if the exposure of this non-existent author is greeted with public outcry and charges of deception, where does that leave postmodernism? The reaction to the LeRoy hoax reveals the unbridgeable chasm that has opened up between the academic celebration and the public reception of postmodern playfulness.[17] As one commentator puts it:

> One could try to defend the deception as a postmodern game in which the author's identity becomes part of the art, but that feels like more charity than the case deserves. The revelations can only leave Leroy's fans disappointed and his works diminished. If it is a game, it's the readers who lose.[18]

Deceitful above all things?

On 17 October 2005 Stephen Beachy published a piece in *New York Magazine* in which he suggested that cult novelist J.T. LeRoy did not exist and that his books were penned by Laura Albert, an outreach worker who supposedly rescued LeRoy from the streets and brought him to live with her and her husband, Geoffrey Knoop. Subsequent articles by Warren St. John of the *New York Times* revealed that while Albert indeed wrote the books attributed to LeRoy, the public role of the writer was played by Savannah Knoop, her twentysomething sister-in-law, who 'bound her breasts, and wore a preposterous blonde wig and sunglasses, affected a West-Virginian accent; and appeared as JT whenever a physical boy was needed.'[19] The case of J.T. LeRoy, then, provides the most perfect symmetry imaginable between passing and authorship, for it emerged that the person who appeared in public as the author of texts fundamentally and persistently concerned with gender b(l)ending was, in fact, a cross-dressed woman.

LeRoy first came to prominence in 1997, when a piece entitled 'Baby Doll', published under the pseudonym 'Terminator', was included in the anthology *Close to the Bone: Memoirs of Hurt, Rage and Desire*.[20] The piece subsequently appeared in his collection of interconnected short stories, *The Heart is Deceitful Above All Things* (2001), which was adapted for the screen in 2004. In the interim, J.T. LeRoy, whose initials stand for Jeremy Terminator, published his first novel, *Sarah* (2000); in 2005 *Harold's End* appeared. LeRoy's work draws upon his own (supposed) traumatic childhood experiences, which include being introduced to heroin and pimped out as a cross-dressed teenage prostitute by his own mother. Although 'packaged as fiction', as Karr notes, LeRoy's books were 'alluded to as fact.'[21] Karr's observation identifies a key distinction because it emphasises the complicity of LeRoy's readers in his passing and the role of the spectator in the act of passing more generally. In other words, it confirms Amy Robinson's point that 'it is the spectator who manufactures a successful pass, whose act of reading (or misreading) constitutes the performance of the passing subject.'[22] That LeRoy's books were 'alluded to as fact' is an act of literal *misreading* on behalf of LeRoy's readers, which positions LeRoy as a passer and a fraud.

If the semi-autobiographical content of his work is borne out by the inclusion of 'Baby Doll' in a collection expressly called 'memoirs', the slippery nature of the category of 'memoir' becomes evident in Michiko Kakutani's *New York Times* review of *Close to the Bone*. Kakutani maintains that although each of the narratives is written in the first person, 'they all have the faintly stylized feel of fiction; indeed in another age – even five years ago, say – such works would have probably been published as short stories.'[23] Similarly, another reviewer notes that 'Baby Doll' is 'as vivid as fiction, and even reads as though it has been embellished for fictional effect.'[24] Thus, LeRoy's 'Baby Doll' reveals the mobility of memoir across literary categories. What might have been a short story in 1992 becomes a memoir in 1997 and a short story again in 2001. What is fascinating about 'Baby Doll' is not only that it reveals the contiguity and interchangeability of memoir and fiction, but that its *content* mirrors so uncannily the boundary crossings that Albert/Knoop-as-LeRoy undertook as author and authorial persona respectively. Mary Karr, whose *The Liar's Club* (1995) is credited by many as having launched the memoir craze, contends after Beachy's revelations that 'Mr. Leroy's whole enterprise was predicated on the tenets of drag – lots of veils and subterfuge.'[25] With hindsight, it is difficult to conceive of the 'real' LeRoy as doing anything but audaciously defying his readers to unmask him by persistently telegraphing references to drag, veils and subterfuge in his writing and, indeed, in his interviews. Almost a year before the appearance of the Beachy article, LeRoy spoke about his reasons for hiding behind a wig and sunglasses in public appearances, claiming that years of therapy have enabled him to shed his image of himself as inherently evil: 'It's been really recent that I could take off the mask.'[26]

In the story 'Baby Doll', the narrator's sadistic mother, Sarah, convinces her son, Jeremiah, that his penis is 'evil' and burns it with a cigarette lighter.[27] Jeremiah, who longs for the intimacy that exists between Sarah and her new boyfriend, Jackson, subsequently glues his penis back between his legs, cross-dresses in Sarah's lingerie and seduces Jackson, only to be discovered by his mother. However, Jeremiah's cross-dressing is not the only, or indeed the first, form of disguise that appears in the story. Towards the beginning, the young protagonist watches his mother apply foundation to cover the freckles on her face. When he asks her to cover his own, she appraises his features, noting his prominent nose: 'Somebody fucked their nigger slave, and you got the nose to prove it' (p. 118). Sarah is referring to the phenomenon of 'atavism', a common fear in narratives of passing. In effect, Sarah is accusing her son of passing as white, his 'nigger nose' evidence of African American ancestry which, with the aid of her make-up brushes, she helps him to 'camouflage' (p. 118). She also claims that if he got the nose, she 'got the lips' and goes about thickening his mouth (p. 119). After Sarah completes her makeover of Jeremiah, which complements the long hair she refuses to let him cut, she tells him, 'I told you you were meant to be a girl' (p. 120). What starts out as an act of *racial* camouflage, then, becomes one of *gender* disguise. The text insists, as so many passing narratives do, upon the slippage between racial and gender masquerade. It is significant, moreover, that in a narrative concerned with multilayered 'category crisis'– especially gender b(l)ending – the story *begins* with a nod to the ultimate form of American disguise, racial passing, for J.T.'s authorial ruse exists in intimate relation to the thematics of his work.

The racial implications of LeRoy's oeuvre have, I would argue, even greater resonance in its depiction of poor whites, and link directly with questions regarding the public appetite for memoir and, indeed, the resurgence of passing in the contemporary moment. Why does the contemporary reading public have a morbid fascination with lurid tales of sexual abuse, incest, drug addiction, AIDS and so on? Why does the reading public want, even need, these stories to be true? For this voyeuristic trend is not only perceptible in the vogue for memoir but also in the immense popularity of true crime novels.[28] If the early twentieth-century narrative of racial passing examines the extent to which race and class intersect (how being identifiable as racially 'black' adversely affected one's socio-economic position), the voyeurism evident in the J.T. LeRoy case betrays an underlying fascination with a demographic which, for the mainstream reading public, embodies both racial and class otherness – 'white trash.' As Matt Wray and Annalee Newitz remind us, the term 'white trash' itself is both 'racialized (i.e., different from "black trash" or "Indian trash") and classed (trash is social waste and detritus).'[29] Equally, Allison Graham argues that

> the centrality of the 'cracker' to our understanding of American racism cannot . . . be overestimated. More than simply a scapegoat, he has functioned in popular culture as a signifier of racial ambiguity, with his class-bound vulgarity consistently representative of contaminated whiteness. As the personification of sullied purity, he is racial debris, white trash.[30]

Throughout *The Heart is Deceitful Above All Things*, Jeremiah – and by extension, J.T. – is coded as 'white trash.' He comes from West Virginia, or 'cracker country' in the popular imagination. He and his mother live in a trailer, when they live anywhere at all. Her parents are bible-bashing religious zealots. If one latter-day mode of passing is 'wigger culture', in which white subjects partake in cultural 'blackness', then, as Dreisinger argues, white hip-hop artists such as Eminem 'legitimate their right to hip-hop by sporting "white trash" as a badge of pride that substitutes race for class.' Similarly, by transforming Jeremiah's 'class position into a kind of race one, one that gives [him] license to speak of suffering', LeRoy both alludes to and revises the relationship between race and class that characterises the traditional passing story.[31]

Audacious though it may be, and true to the demands of post-modernism, the LeRoy ruse is not even original. As Beachy notes, it bears a striking resemblance to the case of Anthony Godby Johnson, the inspiration behind Armistead Maupin's novel, *The Night Listener* (2000). In 1993 Johnson published a memoir entitled *A Rock and a Hard Place: One Boy's Triumphant Story*, in which he described being sexually abused as a child, his rescue by a woman called Vicki Johnson, and his battle with AIDS. Befriended by Maupin, among others, Johnson carried out long telephone conversations with a series of psychologists, authors and publishers, with very few ever managing to meet Johnson in person. In May 1993 Michelle Ingrassia wrote a piece in *Newsweek* entitled 'The Author Nobody's Met', which, through its claim that Tony's soprano voice 'could belong to a woman as convincingly as to a boy', suggested that Vicki Johnson was playing the part of Anthony.[32]

As Beachy observes, Albert could easily have read Ingrassia's piece and drawn inspiration from it in creating J.T. LeRoy. Like Anthony Godby Johnson, LeRoy succeeded in enlisting the help of several published authors, among them Karr, who receives an acknowledgment in *The Heart is Deceitful Above All Things*. (In her response to the exposure of J.T. LeRoy, Karr maintains that LeRoy 'weaseled [her] into taking a call by dropping Mary Gaitskill's name.')[33] He also had several celebrity admirers, including Courtney Love, Winona Ryder and Bono. Could Albert – in creating the fiction that is J.T. LeRoy – have been engaged in a 'critical reworking' of the story of Anthony Godby Johnson?[34] What *is* original about LeRoy is that s/he made public appearances. Like Johnson (and, indeed, Percival Everett's Stagg R. Leigh), who conducted most of his relationships over the telephone, LeRoy did not appear in public until 2001. From that point, he, or evidently Savannah Knoop masquerading as LeRoy, did show up for readings (although the reading was generally undertaken by celebrity friends) and to conduct interviews in person. It is as if Albert and Knoop were attempting to push the boundaries of their deception to their limit and to test exactly how much they could get away with. How they must have laughed when they read interview articles describing LeRoy's 'waifish demeanor' and his 'quiet, girlish voice',[35] his 'androgynous disguise' and 'diminutive' stature.[36]

A million little lies?

Following hot upon the heels of Beachy's LeRoy story was the case of James Frey, whose memoir *A Million Little Pieces* was an Oprah's Book Club selection in December 2005. The memoir recounts Frey's time in a rehabilitation centre in Minnesota battling his addictions to drugs and alcohol. It sold 600,000 copies in the first week after its selection and became the second bestselling book of the year.[37] On 8 January 2006 an investigative website called *The Smoking Gun* published a report disputing many of the events Frey recounts. Among the more choice embellishments were the extent of Frey's involvement in the death of a friend in a train accident and a three-month stint in prison, which turned out to be a few hours in a police cell. Initially, Oprah defended Frey, even telephoning in when he appeared on Larry King Live to reiterate her support. However, she subsequently did an about-turn, invited Frey, a representative of his publisher and several prominent members of the US media onto her show, apologised publicly for her defence of Frey and mounted an assault on Frey and the Doubleday representative. Editions of *A Million Little Pieces*, still marketed as a memoir, are now prefaced with 'A Note to the Reader' in which Frey acknowledges having 'embellished many details about [his] past experiences, and altered others in order to serve what [he] felt was the greater purpose of the book.'[38] Oprah followed her Frey selection with Elie Wiesel's *Night* in January 2006, presumably because it is a memoir whose veracity is deemed indisputable, describing the author's experiences during the Holocaust, the trauma to trump all others.[39]

The connections between embodied (Knoop/LeRoy) and disembodied (Albert/LeRoy) disguise are less obvious in the Frey situation because his exploitation of the slipperiness of memoir/fiction does not have an immediate counterpart in the persona of the author himself. Nonetheless, the controversy bears mentioning not only because it is often discussed alongside that of J.T. LeRoy and, more recently, Margaret B. Jones, but more pertinently, because commentators find it impossible to discuss Frey without deploying metaphors of passing and cross-racial masquerade. As Steve Almond of the *Boston Globe* puts it, Frey 'apes the swagger and vocabulary of hip-hop stars'; he is 'the Vanilla Ice of American letters', thus positioning Frey as a whiteface minstrel. Furthermore, Almond argues that Frey's deception and exposure vindicate Jonathan Franzen's objections to what I would call the memoirification of his novel *The Corrections* in the biographical segment of the Oprah's Book Club programme, mentioned in Chapter 2. In a further use of racially inflected language, Almond describes Franzen as having been 'tarred and feathered' after he aired publicly his reservations concerning his encounter with the Oprah crew.[40] Equally, a *Newsweek* article byline questions: 'When James Frey embellished his rap sheet in his best-selling memoir, did he cross the line into fiction?'[41] 'Crossing the [color] line' is a phrase synonymous with passing as white and provides further evidence of the recourse to passing tropes in cases of fraudulent authorship.

Passing . . . and consequences

If *Erasure* explores the consequences of Monk Ellison's decision to write a ghetto novel under the pseudonym Stagg R. Leigh, an uncanny real-life version of a similar scenario came to light in March 2008 just days after Margaret B. Jones published *Love and Consequences*, a memoir describing her childhood and adolescence as the mixedblood foster child of an African American family living in South Central Los Angeles in the 1980s. Following her foster brothers into involvement with the infamous Bloods gang, Bree, as she is known in the book, escapes their fates (one is murdered in a gang killing; the other endures long periods of incarceration) by gaining admission to the University of Oregon. Just as, in *Erasure*, Juanita Mae Jenkins's book is praised for its 'verisimilitude' and Stagg Leigh's lauded for being 'honest', 'raw', 'real' and 'true', so Jones's memoir was received as an authentic account of African American urban life and was described by reviewers as 'heart-wrenching', 'intimate' and 'visceral.'[42]

According to the *New York Times*, Jones's story began to unravel after she was profiled in that newspaper on 28 February 2008: 'The article appeared alongside a photograph of Ms. Seltzer and her 8-year-old daughter, Rya. Ms. Seltzer's older sister, Cyndi Hoffman, saw the article and called Riverhead to tell editors that Ms. Seltzer's story was untrue.' The *Times* revealed that Seltzer was 'all white and grew up in the well-to-do Sherman Oaks section of Los Angeles, in the San Fernando Valley, with her biological family.' She 'never lived with a foster family, nor did she run drugs for any gang members. Nor did she graduate from the University of Oregon, as she had claimed.'[43] Her publisher, Riverhead (which, as I note in Chapter 4, also publishes Danzy Senna's fiction and memoirs by Rebecca Walker and James McBride), responded by immediately recalling all copies of the book and cancelling a scheduled tour. Just as the author photograph on Monk's book jackets announces his African American identity in a way that the content of his books does not in *Erasure*, so Seltzer's hoax was ultimately uncovered by photographic evidence. In her defence, Seltzer, who works with former gang members, claimed that the memoir provided her with the 'opportunity to put a voice to people who people don't listen to.'[44] In so doing, isn't is possible that Seltzer was merely upholding what Atlas, Staples and Grimes identify as memoir's democratising function?

Recalling the conventions of slave narratives, Jones includes a prefacing 'Author's Note on Language, Dialect, and Kontent' and an 'Afterword', both of which serve to authenticate the main body of the text. In the preface Jones beseeches readers not to 'confuse the use of slang and [her] replacing *c*'s with *k*'s as ignorance or stupidity' because she has done so in the name of 'authenticity.'[45] She explains that the Bloods often change *c*'s to *k*'s as a means of registering their disrespect for their rivals, the Crips. In the afterword she explains her own activism and encourages readers to 'get involved' in organisations that are endeavouring to bring about gang truce (p. 293). Here she adopts a tone that she only occasionally lapses into in the main narrative: a more distanced, 'educated' perspective on the socio-economic condi- tions that have fostered gang violence, as well as the policies that have hindered, rather than helped, the situation (pp. 67, 130). Like the slave narratives, moreover, in which the establishment of a blueprint of authenticity made such authenticity all the easier to reproduce, Jones's book features many staples of black underclass and gangster fiction: an all-suffering black Mammy figure (her foster mother Evelyn, known as 'Big Mom') and local gang leaders who are bulwarks of the community, indeed 'heroes' (pp. 6, 85). As Michiko Kakutani notes in her review of the memoir, as with J.T. LeRoy's work, some of the scenes Jones recreates from her youth 'feel self-consciously novelistic at times.'[46]

The column inches dedicated to LeRoy, Frey and Jones underscore the continuing relevance and importance of 'authenticity' – in terms of the author's racial or gender identity, of his or her professed life experiences and of the words he or she puts down on the page – to the contemporary reading public, no matter how much the academy may insist upon its redundancy. The gap between the perceptions of the scholarly community and the reading public takes us right back to the two cultural notions of passing alluded to in the introduction: the first emphasising authenticity, the assumption of a fraudulent identity, the substitution of a 'black' identity for a white one; the second evincing a mistrust of any sense of a stable self, instead advocating a self that is always already in flux, and an identity that is constituted solely of performance rather than essentialisms. The literary controversies of recent years remind us of the ongoing pertinence of tropes of passing in the contemporary moment because it is the logic of the first cultural notion that characterises the public reception of and reaction to LeRoy, Frey and Jones. More generally, the analogy between passing and writing that many contemporary American writers explore confirms that readers of bodies *and* texts are not so 'postmodern' as they might believe themselves to be.

Notes

1 Tim Carvell, 'A Million Little Corrections', *New York Times* (11 January 2006), A29.
2 William Grimes, 'We All Have a Life. Must We All Write about It?', *New York Times* (25 March 2005), E27.
3 Liz Bury, 'Tugging at Heart Strings', *Bookseller* (23 February 2007), 24.
4 The *Irish Examiner* reports, for example, that seventy-year-old Paddy Malone, who lived four doors down from the McCourts in Limerick, objected so much to the representation of his home city that he tore up a copy of *Angela's Ashes* during a McCourt book signing in Limerick. Tony Purcell, 'Plaudits as Home City gives Film Thumbs Up at Showing', *Irish Examiner* (13 January 2000), http://archives.tcm.ie/irishexaminer/2000/01/13/current/ipage_27.htm (13 May 2006). In the USA, meanwhile, a Limerick-born man called David Crowe organised a book burning at a Long Island bar in March 2000. Eibhear Mulqueen, '"Ashes" to Ashes as McCourt Book Burning Organised in New York', *Irish Times* (19 February 2000), 1.
5 See, for example, Lev Grossman, 'The Trouble with Memoirs', *Time*, 167.3 (23 January 2006), 58.
6 Calvin Sims, 'A Geisha, a Successful Novel and a Lawsuit', *New York Times* (19 June 2001), E2.
7 Linda Hutcheon, *A Poetics of Postmodernism: History, Theory, Fiction* (London: Routledge, 2000), pp. 9–10.
8 Dave Eggers, *A Heartbreaking Work of Staggering Genius* (London: Picador, 2007), p. ix.
9 Mary Karr, 'His So-Called Life', *New York Times* (15 January 2006), 13.
10 Gass, 49.
11 Atlas, 25.
12 Brent Staples, 'Editorial Notebook: Hating It Because It Is True', *New York Times* (27 April 1997), sec. 4, 14.
13 Grimes, E27.
14 Fredric Jameson, 'Postmodernism and Consumer Society', in *Postmodern Culture*, ed. Hal Foster (London: Pluto, 1985), pp. 111–25 (p. 112).
15 Atlas, 25.
16 Jameson, p. 114.
17 Literary critics for newspapers and magazines find themselves caught in between academic and mainstream views of postmodernism. Notably, Michiko Kakutani of the *New York Times* has written a number of articles

over the last decade or so railing against deconstructionist trends in the academy. See, for example, 'Is It Fiction? Is It Nonfiction? And Why Doesn't Anyone Care?', *New York Times* (27 July 1993), C13 and 'Bending the Truth in a Million Little Ways', *New York Times* (17 January 2006), E1.

18 Grossman, 58.

19 Polly Vernon, 'Fooled You All', *Sunday Independent* (23 November 2008), Life, 24–6 (24).

20 Terminator [J.T. LeRoy], 'Baby Doll', in *Close to the Bone: Memoirs of Hurt, Rage, and Desire*, ed. Laurie Stone (New York: Grove, 1997), pp. 14–47.

21 Karr, 13.

22 Robinson, 'Forms of Appearance', p. 241.

23 Michiko Kakutani, 'Woe is Me: Rewards and Perils of Memoirs', *New York Times* (21 October 1997), E8.

24 Jocelyn McClurg, 'Memoirs: Truth is Stranger than Fiction', *Times Union* (26 October 1997), J4.

25 Karr, 13.

26 Warren St. John, 'A Literary Life Born of Brutality', *New York Times* (14 November 2004), Fashion & Style, 1.

27 The text of 'Baby Doll' is that which appears in the collection *The Heart is Deceitful Above All Things* (London: Bloomsbury, 2001), p. 125. Page references hereafter will be included in parentheses in the main body of the text.

28 See Rosemary Herbert, 'Publishers Agree: True Crime Does Pay', *Publishers Weekly* (1 June 1990), 33–6.

29 Matt Wray and Annalee Newitz, 'Introduction', in *White Trash: Race and Class in America*, ed. Matt Wray and Annalee Newitz (New York: Routledge, 1997), pp. 1–12 (p. 4).

30 Allison Graham, *Framing the South: Hollywood, Television, and Race during the Civil Rights Struggle* (Baltimore: Johns Hopkins University Press, 2001), p. 13.

31 Dreisinger, p. 118.

32 Michele Ingrassia, 'The Author Nobody's Met: Is a Young Boy's Book Hard Truth – Or a Ruse?', *Newsweek* (31 May 1993), 63. Tad Friend followed up with an in-depth investigation into the Johnson case for the *New Yorker* in 2001: 'Virtual Love', *New Yorker* (26 November 2001), 88–99.

33 Karr, 13.

34 The phrase 'critical reworking' is from Hutcheon's *Poetics*, p. 4.

35 St. John, 1.

36 Luke Crisell, 'The Lost Boy', *Observer Magazine* (6 March 2005), http://observer.guardian.co.uk/magazine/story/0,11913,1429633,00.html (21 October 2005).

37 Tim Adams, 'Feel the Pain', *Observer* (29 January 2006) www.observer.
    guardian.co.uk/review/story/0,6903,1697020,00.html (1 February
    2006).

38 James Frey, *A Million Little Pieces* (London: John Murray, 2006), p. v.

39 However, amid the fakeries that have emerged in the wake of the memoir
    phenomenon of the past fifteen years are several Holocaust stories:
    Binjamin Wilkomirski's *Fragments: Memoirs of a Childhood* (1995),
    Misha Defonseca's *Misha: A Mémoire of the Holocaust Years* (1997)
    and Herman Rosenblat's *Angel at the Fence: The True Story of a Love
    That Survived*, the publication of which was cancelled in December 2008
    when doubts were raised over the veracity of some of its content.

40 Steve Almond, 'Memoir as Fiction? Not so Fast', *Boston Globe* (22 January
    2006), E7.

41 Marc Peyser, 'The Ugly Truth', *Newsweek* (23 January 2006), 62.

42 Everett, *Erasure*, pp. 46, 155, 288; Mimi Read, 'A Refugee from Gangland',
    New York Times (28 February 2008) www.nytimes.com/2008/02/28/
    garden/28jones.html?ref=books (13 May 2009).

43 Mitoko Rich, 'Gang Memoir, Turning Page, Is Pure Fiction', *New York
    Times* (4 March 2008) www.nytimes.com/2008/03/04/books/04fake.
    html?pagewanted=2&_r=1 (13 May 2009).

44 Ibid.

45 Margaret B. Jones, *Love and Consequences: A Memoir of Hope and
    Survival* (New York: Riverhead, 2008), p. 2. Subsequent references will
    be included in parentheses in the main body of the text.

46 Michiko Kakutani, 'However Mean the Streets, Have an Exit Strategy',
    New York Times (26 February 2008) www.nytimes.com/2008/02/26/
    books/26kaku.html?ref=books (13 May 2009).

Bibliography

Adams, Tim, 'Feel the Pain', *Observer* (29 January 2006), www.observer. guardian.co.uk/review/story/0,6903,1697020,00.html (1 February 2006)

Almond, Steve, 'Memoir as Fiction? Not so Fast', *Boston Globe* (22 January 2006), E7

'American Religious Identification Survey (ARIS): Key Findings' (2001), www. gc.cuny.edu/faculty/research_briefs/aris/key_findings.htm (20 December 2005)

Ashe, Bertram D., 'Paul Beatty's White Boy Shuffle Blues: Jazz, Poetry, John Coltrane, and the Post-Soul Aesthetic', in Lock and Murray, pp. 106–23

Asim, Jabari, 'Grand Slam Champ', *Washington Post* (13 June 1999), X12

Atlas, James, 'Confessing for Voyeurs: The Age of the Literary Memoir is Now', *New York Times Magazine* (12 May 1996), 25

Baker, Aaron, *Contesting Identities: Sports in American Film* (Urbana: University of Illinois Press, 2003)

Baker, Houston A., *Workings of the Spirit: The Poetics of Afro-American Women's Writing* (Chicago: University of Chicago Press, 1991)

Baldwin, James, 'Everybody's Protest Novel', *Collected Essays* (New York: Library of America, 1998), pp. 11–18

Bamboozled, dir. Spike Lee, perf. Damon Wayans, Savion Glover and Jada Pinkett Smith (New Line Cinema, 2000)

Barak, Julie, 'Blurs, Blends, Berdaches: Gender Mixing in the Novels of Louise Erdrich', *Studies in American Indian Literatures* 8.3 (1996), 49–62

Barthes, Roland, 'The Death of the Author', *Image, Music, Text* (New York: Hill and Wang, 1977), rpt.on http://faculty.smu.edu/dfoster/theory/Barthes. htm (29 October 2004)

Baym, Nina, 'The Case for Hannah Vincent', in Gates and Robbins, pp. 315–31

Beatty, Paul, *The White Boy Shuffle* (London: Minerva, 1996)

Bedell, Geraldine, 'He's Not Like Other Girls', *Observer* (6 October 2002), http://books.guardian.co.uk/impac/story/0,14959,1285050,00.html (15 September 2005)

Belluscio, Stephen J., *To Be Suddenly White: Literary Realism and Racial Passing* (Columbia: University of Missouri Press, 2006)

Bennett, Juda, *The Passing Figure: Racial Confusion in Modern American Literature* (New York: Peter Lang, 1996)

—— 'Toni Morrison and the Burden of the Passing Narrative', *African American Review* 35.2 (2001), 205–17

Benston, Kimberly W., 'I Yam What I Yam: The Topos of Un(naming) in Afro-American Literature', in Gates (1984), pp. 151–72

Berlant, Lauren, 'The Face of America and the State of Emergency', in Guins and Cruz, 309–23

Bernier, Celeste-Marie and Judie Newman, '*The Bondwoman's Narrative*: Text, Paratext, Intertext and Hypertext', *Journal of American Studies* 39.2 (2005), 147–65

Bernstein, Richard, 'Books of the Times: Black Poet's First Novel Aims the Jokes Both Ways', *New York Times* (31 May 1996), C25

Berzon, Judith, *Neither White Nor Black: The Mulatto Character in American Fiction* (New York: New York University Press, 1978)

Black. White, perf. Nicholas Sparks, Rose Bloomfield and Carmen Wurgel, (FX, 8 March 2006)

Blackwood, Evelyn, 'Sexuality and Gender in Certain Native American Tribes: The Case of Cross-Gender Females', *Signs* 10 (1984), 27–42

Bloom, John, 'Literary Blackface? The Mystery of Hannah Crafts', in Gates and Robbins, pp. 431–8

Bost, Suzanne, *Mulattas and Mestizas: Representing Mixed Identities in the Americas, 1850–2000* (Athens: University of Georgia Press, 2005)

Boucicault, Dion, *The Octoroon; or, Life in Louisiana 1859* (Upper Saddle River, NJ: Literature House, 1970)

Boudreau, Brenda, 'Letting the Body Speak: "Becoming" White in Caucasia', *Modern Language Studies* 32.1 (2002), 59–70

Brauner, David, *Philip Roth* (Manchester: Manchester University Press, 2007)

Browder, Laura, *Slippery Characters: Ethnic Impersonators and American Identities* (Chapel Hill: University of North Carolina Press, 2000)

Brown, Cecil, *Stagolee Shot Billy* (Cambridge, MA: Harvard University Press, 2003)

Brown, John Gregory, *Decorations in a Ruined Cemetery* (London: Sceptre, 1996)

Brown, William Wells, *Clotel; or the President's Daughter*, in Gates (1990), pp. 3–224

Broyard, Anatole, 'Portrait of the Inauthentic Negro: How Prejudice Distorts the Victim's Personality', *Commentary* 10.4 (1950), 56–64

Bruce, Heather E. and Bryan Dexter Davis, 'Slam: Hip-Hop Meets Poetry – A Strategy for Violence Intervention', *English Journal* 8.5 (2000), 119–27

Bury, Liz, 'Tugging at Heart Strings', *Bookseller* (23 February 2007), 24

Butler, Judith, *Bodies that Matter: On the Discursive Limits of 'Sex'* (New York: Routledge, 1993)

—— *Gender Trouble: Feminism and the Subversion of Identity* (London: Routledge, 1990)

Campbell, Neil, 'Introduction: On Youth Cultural Studies', in *American Youth Cultures*, ed. Neil Campbell (Edinburgh: Edinburgh University Press, 2004), pp. 1–30

Carvell, Tim, 'A Million Little Corrections', *New York Times* (11 January 2006), A29

Castelli, Elizabeth, ' "I Will Make Mary Male": Pieties of the Body and Gender Transformation of Christian Women in Late Antiquity', in Epstein and Straub, pp. 29–49

Cather, Willa, *Sapphira and the Slave Girl* (New York: Knopf, 1940)

Caveney, Graham, 'The Books Interview: Paul Beatty; Sweet Talk and Fighting Words', *Independent* (22 July 2000), 9

Chapman, Alison A., 'Rewriting the Saints' Lives: Louise Erdrich's *The Last Report on the Miracles at Little No Horse*', *Critique* 48.2 (2007), 149–67

Chase-Riboud, Barbara, *The President's Daughter* (New York: Ballantine, 1994)

Chesnutt, Charles W., *The House Behind the Cedars* (1900; London: X Press, 1998)

—— 'The Wife of His Youth', *Tales of Conjure and the Color Line: Ten Stories* (New York: Dover, 1998), pp. 47–56

Child, Lydia Maria, *A Romance of the Republic* (1868), ed. Dana Nelson (Lexington: University Press of Kentucky, 1997)

Chopin, Kate, 'Desirée's Baby', in *The Awakening and Other Stories* (New York: Oxford, 2000), pp. 193–8

Collins, Julia C., *The Curse of Caste; or The Slave Bride* (1865), ed. William L. Andrews and Mitch Kachun (New York: Oxford University Press, 2006)

Comer, Krista, *Landscapes of the New West: Gender and Geography in Contemporary Women's Writing* (Chapel Hill: University of North Carolina Press, 1999)

Couser, G. Thomas, 'Genome and Genre: DNA and Life Writing', *Biography* 24.1 (2001), 185–96

Craft, William and Ellen, *Running a Thousand Miles For Freedom; or the Escape of William and Ellen Craft from Slavery* (London: William Tweedie, 1860), rpt. in *Documenting the American South* (University of North Carolina at Chapel Hill), http://docsouth.unc.edu/neh/craft/menu.html (13 May 2009)

Crafts, Hannah, *The Bondwoman's Narrative*, ed. and intro. Henry Louis Gates, Jr. (London: Virago, 2002)

Crisell, Luke, 'The Lost Boy', *Observer Magazine* (6 March 2005), http://observer.guardian.co.uk/magazine/story/0,11913,1429633,00.html (21 October 2005)

Crouch, Stanley, 'Aunt Jemima Don't Like Uncle Ben', *Notes of a Hanging Judge: Essays and Reviews, 1979–1989* (New York: Oxford University Press), pp. 29–34

Curtis, Tracy, 'Basketball's Demands in Paul Beatty's *The White Boy Shuffle*', in *Upon Further Review: Sports in American Literature*, ed. Michael Cocchiarale and Scott D. Emmert (Westport: Praeger, 2004), pp. 63–73

DaCosta, Kimberly McClain, *Making Multiracials: State, Family, and Market in the Redrawing of the Color Line* (Stanford: Stanford University Press, 2007)

Dearborn, Mary V., *Pocahontas's Daughters: Gender and Ethnicity in American Culture* (New York: Oxford University Press, 1986)

DelRosso, Jeana, *Writing Catholic Women: Contemporary International Catholic Girlhood Narratives* (New York: Palgrave Macmillan, 2005)

Devil in a Blue Dress, dir. Carl Franklin, perf. Denzel Washington, Don Cheadle and Jennifer Beals (1995; DVD, Columbia Tristar Home Video, 2000)

Diner, Hasia R., *In the Almost Promised Land: American Jews and Blacks, 1915–1935* (Baltimore: Johns Hopkins University Press, 1995)

Doctorow, E.L., *The March* (London: Little, Brown, 2006)

Douglass, Frederick, *My Bondage and My Freedom* (1855), ed. and intro. John David Smith (New York: Penguin, 2003)

—— *Narrative of the Life of Frederick Douglass, An American Slave* (1845) in *Narrative of the Life of Frederick Douglass, An American Slave and Incidents in the Life of a Slave Girl*, ed. Kwame Anthony Appiah (New York: Random House, 2000)

Dreger, Alice Domurat, *Hermaphrodites and the Medical Invention of Sex* (Cambridge, MA: Harvard University Press, 1998)

Dreisinger, Baz, *Near Black: White-to-Black Passing in American Culture* (Amherst: University of Massachussetts Press, 2008)

DuBois, W.E.B., *The Souls of Black Folk* (New York: Dover, 1994)

Ducille, Ann, 'Dyes and Dolls: Multicultural Barbie and the Merchandising of Difference', *Differences* 6.1 (1994), 46–68

Dyer, Richard, 'White', *Screen: The Last Special Issue on Race* 29.4 (1988), 44–64

—— *White* (London: Routledge, 1999)

Early, Gerald, *The Culture of Bruising: Essays on Prizefighting, Literature, and Modern American Culture* (Hopewell, NJ: Ecco, 1997)

Eggers, Dave, *A Heartbreaking Work of Staggering Genius* (London: Picador, 2007)

Elam, Michele, 'Passing in the Post-Race Era: Danzy Senna, Philip Roth, and Colson Whitehead', *African American Review* 41.4 (2007), 749–68

Ellis, Trey, *Platitudes* (New York: Random House, 1988)

—— 'The New Black Aesthetic', *Callaloo* 38 (1989), 233–43

Ellison, Ralph, *Invisible Man* (Harmondsworth: Penguin, 1965)

—— *Juneteenth* (London: Penguin, 2000)

—— 'The World and the Jug', *The Collected Essays of Ralph Ellison*, ed. John F. Callahan (New York: Modern Library, 1995), pp. 155–88

Epstein, Julia and Kristina Straub (eds), *Body Guards: The Cultural Politics of Gender Ambiguity* (New York: Routledge, 1991)

Erdrich, Louise, *Four Souls* (New York: HarperCollins, 2004)

—— *Love Medicine* (New York: Bantam, 1987)

—— *The Beet Queen* (London: Flamingo, 1994)

—— *The Bingo Palace* (London: Harper Perennial, 2004)

—— *The Last Report on the Miracles at Little No Horse* (London: Flamingo, 2001)

—— *Tracks* (London: Hamish Hamilton, 1988)

Eugenides, Jeffrey, *Middlesex* (London: Bloomsbury, 2003)

Everett, Percival, *Erasure* (London: Faber and Faber, 2004)

—— 'F/V: Placing the Experimental Novel', *Callaloo* 22.1 (1999), 18–23

Fabi, M. Guilia, *Passing and the Rise of the African American Novel* (Urbana: University of Illinois Press, 2001)

Fabian, Ann, *The Unvarnished Truth: Personal Narratives in Nineteenth-Century America* (Berkeley: University of California Press, 2000)

Faulkner, William, *Absalom, Absalom!* (London: Vintage, 1995)

—— *Light in August* (London: Picador, 1993)

Fauset, Jessie Redmon, *Plum Bun* (1928), ed. Deborah E. McDowell (Boston: Beacon, 1990)

—— *There is Confusion* (New York: Boni and Liveright, 1974)

Feinberg, Leslie, *Trans Liberation: Beyond Pink or Blue* (Boston: Beacon, 1998)

Ferrari, Rita, ' "Where the Maps Stopped": The Aesthetics of Borders in Louise Erdrich's *Love Medicine* and *Tracks*', *Style* 33.1 (1999), 144–65

Fiedler, Leslie A., *Waiting for the End* (New York: Stain and Day, 1964)

Fine, David and Paul Skenazy, 'Introduction', in *San Francisco in Fiction: Essays in a Regional Literature*, ed. David Fine and Paul Skenazy (Albuquerque: University of New Mexico Press, 1995), pp. 1–20

Flynn, Katherine E., 'Jane Johnson, Found! But Is She "Hannah Crafts"? The Search for the Author of *The Bondwoman's Narrative*', in Gates and Robbins, pp. 371–405

Fox-Genovese, Elizabeth, 'Slavery, Race, and the Figure of the Tragic Mulatta, or, The Ghost of Southern History in the Writing of African-American Women', in *Haunted Bodies: Gender and Southern Texts*, ed. Anne

Goodwyn-Jones and Susan V. Donaldson (Charlottesville: University of Virginia Press, 1998), pp. 464–91

Franco, Dean J., 'Being Black, Being Jewish, and Knowing the Difference', *Studies in American Jewish Literature* 23 (2004), 88–103

Franzen, Jonathan, *How to be Alone: Essays* (London: Fourth Estate, 2002)

—— *The Corrections* (London: HarperCollins, 2002)

Frey, James, *A Million Little Pieces* (London: John Murray, 2006)

Friend, Tad, 'Virtual Love', *New Yorker* (26 November 2001), 88–99

Gallego, Mar, *Passing Novels in the Harlem Renaissance: An Alternative Concept of African American Identity* (Munster: Lit Verlag, 2003)

Garber, Marjorie, *Vested Interests: Cross-Dressing and Cultural Anxiety* (London: Penguin, 1993)

Gass, William, 'The Art of Self: Autobiography in an Age of Narcissism', *Harper's Magazine* (May 1994), 43–52

Gates, Henry Louis, Jr., 'Borrowing Privileges', *New York Times* (2 June 2002), 18

—— 'The Passing of Anatole Broyard', *Thirteen Ways of Looking at a Black Man* (New York: Random House, 1997), pp. 180–214

—— (ed.), *Black Literature and Literary History* (New York: Methuen, 1984)

—— (ed.), *Three Classic African-American Novels: Clotel; or the President's Daughter, Iola Leroy, or Shadows Uplifted and The Marrow of Tradition* (New York: Random House, 1990)

—— and Hollis Robbins (eds), *In Search of Hannah Crafts: Critical Essays on The Bondwoman's Narrative* (Cambridge: Perseus, 2004)

Gayle, Addison, *Richard Wright: Ordeal of a Native Son* (New York: Doubleday, 1980)

Gill, Sam D., *Native American Religions: An Introduction* (Belmont, CA: Wadsworth, 1982)

Gilman, Sander L., *Making the Body Beautiful: A Cultural History of Aesthetic Surgery* (Princeton, NJ: Princeton University Press, 1999)

Gilmore, Michael T., *Surface and Depth: The Quest for Legibility in American Culture* (New York: Oxford University Press, 2003)

Ginsberg, Elaine K. (ed.), *Passing and the Fictions of Identity* (Durham, NC: Duke University Press, 1996)

Goellnicht, Donald C., 'Passing as Autobiography: James Weldon Johnson's *The Autobiography of an Ex-Colored Man*', *African American Review* 30.1 (1996), 17–33

Goffman, Ethan, *Imagining Each Other: Blacks and Jews in Contemporary American Literature* (New York: State University of New York Press, 2000)

Golden, Arthur, *Memoirs of a Geisha* (1997; London: Vintage, 2005)

Goldschmidt, Henry, 'Introduction: Race, Nation, and Religion', in *Race, Nation, and Religion in the Americas*, ed. Henry Goldschmidt and Elizabeth McAlister (New York: Oxford University Press, 2004), pp. 3–31

Graham, Allison, *Framing the South: Hollywood, Television, and Race during the Civil Rights Struggle* (Baltimore: Johns Hopkins University Press, 2001)

Grice, Helena, Candida Hepworth, Maria Lauret and Martin Padget, *Beginning Ethnic American Literatures* (Manchester: Manchester University Press, 2001)

Griffin, John Howard, *Black Like Me* (New York: Signet, 1976)

Griffin, Susan M., *Anti-Catholicism and Nineteenth-Century Fiction* (Cambridge: Cambridge University Press, 2004)

—— 'Awful Disclosures: Women's Evidence in the Escaped Nun's Tale', *PMLA* 111.1 (1996), 93–107

Grim, John A., *The Shaman: Patterns of Religious Healing Among the Ojibway Indians* (Norman: University of Oklahoma Press, 1987)

Grimes, William, 'We All Have a Life. Must We All Write about It?', *New York Times* (25 March 2005), E27

Grossman, Lev, 'The Trouble with Memoirs', *Time*, 167.3 (23 January 2006), 58

Guins, Raiford and Omayra Zaragoza Cruz (eds), *Popular Culture: A Reader* (London: Sage, 2005)

Hackett, David G., 'Gender and Religion in American Culture', *Religion and American Culture* 5.2 (1995), 127–57

Haizlip, Shirlee Taylor, *The Sweeter the Juice* (New York: Simon and Schuster, 1995)

Halberstam, Judith, *Female Masculinity* (Durham, NC: Duke University Press, 1998)

Hannah, Norman B., 'The Open Book Memorial', *National Review* (11 December 1981), 1476

Harper, Frances E.W., *Iola Leroy, or Shadows Uplifted*, in Gates (1990), pp. 227–463

Harper, Phillip Brian, *Are We Not Men? Masculine Anxiety and the Problem of African-American Identity* (New York: Oxford University Press, 1996)

—— 'Passing for What? Racial Masquerade and the Demands of Upward Mobility', *Callaloo* 21.2 (1998), 381–97

Harrison-Kahan, Lori, 'Passing for White, Passing for Jewish: Mixed Race Identity in Danzy Senna and Rebecca Walker', *MELUS* 30.1 (2005), 19–48

Hausknecht, Gina, 'Self-Possession, Dolls, Beatlemania, Loss: Telling the Girl's Own Story', in *The Girl: Constructions of the Girl in Contemporary Fiction by Women*, ed. Ruth O. Saxton (London: Macmillan, 1998), pp. 21–42

Hedin, Raymond, 'Strategies of Form in the American Slave Narrative', in *The Art of the Slave Narrative: Original Essays in Criticism and Theory*, ed. John Sekora and Darwin T. Turner (Macomb: Western Illinois University Press, 1982), pp. 25–35

Herbert, Rosemary, 'Publishers Agree: True Crime Does Pay', *Publishers Weekly* (1 June 1990), 33–6

Hildreth, Richard, *The Slave; or Memoirs of Archy Moore* (Upper Saddle River, NJ: Gregg Press, 1968)

Hopkins, Pauline, *The Magazine Novels of Pauline Hopkins* (1901–3), ed. Hazel V. Carby (New York: Oxford University Press, 1988)

Howe, Irving, *A World More Attractive: A View of Modern Literature and Politics* (New York: Horizon, 1963)

—— 'Philip Roth Reconsidered', in *Philip Roth*, ed. Harold Bloom (New York: Chelsea, 1986), pp. 71–88

Howells, William Dean, *An Imperative Duty* (New York: Harper & Brothers, 1891), rpt. The William Dean Howells Society, Washington State University, www.wsu.edu/~campbelld/wdh/imd.html (13 May 2009)

Hughes, Langston, 'Passing', *The Ways of White Folks* (London: Vintage, 1990), pp. 51–5

Hughes, Sheila Hassell, 'Tongue-Tied: Rhetoric and Relation in Louise Erdrich's *Tracks*', *MELUS* 25.3/4 (2000), 87–116

Hunter, Michele, 'Revisiting the Third Space: Reading Danzy Senna's *Caucasia*', in *Literature and Racial Ambiguity*, ed. Teresa Hubel and Neil Brooks (Amsterdam: Rodopi, 2002), pp. 297–316

Hurston, Zora Neale, *Their Eyes Were Watching God* (New York: Harper Perennial, 1990)

Hutcheon, Linda, *A Poetics of Postmodernism: History, Theory, Fiction* (London: Routledge, 2000)

—— *The Politics of Postmodernism* (London: Routledge, 1991)

Hutchison, Anthony, *Writing the Republic: Liberalism and Morality in American Political Fiction* (New York: Columbia University Press, 2007)

Ibrahim, Habiba, 'Canary in a Coal Mine: Performing Biracial Difference in *Caucasia*', *Literature Interpretation Theory* 18.2 (2007), 155–72

Ignatiev, Noel, *How the Irish became White* (New York: Routledge, 1995)

Illouz, Eva, *Oprah Winfrey and the Glamour of Misery: An Essay on Popular Culture* (New York: Columbia University Press, 2003)

Ingrassia, Michelle, 'The Author Nobody's Met: Is a Young Boy's Book Hard Truth – Or a Ruse?', *Newsweek* (31 May 1993), 63

Iovannone, J. James, '"Mix-Ups, Messes, Confinements, and Double-Dealings": Transgendered Performances in Three Novels by Louise Erdrich', *Studies in American Indian Literatures* 21.1 (2009), 38–68

Itzkovitz, Daniel, 'Passing Like Me: Jewish Chameleonism and the Politics of Race', in Sánchez and Schlossberg, pp. 38–63

Jackson, Holly, 'Identifying Emma Dunham Kelley: Rethinking Race and Authorship', *PMLA* 122.3 (2007), 728–41

Jacobs, Connie A., *The Novels of Louise Erdrich: Stories of her People* (New York: Peter Lang, 2001)

Jacobson, Matthew Frye, *Whiteness of a Different Color: European Immigrants and the Alchemy of Race* (Cambridge, MA: Harvard University Press, 2000)

Jameson, Fredric, 'Postmodernism and Consumer Society', in *Postmodern Culture*, ed. Hal Foster (London: Pluto, 1985), pp. 111–25

Japtok, Martin, *Growing Up Ethnic: Nationalism and the Bildungsroman in African American and Jewish American Fiction* (Iowa City: University of Iowa Press, 2005)

Jen, Gish, 'An Ethnic Trump', *New York Times Magazine* (7 July 1996), 50

Johnson, Anthony Godby, *A Rock and a Hard Place: One Boy's Triumphant Story* (1993; New York: Signet, 1994)

Johnson, Charles, *Being and Race: Black Writing since 1970* (London: Serpent's Tail, 1988)

—— *Oxherding Tale* (New York: Plume, 1995)

Johnson, James Weldon, *Along This Way: The Autobiography of James Weldon Johnson* (Harmondsworth: Penguin, 1990)

—— *The Autobiography of an Ex-Colored Man* (New York: Dover, 1995)

Johnson, Mat and Warren Pleese, *Incognegro* (London: Titan, 2009)

Jones, Lisa, *Bulletproof Diva: Tales of Race, Sex, and Hair* (London: Penguin, 1995)

Jones, Margaret B., *Love and Consequences: A Memoir of Hope and Survival* (New York: Riverhead, 2008)

Jones, Suzanne, *Race Mixing: Southern Fiction Since the Sixties* (Baltimore: Johns Hopkins University Press, 2006)

Kakutani, Michiko, 'Bending the truth in a Million Little Ways', *New York Times* (17 January 2006), E1

—— 'Confronting the Failures of a Professor Who Passes' (review of *The Human Stain*), *New York Times* (2 May 2000), E1

—— 'However Mean the Streets, Have an Exit Strategy', *New York Times* (26 February 2008), www.nytimes.com/2008/02/26/books/26kaku. html?ref=books (13 May 2009)

—— 'Is It Fiction? Is It Nonfiction? And Why Doesn't Anyone Care?', *New York Times* (27 July 1993), C13

—— 'Woe is Me: Rewards and Perils of Memoirs', *New York Times* (21 October 1997), E8

Kane, Paula M., 'American Catholic Culture in the Twentieth Century', in *Perspectives on American Religion and Culture: A Reader*, ed. Peter W. Williams (Malden, MA: Blackwell, 1999), pp. 390–404

Kaplan, Brett Ashley, 'Anatole Broyard's Human Stain: Performing Postracial Consciousness', *Philip Roth Studies* 1.2 (2005), 125–44, 190

—— 'Reading Race and the Conundrums of Reconciliation in Philip Roth's *The Human Stain*', in *Turning Up the Flame: Philip Roth's Later Novels*, ed. Jay L. Halio and Ben Siegel (Newark: University of Delaware Press, 2005), pp. 172–93

Kaplan, Sidney, 'The Miscegenation Issue in the Election of 1864', in Sollors (2000), pp. 219–65

Karr, Mary, 'His So-Called Life', *New York Times* (15 January 2006), 13

Kawash, Samira, 'Haunted Houses, Sinking Ships: Race, Architecture, and Identity in *Beloved* and *Middle Passage*', *New Centennial Review* 1.3 (2001), 67–86

Keenan, Deirdre, 'Unrestricted Territory: Gender, Two Spirits, and Louise Erdrich's *The Last Report on the Miracles at Little No Horse*', *American Indian Culture and Research Journal* 30.2 (2006), 1–15

Kennedy, Randall, *Interracial Intimacies: Sex, Marriage, Identity, and Adoption* (New York: Pantheon, 2003)

King, Richard H., *Race, Culture, and the Intellectuals, 1940–1970* (Baltimore: Johns Hopkins University Press, 2004)

Kinney, James, *Amalgamation!: Race, Sex, and Rhetoric in the Nineteenth-Century Novel* (Westport, CT: Greenwood, 1985)

Lane, Jeffrey, *Under the Boards: The Cultural Revolution in Basketball* (Lincoln: University of Nebraska Press, 2007)

Larsen, Nella, *Quicksand* & *Passing* (London: Serpent's Tail, 1989)

LeRoy, J.T. [Terminator], 'Baby Doll', in *Close to the Bone: Memoirs of Hurt, Rage, and Desire*, ed. Laurie Stone (New York: Grove, 1997), pp. 14–47

—— *The Heart is Deceitful Above All Things* (London: Bloomsbury, 2001)

Leseur, Geta, *Ten is the Age of Darkness: The Black Bildungsroman* (Columbia: University of Missouri Press, 1995)

Lewis, James R., ' "Mind-Forged Manacles": Anti-Catholic Convent Narratives in the Context of the American Captivity Tale Tradition', *Mid-America: An Historical Review* 72.3 (1990), 149–67

Lewis, Valerie, 'Build the Virtual Wall', *America's Network* (November 2000), 38–9

Lhamon, W.T., Jr., *Raising Cain: Blackface Performance from Jim Crow to Hip Hop* (Cambridge, MA: Harvard University Press, 1998)

'Listen Up', *The L Word*, Showtime, 7 March 2004

Lively, Adam, *Masks: Blackness, Race and the Imagination* (London: Vintage, 1999)

Lock, Graham and David Murray (eds), *Thriving on a Riff: Jazz and Blues Influences in African American Literature and Film* (Oxford: Oxford University Press, 2008)

Long, Angela, 'The Idea of the Home as a Safe Place is Lost to us Now – in the US More than in Other Places' (interview with Sue Miller), *Irish Times* (18 March 2002), 12

Lott, Eric, *Love and Theft: Blackface Minstrelsy and the American Working Class* (New York: Oxford University Press, 1993)

Mailer, Norman, 'The White Negro: Superficial Reflections on the Hipster' (1959), in *Advertisements for Myself* (London: Panther, 1972)

Maitland, Sara, *A Map of the New Country: Women and Christianity* (London: Routledge and Kegan Paul, 1983)

Maslan, Mark, 'The Faking of the Americans: Passing, Trauma, and National Identity in Philip Roth's *The Human Stain*', *Modern Language Quarterly* 66.3 (2005), 365–89

Max, D.T., 'The Oprah Effect', *New York Times Magazine* (26 December 1999), 36–9

Maupin, Armistead, *The Night Listener* (London: Black Swan, 2001)

McBride, James, *The Color of Water* (New York: Riverhead, 1996)

McCaig, Donald, *Jacob's Ladder* (Harmondsworth: Penguin, 1999)

McClain DaCosta, Kimberly, *Making Multiracials: State, Family, and Market in the Redrawing of the Color Line* (Stanford: Stanford University Press, 2007)

McClure, John A., *Partial Faiths: Postsecular Fiction in the Age of Pynchon and Morrison* (Athens: University of Georgia Press, 2007)

McClurg, Jocelyn, 'Memoirs: Truth is Stranger than Fiction', *Times Union* (26 October 1997), J4

McCourt, Frank, *Angela's Ashes* (London: HarperCollins, 1996)

McDowell, Deborah E., '"It's Not Safe. Not Safe at All": Sexuality in Nella Larsen's *Passing*', in *The Lesbian and Gay Studies Reader*, ed. Henry Abelove, Michèle Ana Barale and David M. Halperin (New York: Routledge, 1993), pp. 616–25

McKay, Claude, 'Near-White', in Sollors (2004), pp. 559–72

McKenzie, James, '"Sharing What I Know": An Interview with Francis Cree', *North Dakota Quarterly* 59.4 (1991), 98–112

Melnick, Jeffrey, *A Right to Sing the Blues: African Americans, Jews, and American Popular Song* (Cambridge, MA: Harvard University Press, 2001)

Michaels, Walter Benn, *The Trouble with Diversity: How We Learned to Love Idenity and Ignore Inequality* (New York: Henry Holt, 2007)

Miller, Laura, '"Middlesex": My Big Fat Greek Gender Identity Crisis' (review of *Middlesex*), *New York Times* (15 September 2002), www.nytimes. com/2002/09/15/books/my-big-fat-greek-gender-identity-crisis.html (15 September 2005)

—— 'Sex, Fate, and Zeus and Hera's Kinkiest Argument' (interview with Jeffrey Eugenides), *Salon.com* (8 October 2002), www.archive.salon.com/books/int/2002/10/08/eugenides/print.html (14 September 2005)

Moore, Lorrie, 'The Wrath of Athena' (review of *The Human Stain*), *New York Times Book Review* (7 May 2000), 7–8

Morrison, Toni, *Paradise* (London: Vintage, 1999)

—— 'Recitatif' (1983), rpt. in *Norton Anthology of American Literature*, Vol. 2, 2nd ed., ed. Nina Baym et al. (New York: Norton, 1998), pp. 2078–92

—— 'Talk of the Town', *New Yorker* (6 October 1998), 31–2

—— *The Bluest Eye* (London: Picador, 1994)

Mulqueen, Eibhear, '"Ashes" to Ashes as McCourt Book Burning Organised in New York', *Irish Times* (19 February 2000), 1

Murray, David, 'Spreading the Word: Missionaries, Conversion and Circulation in the Northeast', in *Spiritual Encounters: Interactions between Christianity and Native Religions in Colonial America*, ed. Nicholas Griffiths and Fernando Cervantes (Birmingham: University of Birmingham Press, 1999), pp. 43–64

'Nanabozho', *Encyclopedia of North American Indians*, http://college.hmco. com/history/readerscomp/naind/html/na_024700_nanabozho.htm (14 July 2004)

Nickell, Joe, 'Searching for Hannah Crafts', in Gates and Robbins, pp. 406–16

Nickerson, Catherine, *The Web of Iniquity: Early Detective Fiction by Women* (Durham, NC: Duke University Press, 1998)

Norment, Lynn, 'Who's Black And Who's Not?: New Ethnicity Raises Provocative Questions about Racial Identity', *Ebony* (March 1990), 134–9

Obama, Barack, *Dreams from My Father* (Edinburgh: Canongate, 2008)

O'Hagan, Sean, 'Color Bind' (interview with Percival Everett), *Observer* (16 March 2003), http://books.guardian.co.uk/departments/generalfiction/ story/ 0,6000,914871,00.html (11 August 2005)

Oikonnen, Venla, '"The Final Clause in a Periodic Sentence": Sexing Difference in *Middlesex*', in *Masculinities, Femininities and the Power of the Hybrid in U.S. Narratives: Essays on Gender Borders*, ed. Nieves Pascual, Laura Alonso-Gallo and Francisco Collado-Rodríguez (Heidelberg: Universitätsverlag, 2007), pp. 245–59

'Oprah's Book Club 43rd Selection: *The Corrections*' (22 October 2001), www. oprah.com/obc/pastbooks/jonathan_franzen/obc_user_ communication. jhtml (28 July 2005)

Owens, Louis, *Mixedblood Messages: Literature, Film, Family, Place* (Norman: University of Oklahoma Press, 1998)

Pagliarini, Marie Anne, 'The Pure American Woman and the Wicked Catholic Priest: An Analysis of Anti-Catholic Literature in Antebellum America', *Religion and American Culture* 9.1 (1999), 97–128

Parrish, Timothy L., 'Ralph Ellison: The Invisible Man in Philip Roth's *The Human Stain*', *Contemporary Literature* XLV.3 (2004), 421–59

Peterson, Nancy J., *Against Amnesia: Contemporary Women Writers and the Crises of Historical Memory* (Philadelphia: University of Pennsylvania Press, 2001)

Peyser, Marc, 'The Ugly Truth', *Newsweek* (23 January 2006), 62

Pfeiffer, Kathleen, *Race Passing and American Individualism* (Amherst: University of Massachusetts Press, 2003)

Pope John Paul II, *The Theology of the Body: Human Love in the Divine Plan* (Boston: Pauline Books, 1997)

Posnock, Ross, *Philip Roth's Rude Truth: The Art of Immaturity* (Princeton, NJ: Princeton University Press, 2006)

—— 'Purity and Danger: On Philip Roth', *Raritan* 21.2 (2001), 85–101

Powers, William, 'Sapphire's Raw Gem', *Washington Post* (6 August 1996), B1–4

Purcell, Tony, 'Plaudits as Home City gives Film Thumbs Up at Showing', *Irish Examiner* (13 January 2000), http://archives.tcm.ie/irishexaminer/2000/01/13/current/ ipage_27.htm (13 May 2006)

Rader, Pamela J., 'Dis-robing the Priest: Gender and Spiritual Conversions in Louise Erdrich's *The Last Report on the Miracles at Little No Horse*', in *The Catholic Church and Unruly Women Writers: Critical Essays*, ed. Jeana DelRosso, Leigh Eicke and Ana Kothe (Basingstoke: Palgrave Macmillan, 2007), pp. 221–35

Read, Mimi, 'A Refugee from Gangland', *New York Times* (28 February 2008), www.nytimes.com/2008/02/28/garden/28jones.html?ref=books (13 May 2009)

Reed, Ishmael, *Reckless Eyeballing* (London: Allison and Busby, 1989)

Rich, Mitoko, 'Gang Memoir, Turning Page, Is Pure Fiction', *New York Times* (4 March 2008), www.nytimes.com/2008/03/04/books/04fake.html?pagewanted=2&_r=1 (13 May 2009)

Robinson, Amy, 'Forms of Appearance and Value: Homer Plessy and the Politics of Privacy', in *Performance and Cultural Politics*, ed. Elin Diamond (London: Routledge, 1996), pp. 237–61

—— 'It Takes One to Know One: Passing and Communities of Common Interest', *Critical Inquiry* 20.4 (1994), 715–36

Roediger, David, *The Wages of Whiteness: Race and the Making of the American Working Class* (London: Verso, 1991)

Rogin, Michael, *Blackface, White Noise: Jewish Immigrants in the Melting Pot* (Berkeley: University of California Press, 1998)

Rolo, Mark Anthony, Interview with Louise Erdrich, *The Progressive* (April 2002), www.findarticles.com/p/articles/mi_m1295/is_4_66/ai_84866888 (2 July 2004)

Roscoe, Will, *Changing Ones: Third and Fourth Genders in Native North America* (New York: St. Martin's Press, 1998)

Roth, Philip, *The Human Stain* (London: Vintage, 2001)

—— 'Writing American Fiction', in *The Novel Today: Contemporary Writers on Modern Fiction*, ed. Malcolm Bradbury (London: Fontana, 1977), pp. 32–47

Rottenberg, Catherine, *Performing Americanness: Race, Class, and Gender in Modern African-American and Jewish-American Literature* (Lebanon, NH: University Press of New England, 2008)

Safer, Elaine B., 'Tragedy and Farce in Roth's *The Human Stain*', *Critique* 43.3 (2002), 211–27

Saks, Eva, 'Representing Miscegenation Law', in Sollors (2000), pp. 61–81

Sánchez, María Carla and Linda Schlossberg (eds), *Passing: Identity and Interpretation in Sexuality, Race, and Religion* (New York: New York University Press, 2001)

Sapphire, *Push* (London: Vintage, 1998)

—— 'Sapphire's Big Push' (interview with Mark Marvel, June 1996), www.findarticles.com/p/articles/mi_m1285/is_n6_v26/ai_18450196 (31 October 2004)

Sartre, Jean-Paul, 'Portrait of the Inauthentic Negro', *Commentary* 5.5 (1948), 389–97

Schultz, Nancy Lusignan, 'Introduction', *Veil of Fear: Nineteenth Century Convent Tales* (West Lafayette, IN: Purdue University Press, 1999), pp. vii–xxxiii

Sekora, John, 'Black Message/White Envelope: Genre, Authenticity, and Authority in the Antebellum Slave Narrative', *Callaloo* 32 (1987), 482–515

Senna, Danzy, Interview with Claudia M. Milian Arias, *Callaloo* 25.2 (2002), 447–52

—— *From Caucasia, with Love* (London: Bloomsbury, 2001)

—— 'Mulatto Millennium', in *Half and Half: Writers on Growing Up Biracial and Bicultural*, ed. Claudine Chiawei O'Hearn (New York: Pantheon, 1998), pp. 12–27, rpt.on *Salon.com* (24 July 1998), http://archive.salon.com/mwt/feature/1998/07/24feature.html (3 July 2004)

—— 'Novel Companions: Books for the 21st Century' (interview with Amy Aronson), *Ms. Magazine* (December 1999), www.msmagazine.com/dec99/books-senna.html (10 January 2005)

Sifuentes, Zachary, 'Strange Anatomy, Strange Sexuality: The Queer Body in Jeffrey Eugenides' *Middlesex*', in *Straight Writ Queer: Non-Normative Expressions of Heterosexuality in Literature*, ed. Richard Fantina (Jefferson, NC: McFarland, 2006), pp. 145–57

Silko, Leslie Marmon, 'Here's an Odd Artifact for the Fairy-Tale Shelf', *Studies in American Indian Literature* 10.4 (1986), 178–84

Sims, Calvin, 'A Geisha, a Successful Novel and a Lawsuit', *New York Times* (19 June 2001), E2

Smith, Jeanne Rosier, *Writing Tricksters: Mythic Gambols in American Ethnic Literature* (Berkeley: University of California Press, 1997)

Smith, Theresa S., 'The Church of the Immaculate Conception: Inculturation and Identity among the Anishnaabeg of Manitoulin Island', in *Native American Spirituality: A Critical Reader*, ed. Lee Irwin (Lincoln: University of Nebraska Press, 2000), pp. 145–56

Sollors, Werner, *Neither Black Nor White Yet Both: Thematic Explorations of Interracial Literature* (New York: Oxford University Press, 1997)

—— (ed.), *An Anthology of Interracial Literature: Black-White Contacts in the Old World and the New* (New York: New York University Press, 2004)

—— (ed.), *Interracialism: Black-White Intermarriage in American History, Literature, and Law* (New York: Oxford University Press, 2000)

Somerville, Siobhan, *Queering the Color Line: Race and the Invention of Homosexuality in American Culture* (Durham, NC: Duke University Press, 2000)

Soskis, Benjamin, 'Freedoms and Fictions', *New Republic* (3 June 2002), 36–40

Soul Man, dir. Steve Miner, perf. C. Thomas Howell, Rae Dawn Chong and James Earl Jones (Balcor Film Investors, 1986)

Spickard, Paul R., 'The Subject is Mixed Race: The Boom in Biracial Biography', in *Rethinking 'Mixed Race'*, ed. David Parker and Miri Song (London: Pluto, 2001), pp. 76–98

Staples, Brent, 'Editorial Notebook: Hating It Because It Is True', *New York Times* (27 April 1997), sec. 4, 14

St. John, Warren, 'A Literary Life Born of Brutality', *New York Times* (14 November 2004), Fashion & Style, 1

Sternbergh, Adam, 'Back in a Flash', *New York Magazine* (21 February 2005), http://newyorkmetro.com/nymetro/arts/tv/11057/ (27 May 2006)

Stowe, Harriet Beecher, *Uncle Tom's Cabin* (Ware, Herts.: Wordsworth, 2002)

Sundquist, Eric J., *Strangers in the Land: Blacks, Jews, Post-Holocaust America* (Cambridge, MA: Harvard University Press, 2005)

Tate, Andrew, *Contemporary Fiction and Christianity* (London: Continuum, 2008)

Taylor, Gordon O., 'Past as Prologue', *Genre* 21.4 (1998), 579–84

The Associate, dir. Donald Petrie, perf. Whoopi Goldberg, Dianne Wiest and Eli Wallach, (Buena Vista, 1996)

The Holy Bible, containing the Old and New Testaments (Cambridge, 1800), http://galenet.galegroup.com/servlet/ECCO (6 February 2006)

'The Leopoldine Society', *Catholic Encyclopedia*, www.newadvent.org/cathen/16052a.htm (2 February 2005)

'The Week: Stop that Monument', *National Review* (18 September 1981), 1064

Time Warner Press Release, *The Bondwoman's Narrative* by Hannah Crafts (2 April 2002) www.twbookmark.com/books/48/0446530085/press_release.html, (22 November 2004)

'Top Grossing Movies for 2004 in the USA', www.imdb.com/Sections/Years/2004/top-grossing (1 December 2005)

Transamerica, dir. Duncan Tucker, perf. Felicity Huffman, Kevin Zegers and Fionnula Flanagan (Belladonna Productions, 2005)

Twain, Mark, *Pudd'nhead Wilson* (New York: Dover, 1999)

TWIZ TV, *The L Word* Transcripts, www.twiztv.com/cgi-bin/thelword.cgi?episode=http://www.l-word.com/transcripts/tx/1x08listenup.html (26 May 2006)

Tyler, Carole Anne, 'Passing: Narcissism, Identity, and Difference', *Differences* 6:2+3 (1994), 212–48

Van Thompson, Carlyle, *The Tragic Black Buck: Racial Masquerading in the American Literary Imagination* (New York: Peter Lang, 2004)

Vernon, Polly, 'Fooled You All', *Sunday Independent* (23 November 2008), Life, 24–6

Von Eckhardt, Wolf, 'Storm over a Viet Nam Memorial: An Eloquently Simple Design for Washington's Mall Draws Fire', *Time* (9 November 1981), 103

Vourvoulias, Bill, 'Talking with Danzy Senna: Invisible Woman', *Newsday* (29 July 1998), B11

Wald, Gayle, *Crossing the Line: Racial Passing in Twentieth Century U.S. Literature and Culture* (Durham, NC: Duke University Press, 2000)

Walker, Alice, *The Color Purple* (London: Women's Press, 1992)

Walker, Rebecca, *Black, White and Jewish: Autobiography of a Shifting Self* (New York: Riverhead, 2001)

Walsh, Dennis, 'Catholicism in Louise Erdrich's *Love Medicine* and *Tracks*', *American Indian Culture and Research Journal* 25.2 (2001), 107–27

Washington, Mary Helen, *Invented Lives: Narratives of Black Women, 1860–1960* (London: Virago, 1989)

Watermelon Man, dir. Melvin Van Peebles, perf. Godfrey Cambridge, Estelle Parsons and Howard Caine (Columbia Pictures, 1970)

Watson, Reginald, 'The Changing Face of Biraciality: The White/Jewish Mother as Tragic Mulatto Figure in James McBride's *The Color of Water* and Danzy Senna's *Caucasia*', *Obsidian III: Literature in the African Diaspora* 4.1 (2002), 101–13

Webb, Frank J., *The Garies and their Friends* (Baltimore: Johns Hopkins University Press, 1997)

Weedon, Chris, *Feminist Practice and Poststructuralist Theory* (Oxford: Blackwell, 1997)

White, Barbara E., *Growing up Female: Adolescent Girlhood in American Fiction* (Westport, CT: Greenwood, 1985)

White Chicks, dir. Keenen Ivory Wayans, perf. Shawn Wayans and Marlon Wayans (Columbia, 2004)

Williamson, Joel, *New People: Miscegenation and Mulattoes in the United States* (New York: Macmillan, 1980)

Willis, Susan, 'I Shop Therefore I Am: Is There a Place for Afro-American Culture in Commodity Culture?', in *Changing Our Own Words: Essays on Criticism, Theory, and Writing by Black Women*, ed. Cheryl A. Wall (London: Routledge, 1990), pp. 173–95

Wilson, Harriet E., *Our Nig; or, Sketches from the Life of a Free Black, In a Two-Story White House, North. Showing that Slavery's Shadows Fall Even There. By 'Our Nig'* (1859), intro. R. J. Ellis (Nottingham: Nottingham Trent University Press, 1998)

Wray, Matt and Annalee Newitz, 'Introduction', *White Trash: Race and Class in America*, ed. Matt Wray and Annalee Newitz (New York: Routledge, 1997), pp. 1–12.

Wright, Richard, *Native Son* (London: Picador, 1995)

Wynter, Leon E., *American Skin: Pop Culture, Big Business, and the End of White America* (New York: Crown, 2002)

Yellin, Jean Fagan, *The Intricate Knot: Black Figures in American Literature, 1776–1863* (New York: New York University Press, 1972)

—— *Women and Sisters: The Antislavery Feminists in American Culture* (New Haven: Yale University Press, 1989)

Young, John K., *Black Writers, White Publishers: Marketplace Politics in Twentieth-Century African American Literature* (Jackson: University Press of Mississippi, 2006)

Yu, Henry, 'How Tiger Woods Lost his Stripes: Post-Nationalist American Studies as a History of Race, Migration, and the Commodification of Culture', in Guins and Cruz, pp. 197–210

Index